About the author

Bob Pease is chair of social work in the School of Health and Social Development at Deakin University in Geelong, Australia. He has published widely in the fields of masculinity studies and critical approaches to social work practice and is the author or co-editor of ten previous books. His most recent co-edited books are the *International Encyclopedia of Men and Masculinities* (2007), *Migrant Men: Critical Studies of Masculinities and the Migration Experience* (2009) and *Critical Social Work: Theories and Practices for a Socially Just World* (2nd edition 2009). He has been involved in pro-feminist masculinity politics for many years and actively engaged in campaigns to end men's violence against women.

UNDOING PRIVILEGE

unearned advantage in a divided world

Bob Pease

Zed Books
LONDON · NEW YORK

Undoing Privilege: Unearned advantage in a divided world was first published in 2010 by Zed Books Ltd, 7 Cynthia Street, London N1 9JF, UK, and Room 400, 175 Fifth Avenue, New York, NY 10010, USA

www.zedbooks.co.uk

Set in Monotype Sabon and Gill Sans Heavy by Ewan Smith, London
Index: ed.emery@thefreeuniversity.net
Cover designed by Rogue Four Design
Printed and bound in Great Britain by MPG Books Group, Bodmin and King's Lynn

Distributed in the USA exclusively by Palgrave Macmillan, a division of St Martin's Press, LLC, 175 Fifth Avenue, New York, NY 10010, USA

A catalogue record for this book is available from the British Library
Library of Congress Cataloging in Publication Data available

ISBN 978 1 84813 028 9 hb
ISBN 978 1 84813 029 6 pb
ISBN 978 1 84813 537 6 eb

Contents

Acknowledgements

A book like this is always a collective effort. The ideas have been developed over many years by engaging with allies and opponents in political struggles, through reading the work of others and testing ideas out in conversations and teaching. I have been very fortunate to have the support of so many people in working through my ideas. I have also been buoyed by the encouragement I have received and the belief by others that the ideas in this book were important to share more widely.

In the first instance, I want to thank Stephen Fisher and Maria Pallotta-Chiarolli who read the early chapters of the book when I was developing my conceptual framework for interrogating privilege. Their comments reminded me of the importance of writing a book that would reach beyond the academy if I wanted to motivate people to take action against social injustice.

This book took me outside my comfort zone and I faced many challenges in writing it. This is as it should be. Writing a book such as this required me to immerse myself in multiple areas of scholarship, including development studies, Marxism and post-Marxism, feminist theory and masculinity studies, critical race theory and whiteness studies, sexuality studies and disability studies. I do not claim to be an expert in all of these fields. So I am immensely grateful to the following people who generously commented on draft chapters in their areas of expertise: Jacques Boulet (development studies); Keith Abbott, Mike Donaldson and Iain Ferguson (Marxism and post-Marxism); Cathy Bettman, Sarah Epstein and Carole Wright (feminist theory); Veronica Arbon, Clare Land and Selma Macfarlane (critical race theory and whiteness studies); Maxwell Clarke, Gary Dowsett, Steven Hicks (sexuality studies); Barbara Fawcette, Kelley Johnson, Jane Maidment and Erin Wilson (disability studies). Heather D'Cruz also read and commented on a draft of the final chapter. They all provided extremely useful and very thoughtful comments and suggestions that enabled me to strengthen earlier drafts of these chapters. Without their critical feedback, there would have been embarrassing errors of omission and misinterpretation.

I am also indebted to Heather Fraser, Mel Gray, Jim Ife and Silvia Starc, who read and commented on the full draft of the manuscript. I have benefited greatly from their salient comments and suggestions; they have all made this a much better book. I want to thank the non-anonymous reviewer for Zed Books, Ravindra Rukmini Pandharinath, who read and commented on the original manuscript and whose critical comments were very useful in identifying some important gaps in the book. It is, of course, important to say that any flaws or limitations remaining in the argument are mine.

This book has also been strengthened by responses from audiences at a number of seminars and conferences in Australia and Sweden. I would like to thank Keith Pringle and Mona Livholts for their Swedish hospitality and for organising a number of public forums where I tested out many of the ideas in the book.

I would like to acknowledge the support of Deakin University for granting me study leave to complete the book. Part of this book was written during a period of leave at the University of Bradford. I would like to thank Brid Featherstone and her colleagues for providing me with collegial support and the facilities to write.

I would like to thank Ellen McKinlay at Zed Books, who commissioned the book and regularly checked in with me to see how it was going. After Ellen left the company, Ken Barlow took over as commissioning editor and he generously provided me with an extra three months to finish the book when I needed it.

Writing a book always involves an intense commitment of time and energy and these limited resources have to be found amid competing pressures and demands, and invariably such a project impacts on family life. So, finally, I want to express my special appreciation to Silvia Starc who, in addition to reading the full manuscript, supported me in the writing endeavour when I was struggling under the pressure of these other demands.

Preface

I can trace many of the ideas in this book back to 1990 when I presented a paper at an international social work conference in Peru. The theme of the conference was eliminating poverty. With hundreds of thousands of very poor people in the capital city of Lima, it seemed like a good place to hold an international conference on poverty. I remember vividly the experience of passing by the shanty towns and the beggars on the way to the hotel from the airport. When I checked into the five-star hotel where the conference was being held, I was acutely aware of the tension of discussing poverty in such luxurious surroundings. Is it an irony or a contradiction that professional educators travel to 'exotic' locations and deliver papers on poverty?

At the conference, I talked about some of the dilemmas and contradictions facing those who of us who were privileged, but who positioned ourselves on the side of those who were marginalised and oppressed. For those of us who are male, white and professional in the 'developed world', it seemed to me that we were very much part of the problem that needed to be addressed. How could people such as myself, who are members of privileged groups, develop a consciousness of our privilege and challenge the ideas that lead us to participate in the oppression of others? Was it possible for members of privileged groups to overcome the interests of our own group? Could we form meaningful alliances with oppressed groups? I remember that I raised more questions than I provided answers in that paper. Twenty years later, these questions are still with me.

In most of my research, writing and activism since then, I've addressed these questions primarily in relation to men's work in challenging male privilege and dominant forms of masculinity.[1] Where do men who are supportive of gender equality stand in relation to feminism? How can we challenge other men's sexism and violence without colluding with them? How do we make sure

1. See, for example, Pease (2000), Pease and Pringle (2001) and Pease (2002a).

that our work against sexism is accountable to women? But in focusing my work primarily on male privilege, I became increasingly concerned that I was allowing other aspects of my privileged identity, in relation to whiteness, heterosexuality, the class-elitist world of academia and my location in the West to go unchallenged. It seemed then that an obvious and necessary next step was for me to extend my research, writing and activism into other dimensions of privilege. This book is an outcome of that project. It is one stage of a journey to give voice to some of the dilemmas and experiences of inhabiting many privileged social positions, while being opposed to the underpinnings of that privilege.

The emphasis of this book on 'undoing privilege' makes it different from those books that challenge social dominance by focusing on what the oppressed can do. Many of these books are written by class-privileged, white heterosexual men who say nothing about their own stake in the political project they advocate. I argue that we cannot understand oppression unless we understand privilege. I believe that too much attention has been focused on the responsibility of those who are oppressed and too little attention has been given to how those in privileged groups reproduce inequality.

On the surface, it would seem that the concept of privilege has been discussed for some time in political science and sociology. Certainly, elite studies is a well-established area of social inquiry, along with the considerable literature on social inequality, social divisions, social exclusion, social problems, discrimination and oppression. However, I maintain that much of this literature does not adequately examine the complex nature of privilege and how it is reproduced daily by members of privileged groups.

Part of the problem is that it is very difficult to get the issue of privilege on the agenda because it is so well legitimated. Privilege is not recognised as such by many of those who have it. Privilege structures the world so that its mechanisms are either invisible or appear to be natural. Therefore, it is necessary to 'unmask' privilege and make it more visible so that its consequences can be addressed.

Every book has an intended audience and is often written with an ideal audience in mind. Of course, books are read by diverse audiences and this is sometimes regarded as problematical. In the 1970s, I was part of a profeminist reading group who read and discussed major feminist texts of the time. We endeavoured to locate our experiences in a context of feminist theory; although we recognised that we read such theory as men. Some feminists regarded men reading feminist books with scepticism and concern. Women wrote these books for women and some feminists were concerned that we might use what we gained from the books to further oppress women. These were not unfounded fears.

I do not expect that those who gain the most from privilege are likely to read a book with the title *Undoing Privilege*. It is unlikely that white men in the capitalist class, who constitute the most powerful and privileged group in Western societies, will read it. However, I believe that there are many people with privilege who are opposed to social inequalities but may be unaware of how they reproduce those inequalities in their daily lives. They may be whites challenging racism, for example, but not be aware of how they gain privilege by being white. This book is addressed primarily to those who share at least one or more of the sites of privilege examined here and who are open to exploring the impact of this privilege on people's lives.

As I am a white, heterosexual, able-bodied academic man in the developed world, I write from within multiple positions of privilege. Since I am writing a book on privilege from within and I want to engage readers who have privilege, I write in the form of a first person narrative. I have a dilemma, though, in using the first person plural 'we', when discussing privilege. It is important to clarify at the outset who the 'we' is that I am referring to. When I write about gender as a man, a woman will clearly not identify herself as part of the 'we'. However, that same woman, if she is white, may identify herself as part of the 'we' when I am writing about white privilege. A male, black heterosexual activist in Africa will feel excluded from the 'we' category when I am discussing Western and white privilege. However, he may see elements of himself within the 'we' when I discuss male and heterosexual privilege. Thus many readers will at times be included and excluded by my use of 'we'.

Pennycook (1994) argues that the use of 'we' is never unproblematic and that all use of pronouns reflects power relations. More often than not, 'we' is used with a lack of consciousness about relations of power. Often, the use of 'we' assumes a white, heterosexual, able-bodied, middle-class man without having been marked as such. I hope that by the naming of privilege from within, I will have avoided 'othering' those who do not have access to this privilege.

I assume a social change and social justice orientation in this book. I locate myself within the critical sociological tradition. Hence, I argue that unearned privilege is a source of oppression and that it entrenches social inequality and damages the lives of people who do not have access to it. Since the book is an argument against unearned privilege, I invite the reader to be part of a collective endeavour against such privilege and I hope that he or she will find some resonance with the argument advanced here. It goes without saying that some readers will disagree with some of the imperatives in the book and I hope that it will stimulate a much-needed debate about the possible role of the privileged in struggles against oppression.

Finally, in relation to representation, I am institutionally located within the field of social work education. Although this is clearly not a social work book, invariably at times I will draw upon social work literature and examples to illuminate some aspect of privilege and oppression. While the book should be of interest to students of social work and community development, it should also interest students of gender, race, sexuality, disability and development studies. Some students in courses on therapy and counselling will also be interested, as increasingly such courses are becoming more alert to issues of privilege and power in the counselling process. Students in the field of critical psychology will also be interested in the psychological processes underpinning privilege. Beyond the academic market, the book will be of interest to social activists and practitioners in the human services, community development, social movements and human rights, who are challenging privilege and oppression in their work.

Can privileged individuals overcome their own self-interest in the maintenance of privilege in order to challenge it? Is this just wishful thinking in the current political climate? While I argue against the notion that privileged individuals can somehow simply give up their privilege, I do maintain that members of privileged groups can make choices about whether they want to hold on to their privilege or challenge it. All readers are invited to critically reflect upon their own position in relation to the sites of privilege examined. I hope this book challenges and unsettles those who are willing to face the role that they play, often unconsciously, in reproducing the very social divisions they oppose.

This book is written at a particular historical moment. Throughout history, members of the middle class supported the rights of working people, European and North American whites opposed slavery, men supported equal rights for women and heterosexual people opposed homophobia.

Kimmel and Mosmiller (1992) undertook a documentary history of profeminist men's involvement in women's struggles in the United States. They demonstrate a long history of men's support for feminist causes. In particular, they note the ability of African-American and gay men who struggled against racism and homophobia to examine the links between their subordination as marginalised men and male privilege and entitlement. There have been similar historical accounts of anti-racist whites in North America (Aptheker 1975; Loewen 2003).

Hochschild's (2005) history of the British struggle to abolish slavery illustrates striking parallels with recent attempts to challenge privilege from within. Like privilege, slavery was seen to be normal and was deeply entrenched in the social order of the time. It is well known that even Thomas Jefferson, who supported struggles for human rights, was a slave owner (Ife 2010). However, as people came to understand the suffering caused by slavery, they increasingly opposed it and created a large-scale abolitionist movement. Similarly, as people come to recognise the damage caused by unearned privilege, more people may become distressed by its existence.

So how will I explore these issues? In Chapter 1, I outline how much of the literature on social and political inequality fails to adequately address the processes by which privilege is reproduced and I examine the characteristics of privilege. In Chapter 2, I examine the intersections and social dynamics of privilege and I explore how privilege is constructed through the daily activities of privileged individuals and groups.

Chapters 3 to 8 explore particular dimensions of privilege in the intersecting sites of 'the West', political economy, gender order, racial formations, institutionalised heterosexuality and ableist relations.[2] By naming specific systems of dominance such as

2. The forms of privilege examined in this book are not exhaustive of the various social divisions. I have not, for example, examined the organising logic of privilege and oppression in relation to age, intellectual disability, ethnicity, religion, mental health status or human species. Since completing the book, and discussing the ideas within it, I have been specifically challenged about giving insufficient attention to human privilege in relation

colonialism, capitalism, patriarchy, white supremacy, heterosexism and able-bodiedness, I face the danger of portraying each form of privilege as separate and isolated systems of power that are not connected to each other. To avoid this danger of presenting each site of privilege in isolation, I explore each particular form of privilege from an intersectional perspective that recognises the heterogeneity and multiple identities within each dominant group. However, I think that it is important to interrogate and analyse the specific features of particular forms of dominance. Since each site has its own organising logic, it is necessary to examine the way in which privilege is reproduced by social structures and processes in particular contexts and locations. For analytical purposes, I have thus found it useful to place specific intersecting sites of privilege in the foreground rather than to interrogate privilege without reference to specificity and context.

While working within an intersectionality framework that recognises the intersections between diverse forms of privilege and oppression, I also focus on the similarities and the distinctiveness of each socially situated form of dominance. If intersectionality is taken to the extreme, it is not possible to talk at all about class, gender and race from this perspective because they are always enmeshed (Cooper 2004).

In Chapter 9, I explore strategies for members of dominant groups to challenge the reproduction of internalised dominance. The chapter also examines the limitations and potential of dialogue and alliances across structural power differences when members of dominant groups act as allies in challenging privilege.

I hope that this book encourages readers who are new to these ideas to engage with the wider scholarship of critical theory and writings on oppression from below. I could not have written the book without immersing myself in postcolonial studies, Marxism, feminism, critical race studies, queer theory and disability studies. Thus it should not be read as an alternative to the extensive scholarship that is grounded in the experiences of those who are oppressed.

---

to the non-human world and adult privilege in relation to children and young people. As an ecologically aware citizen and as a parent, these are uncomfortable omissions to acknowledge and they no doubt reflect elements of unexamined privilege in my own life. I can only make a commitment to address them in my future work.

The identities of those of us who are privileged are often shaped by our experiences of unquestioned advantages. Thus challenging privilege can be experienced as undermining the basis of who we are. I am expecting some resistance to many of my arguments in this book. As a teacher who raises these issues in university classrooms and as an activist who challenges members of privileged groups to think about their unearned benefits, I have encountered a range of defensive responses to these arguments. I hope that readers will seriously consider the many contradictory ways in which we are all affected by privilege. In the end, I believe that we have much to gain in becoming aware of the costs of our privileges for ourselves and for those around us.

PART ONE

Theoretical and conceptual foundations

ONE
Oppression, privilege and relations of domination

We live in an unequal world structured along the relational divisions of class, race, gender, sexuality and other social divisions. How that inequality is understood and the extent to which it is justified has been the subject of a considerable amount of debate in popular culture and in the social sciences. Numerous books have documented various forms of social inequality in Western societies, including economic inequality, status inequality, sex and gender inequality, racial and ethnic inequality and inequalities between different countries. Many of these books concerned with sociological inquiry have also examined the sources of social and political inequality in modern capitalist societies and the ways in which social and political arrangements reproduce those inequalities.

To help understand the costs of inequality, other key concepts in the social sciences have also been used to explain the dynamics of modern capitalist societies, including: social exclusion, social divisions, social problems, discrimination, disadvantage, powerlessness, exploitation, oppression and, to a lesser extent, the concept of elites. While each of these concepts is important in illustrating the structural dimensions of unequal social relations and examining the costs of these relations for marginalised and oppressed groups, they do little to address the role played by those of us who benefit most from existing social divisions and inequalities. Nor do most of these books examine how these inequalities are reproduced by and through the daily practices of privileged groups.

Many writers on social inequality demonstrate the structural and institutional dimensions of social inequality and how it is reflected in political and legal institutions. Such theories of social dominance emphasise the importance of locating inequality within the context of institutional and structural arrangements. These theories have been significant in explaining the continuation of social inequality. They have certainly informed my own understanding of modern capitalist societies and they have shaped my own critical consciousness of structural inequalities.

However, most inequality theorists do not explore the responsibility of privileged groups for maintaining these social arrangements. Perhaps they consider it to be self-evident. But it is this self-evidence that, in part, lessens the responsibility that members of such groups have to challenge these unequal arrangements.

The other side of discrimination and oppression

One concept that would seem to provide a basis for holding privileged groups responsible is that of discrimination, whether this be in the form of class, race, sexuality, age or gender discrimination. There has been an explosion of social science literature dealing with the experiences of discrimination. While much of this literature acknowledges the structural basis of discrimination based on race, gender, class, sexuality and so forth, it is usually presented in terms of personal or group attitudes and prejudices. Terms like 'racist' and 'sexist' are used to describe people who stereotype and discriminate against others. However, such terms focus on the behaviour of individuals and groups and usually ignore the wider social context in which discrimination takes place. Mostly, the individual is blamed for being prejudiced rather than identifying the ways in which their behaviour is socially reinforced and normalised (Wildman and Davis 2000). In this way, these descriptions often hide the flipside of discrimination, which is privilege. We need to make privilege more visible rather than focusing on only one half of the system of inequality. The concept of discrimination places too much emphasis on prejudice and is too narrowly focused to address the complexity of dominant–subordinate relations.

In relation to the concept of oppression, there is a considerable amount of literature that focuses on the oppression of particular groups: women, gays, people of colour, and so forth. While it is usually recognised that dominant groups gain from the oppression of others, most books on oppression are concerned with changing the way the oppressed think and act. Considerable attention is given to how oppressed groups reproduce their own oppression.

Such writers emphasise how inequality is legitimated through a belief in the 'rightfulness' of existing social inequalities. However, when discussing which groups believe in the 'rightfulness' of the unequal distribution of rewards and resources, most social theorists emphasise the role played by the marginalised. It is suggested that subordinated individuals perpetuate their own marginalisation and oppression by internalising the ideas from the dominant culture into their psyches. Many people blame themselves for not achieving more in their lives because they are actively encouraged to do so.

One way that has been used to explain this accommodation is 'internalised oppression', which Pheterson (1986: 148) describes as 'the incorporation and acceptance by individuals within an oppressed group of the prejudices against them within the dominant society'. For example, some gay men may internalise homophobia and feel a lack of pride in their identity and their history.

This leads often to a concern with strategies to assist marginalised groups to challenge their oppression. Oppressed groups may accept, accommodate to or reject their subordination. The latter response is what Mansbridge (2001) refers to as 'oppositional consciousness'. Subordinate groups are said to 'have an oppositional consciousness when they claim their previously subordinate identity as a positive identification, identify injustices done to their group and demand changes in the polity, economy or society' (ibid.: 1). Such a term is seen to embrace race, class and other forms of consciousness of subordination. Oppositional consciousness encourages subordinate groups to identify dominant groups as oppressors. During the rise of second-wave feminism, gay liberation and anti-racist struggles by indigenous peoples in the 1970s, this critical consciousness of oppression was the basis of much social activism.

The concern is with the opportunities and capacity of the excluded to resist the forces of their exclusion. There is a danger here that those seen as socially excluded may be portrayed as reproducing their own marginalisation. This notion comes close to blaming victims for their own victimisation. To what extent can we charge those who are oppressed with not doing enough to challenge their oppression, while those who are privileged have barely begun to acknowledge the role they play in oppressing others?

The role of dominant groups in legitimating social discourse through the control of ideology is well known in Marxist theory, whether it is in the form of producing 'false consciousness' or, in Antonio Gramsci's (1957) words, 'ideological hegemony'. The argument is that dominant groups maintain their position by winning over the hearts and minds of those who are exploited by the existing system. This lack of consciousness of inequality is thus presented as a way of explaining its continuance. So the focus is on how those who are marginalised are unaware of or do not acknowledge the structural basis of social inequality. While these writers acknowledge the existence of dominant groups, the self-interest of these groups in maintaining the existing inequalities is usually taken as a given and is not critically examined.

One of the main factors in encouraging oppositional consciousness is seeing unequal relations as unjust. Why should this concern be directed only at those who are on the receiving end of injustice and subordination? If we focus only on discrimination and oppression, we reinforce the invisibility of privilege. If we are really going to understand the sources of discrimination and oppression in society, we must understand how privilege is constructed and maintained. Furthermore, as Bailey (1998: 117) comments, we need to be 'attentive to the ways in which complex systems of domination rely on the oppression of one group to generate privilege for another'.

To put it another way, why do sociologists focus primarily on the bottom of the social divisions and not on the dominant group? It is often noted that academics are more likely to study 'down' rather than 'up'. There are numerous sociological studies of oppressed and marginalised groups, but few studies of powerful and privileged groups. Why is this so? Is it simply because it implicates those in power? If we focus exclusively upon the oppressed and the socially excluded, we get a one-sided picture that reinforces the invisibility of privilege. Understanding the construction of privilege is necessary for a complete understanding of how oppression and discrimination are sustained.

Privileged groups may also come to see the injustice in systems of domination. For example: men can challenge patriarchy; white people can challenge racism; heterosexuals can confront homophobia. This consciousness of inequality is particularly more likely if people have an oppositional consciousness about their own subordination on one dimension of stratification. Such people may be able to more easily empathise with the experiences of another group's oppression. For example, it might be expected that black men would be more likely than white men to support feminism because they have experienced oppression. Sandoval (2000) refers to this as 'differential oppositional consciousness'. However, while groups who are dominant on one dimension of inequality and oppressed on another may, in some instances, identify more closely with oppressed groups, on other occasions they may identify their interests with dominant and privileged groups. I examine the complexity of people experiencing both oppression and privilege more fully in Chapter 2.

While it is important to recognise the structural constraints on challenging inequality and it is equally important to explore the potential of subordinated groups to mobilise collective actions against inequality, I am arguing that those who benefit from existing inequalities are often 'let off the hook' and that the role they play in reproducing inequalities is neglected. This book talks about the ways in which members of dominant groups reproduce their dominance, sometimes consciously but often unconsciously as well.

We need to develop a new vocabulary to understand the ways in which various dimensions of privilege are interconnected and reproduced. This means that the very naming of privilege as opposed to discrimination, social exclusion, oppression and so forth gives us another perspective from which to understand social inequality.

Elite studies and studying up

An exception to the focus on the oppressed and marginalised is elite studies that *do* study upwards. The concept of elites is commonly acknowledged in the social sciences, but there are considerably fewer studies of them. Elites are those who have considerable wealth and power usually located in politics and business. More than forty years ago, for example, Lenski (1966: 43) tried to answer the question of 'who gets what and why', and argued that 'privilege is largely a function of power'. Similarly, just over twenty-five years ago, Daniel (1983: 12) argued that '(t)he status of occupations provides a useful reflection of the way [in which] power and privilege is held in society'. Her focus was on how those at the top of the occupational hierarchy constituted an upper-class elite.

I find that the concept of privilege is inadequately explored in elite studies. The problem with elite studies is that there is often little critical examination of the legitimacy of elite power. The classical elite theorists, Pareto (1935), Mosca (1939) and Michels (1962) all approved of elite domination, arguing that elites were inevitable in all societies because people with superior abilities would excel and achieve high status. Back in 1956 C. Wright Mills noted that 'ordinary men [sic], even today, are prone to explain and to justify power and wealth in terms of knowledge and ability' (Mills 1956: 351). Conservatives have long argued that people reach the top strata of society by hard work and in doing so continue to win the ideological battle over the legitimacy of the power of the elite. Thus I argue that Mills's phrase of 'even today' still applies, more than fifty years later.

Many of those who advocate elitism do not see any incompatibility with democracy. Carlton (1996: 204), in a contemporary revision of elite theory, argues that elite status arises out of 'necessary role differentiation in society', and so he regards elitism as inevitable. Woods (1998) also notes that all elite theorists, in portraying an elite at the top of a pyramid above the masses below, end up reproducing the idea of the elite possessing superior qualities and abilities. So, many elite theorists do not explicitly challenge the legitimacy of the elite but are instead more interested in the functions of elitism.

Since elite theories identify privilege and power as being based upon considerable wealth and political and bureaucratic positions of authority, everyone else constitutes the 'non-elite'. In this way, many of us who have particular dimensions of privilege are encouraged to see ourselves as part of the 'non-elite' because we are not in the upper class. This drawing of the boundaries between the elite and the non-elite conceals the multifaceted nature of privilege that I examine in this book.

Bailey (1998: 109) describes privilege as 'systematically conferred advantages individuals enjoy by virtue of their membership in dominant groups with access to resources and institutional power that are beyond the common advantages of marginalised citizens'. Sidanius and Pratto (1999: 31–2) identify the main benefits that accrue from privilege:

> possession of a disproportionately large share of positive social value or all those material and symbolic things for which people strive. Examples of positive social value are such things as political authority and power, good and plentiful food, splendid homes, the best available health care, wealth and high social status'. Individuals come to possess these benefits by virtue of his or her prescribed membership in a particular socially constructed group such as race, religion, clan, tribe, ethnic group or social class.

What is important here is that the groups to which people belong are more likely to make them privileged than their individual abilities. Privilege is usually thought of as positive state brought about by either hard work or luck. However, even many of those forms of privilege that people believe that they have earned through their own efforts are often complicated by unearned systems of dominance of which they are unaware. When privilege is systematically conferred, rather than earned, it gives one group of people the power to feel superior over another. While some forms of privilege need to be extended to become the norm in a socially just society, other forms of privilege need to be rejected because they reinforce hierarchy and damage people's lives.

One of the first writers to relate the concept of privilege to the specific benefits individuals receive was Peggy McIntosh. She distinguished between 'earned strength and unearned power conferred systematically' (McIntosh 1992: 78). McIntosh constructed a list of fifty advantages that were available to her as a white person that were not available to people of colour under racism.[1] To make sense of how individuals gain these benefits, we need to identify the key dimensions of privilege: the invisibility of privilege by those who have it; the power of the privileged group to determine the social norm; the naturalisation of privilege and the sense of entitlement that accompanies privilege.

The invisibility of privilege

Most privilege is not recognised as such by those who have it. In fact, 'one of the functions of privilege is to structure the world so that mechanisms of privileges are invisible – in the sense that they are unexamined – to those who benefit from them' (Bailey 1998: 112). Not being aware of privilege is an important aspect of privilege. A. Johnson (2001) observes how members of privileged groups either do not understand what others mean when they refer to them as privileged or they tend to get angry and defensive. When well-meaning members of privileged groups offer to support the struggles of oppressed groups, they often cannot understand why those groups might be suspicious or even hostile towards them. Many men challenging male violence wonder why women do not embrace and applaud their efforts. Also, many whites who are opposed to racism wonder why indigenous people are not more supportive of their stand. Members of privileged groups usually do not see how they benefit from the practices that they claim to oppose. Some argue that privilege does not necessarily bring happiness and fulfilment. This may then be used to deny the

1. See Chapter 6 for an extended discussion of McIntosh and a detailed analysis of white privilege.

existence of privilege, compounding the challenge of recognising the power of privilege. These responses represent significant obstacles to the struggle for equality.

Michael Kimmel (2003), a profeminist academic in the United States, tells a story about a graduate seminar on feminist theory he participated in some years ago. He overheard a conversation between a white woman and a black woman about whether their common experiences as women were more or less significant than their cultural differences. The white woman was trying to convince the black woman that their shared experiences as women created a bond between them that overcame their racial differences. In response the black woman asked: 'When you wake up in the morning and look in the mirror, what do you see?'

'I see a woman.'

'That's precisely the issue,' replied the black woman. 'I see a black woman. For me, race is visible every day, because it is how I am not privileged in this culture. Race is invisible to you, which is why our alliance will always seem somewhat false to me.'

Kimmel was startled by this exchange because he realised that when he looked in the mirror in the morning he saw 'a human being'. He regarded himself as 'the generic person'. His race and gender were invisible to him (Kimmel 2003: 6–7). His class and his sexuality were also invisible to him at this time, although he does address these dimensions of privilege in his later work.

Kimmel's story suggests that people are more likely to be aware of experiences of oppression than they are likely to be conscious of aspects of their privilege. Oppressed people are continually reminded of how their gender or their class or their race are sources of discrimination. As a result, they are likely to have a heightened consciousness of their oppression, whereas those privileged by prized statuses often remain blithely unaware of them.

As Rosenblum and Travis (1996) note, members of privileged groups have what they call an 'unmarked status'. By this they mean that people in unmarked categories do 'not require any special comment. The unmarked category tells us what a society takes for granted' (ibid.: 142). One of the consequences of this is that members of privileged groups are unlikely to be aware of how others do not have access to the benefits that they receive. Thus they are unlikely to be able to acknowledge the experiences of those who are marginalised. Consequently, many privileged individuals may oppress people without being aware of it. By simply exercising their prerogatives in everyday life, they can easily ignore how others are denied the same opportunities.

When people are unable to recognise their privilege because they are so focused on their oppression, they are unable to see their role in keeping others subordinated. They make a claim to what Razack (1998) calls 'the race to innocence'. Razack levels this charge at white middle-class feminists for being insufficiently aware of their complicity in reproducing oppression. She argues that some feminist women have emphasised their marginalised status 'to avoid addressing our position within dominant groups and to maintain our innocence or belief in our non-involvement in the subordination of others' (ibid.: 132). While there are certainly some examples of this lack of awareness in women's history, increasingly, feminists have adopted multi-racial perspectives on gender domination in the last two decades.

While some men are willing to acknowledge that women are oppressed, they are less willing to recognise that they are correspondingly 'privileged'. McIntosh identifies parallels between the unwillingness of men to come to terms with their male privilege and white women's reluctance to accept their white privilege. She refers to white privilege as being like 'an invisible weightless knapsack' (McIntosh 1992: 71). As a result of this, much oppressive behaviour can be quite unconscious. It is easy to recognise blatant sexism or racism when someone puts another person down because of their gender or their race. But it is much harder to recognise how in everyday interactions dominance may be reinforced just because of belonging to a dominant group by birth.

McIntosh says that she did not regard herself as racist because she was taught 'to recognise racism only in individual acts of meanness by members of my group, never in invisible systems conferring racial dominance on my group from birth' (ibid.: 81). Most people seem to have some difficulty in accepting their own involvement in the day-to-day oppression of others and how many of the benefits they receive have been derived from the continued subordination of others. Members of dominant groups are conditioned not to see themselves as privileged or prejudiced because they are able to identify only the more blatant forms of discrimination enacted against marginalised groups. They do not recognise the ways in which society gives them privileges that come with their gender, class, race and sexuality.

J. Harvey (1999) used the term 'civilised oppression' to describe the way in which processes of oppression are normalised in everyday life. Because civilised oppression is also embedded in cultural norms and bureaucratic institutions, many of these practices are habituated and unconscious. Many of the injustices people suffer are a result of the attitudes and practices of ordinary people going about their daily lives who are not aware of how their assumptions of superiority impact on the lives of others. Such people do not understand themselves as having unearned privilege. Nor do they see themselves as oppressing others. Civilised oppression can be used to describe many of the specific uses of privilege documented in the different sites in this book. In making privilege more visible, we will also make civilised oppression more recognisable.

While members of dominant groups may intentionally oppress others, not all members of dominant groups behave in oppressive ways. The reproduction of oppression does not require active consciousness on the part of the privileged. Ferree et al. (1999: 11) illustrate how 'the lives of different groups are interconnected even without face to face relations'. They discuss how, for example, white people gain privileges through the oppression of people of colour, even if they are not personally exploiting or taking advantage of them (ibid.: 11). So, while it is important to disapprove of these 'unearned advantages', and even to become distressed by them, this disapproval and distress will not, in itself, be enough to change them. Unearned privileges are conferred on members of privileged groups because they belong to those groups. Yet our disapproval of inequalities does not stop us from continuing to benefit from them.

The normativity of privilege

People in privileged groups feel that their lives are normal. In fact, they have become the model for idealised human relations and this partly explains why most do not want to know about the experiences of the oppressed. Perry (2001: 192) notes that the privileged group comes to represent the dominant norm (the rules regulating our behaviour), whereby 'white, thin male young heterosexual Christian and financially secure people come to embody what it means to be normal'.

Ife (2010) locates the normative framework that entrenches privilege as a legacy of the Enlightenment and Western humanism, whereby the human was exalted over and above nature. As he points out, it was a particular construction of the human that was idealised, namely European, white, adult, able-bodied and highly educated males. Thus humanism was used to defend a Western, patriarchal and colonialist world view.

Perry observes that, through the positioning of self and other, various forms of difference are devalued because they are seen as inferior, weak or subordinate in relation to the norm, which is presented as superior, strong and dominant. In other words, 'racism, sexism, homophobia are all predicated upon such negative valuations of difference' (Perry 2001: 46). The normativity of privilege means that this becomes the basis for measuring success and failure. Those who are not privileged deviate from the norm. Normative standard leads to the negative valuation of difference. Since the privileged are regarded as normal, they are less likely to be studied or researched because the norm does not have to be marked. Gender, for example, becomes a code word for women and race always seem to refer to people of colour.

The normativity of privilege provides some insight to the process of 'othering'. Othering is a method of portraying difference as if it were in some way alien to that which is normal. The flipside of the 'other' are the insiders who constitute the privileged group. Pickering (2001: 73) reminds us 'that those who are "othered" are unequally positioned in relation to those who do the "othering". The latter occupy a privileged space in which they define themselves in contrast to the others who are designated as different.' Thus some social statuses are valued, while others are devalued. For example, in Western society:

	VALUED	DEVALUED
Gender	male	female
Race	white	non-white
Language	English	other
Religion	Christian	Muslim
Sexuality	heterosexual	homosexual
Life cycle	adult	child and senior citizen
Education	educated	illiterate
Physical health	healthy	unhealthy
Ability	able-bodied	disabled
Mode of income	work	state benefits

	VALUED	DEVALUED
Housing	home owner	tenant
Marital status	married	unmarried
Family size	two children	childless or four plus children

It is necessary to untangle the processes by which this valuing and devaluing takes place to understand how particular social statuses come to be valued over others across time and social contexts. Otherwise, the normative basis of privilege remains untouched.

The naturalisation of privilege

The social divisions between the privileged and the oppressed are further reproduced through what is constituted as natural. Rather than seeing difference as being socially constructed, gender, race, sexuality and class are regarded as flowing from nature. Even gender and race, which one might suggest are surely natural differences, are socially formed. A belief about social hierarchy as being natural justifies social dominance and lets dominant groups off the hook for addressing social inequalities (Gould 2000).

In Part Two of this book, I will show how the various forms of privilege are socially constructed through the interactions between people in historical and cultural contexts and argue that it is the belief in the 'God-given' or biological basis of dominance that reproduces social inequality. Members of privileged groups either believe they have inherited the characteristics which give them advantages (for example, gifted intelligence or the will to compete) or they set out to consciously cover up the socially constructed basis of their dominance (Wonders 2000). This belief in the naturalness of inequality leads most people to accept and live with existing inequalities in the same way that we live within the laws of gravity. It is only when we understand that social inequalities are human creations designed to benefit a few that we can see the possibilities for challenging inequality.

Western culture rests on the idea that differences between people are based on essences (Martin 1994); that is, the belief that people have fixed, innate characteristics that we are born with. This may partly explain why oppositional groups in Western societies will sometimes essentialise dominance, as for example, in the radical feminist assertion that 'all men are oppressors'. Such a notion portrays men as unchanging and as inevitably oppressive just by virtue of the fact that they are men.

Part of the process of exploring dominant identities is to question how and why they appear natural: 'It means to lay open . . . their dependency on power relations and to particularise them' (Tillner 1997: 3). Perhaps, as Tillner suggests, it may be useful to represent non-dominant identities as 'normal' and dominant identities as 'particular' as a way of subverting the tendency for dominant groups always to represent themselves as 'the universal'. For example, naming of straight, white, middle- to upper-class men as a particular group of men will make it more difficult for them to universalise their human experience.

Privilege and the sense of entitlement

Members of privileged groups usually have a sense of entitlement to the privileges they enjoy. As Rosenblum and Travis (1996: 141) state: 'The sense of entitlement that one has a right to be respected, acknowledged, protected and rewarded – is so much taken for granted by those of us in non-stigmatised statuses, that they are often shocked and angered when it is denied them.'

Men's sense of entitlement can result in violence against women. As Connell (2000b: 3) puts it: 'From a long history of gender relations, many men have a sense of entitlement to respect, deference, and service from women. If women fail to give it, some men will see this as bad conduct which ought to be punished.' Some men will experience women's challenge to their entitlement as a threat to their masculinity.

It is necessary to understand more clearly how privileged group members' sense of entitlement is experienced and socially constructed. Adams et al. (1995), for example, identify the ways in which men use language to reinforce their assumptions about male dominance. Men construct what Adams et al. call a 'discourse of natural entitlement' that enables them to believe that they are designed to dominate women. These discourses are then used to legitimate men's use of violence against women.[2]

In reflecting upon my own situation as a white, academic man from a working-class background, I had come to believe that I deserved whatever benefits and status I had attained because I had struggled for them. As an academic whose background is working class, I was very conscious of the class barriers that I had to overcome, but I did

2. This issue is explored more fully in Chapter 5.

not recognise how my gender and race facilitated my achievements. We all need to critically reflect upon the ways in which we receive unearned advantages in our lives because of the consequence of those advantages for the reproduction of oppression. One of the purposes of this book is to encourage that process of reflection.

TWO

The matrix and social dynamics of privilege

This book emphasises how privilege is actively reproduced by members of privileged groups. Unless we examine the ways in which the privileged reproduce or resist their dominant positions, we avoid one of the most significant dimensions of personal, cultural and structural change. Towards this end, it is important to move beyond those analyses that focus on single strands of oppression and privilege. What is notable about much of the discussion about social inequality is that there is very little attention given to the intersections of class, race, sexuality and gender in the context of a globalised world. There are, of course, some important exceptions to this general neglect. At the time of writing (2009), it is twenty-five years since Wineman (1984) first criticised what he called 'single cause' and 'parallel' theories of oppression. It is worth revisiting his work at some length because I think that Wineman's critique of single strand theories of oppression has important implications for theorising the intersectional nature of unearned privilege.

Single cause theories of oppression view all forms of oppression as arising from one fundamental source. An example of this approach is the conventional Marxist analysis that places economic organisation and class oppression at the centre of the political world. Historically, Marxists have viewed all other forms of oppression, including sexism, racism and homophobia, as deriving from working-class class oppression. They are seen as 'secondary forms of oppression', used by the ruling class to divide the working class and fragment and prevent political mobilisation. Yet, class privilege is not the only form of privilege. I believe that this form of analysis lets many relatively privileged groups off the hook. For example, in this view, working-class men are not held responsible for their sexism or their homophobia.

Some people reject the centrality of class oppression, but they replace it with another single form of oppression. Some radical feminists may argue, for example, that male domination is the cause of inequality in economic, social and political relations. In this view, the most critical form of privilege is male privilege. White women's racial privilege could be overlooked in this view. These perspectives all claim that a single factor explains all forms of oppression. However, there is ongoing contestation between, for example, Marxists and radical feminists about which factor constitutes the primary dynamic.

Parallel theories suggest that different kinds of oppression run on distinct and parallel tracks from one another. According to this approach, diverse forms of oppression all involve comparable dynamics of domination and subordination. However, each form of oppression is caused and sustained by an autonomous set of political, economic, cultural and social factors that has a major effect on a distinct group of oppressed people. So class oppresses working people, racism oppresses people of colour, sexism oppresses women, and heterosexual dominance oppresses gay men and lesbians. The political implications here are to create single-issue movements that challenge only one form of oppression. This type of organising is sometimes referred to as identity politics. The flipside of this in terms of privilege would be to regard men, whites and heterosexuals as homogeneous privileged groups. The problem with this view is the inability to acknowledge the multiplicity of people's identities and the myriad of oppressions that confront them as a result.

An intersectional model recognises that different oppressions are distinct, but acknowledges that they are interrelated and mutually reinforcing. In this approach, any one form of oppression cannot be addressed alone. Since this intersectional approach has important implications for understanding the way in which different forms of privilege intersect with each other and with other forms of oppression, I will examine it in more detail here.

Towards an intersectional theory of oppression: anti-oppressive theory

African-American feminists and Third World scholars have extended the concepts of 'intersectionality' and interlocking systems of oppression (Collins 1991; Mohanty 1991). Many of these perspectives arose out of a critique of white Western middle-class feminism.

In the early 1990s, African-American and postcolonial feminists argued that white middle-class feminists gave insufficient attention to women of colour and working-class women and that they were unable to analyse the complexity of women's lives (Collins 1991;

Mohanty 1991). By failing to sufficiently acknowledge the experiences of marginalised women, gender relations were granted a primary status and other forms of inequality are seen as secondary. One of the results of this neglect is that women who were relatively privileged were insufficiently aware of the problems faced by working-class and black women (Zinn et al. 1986). To understand gender inequality, it is necessary to move beyond the experiences of middle-class white women to explore the impact of class and race on women's lives.

During the 1980s and 1990s, African-American sociologists explored how the intersections of race, gender and class impacted on the lives of marginalised people. The most sophisticated expression of the black feminist standpoint is the work of Patricia Hill Collins (1991); she documented the forms of resistance by white feminist women to black women's ideas and experiences. The black women's standpoint was based upon an Afrocentric feminist theory of knowledge that challenged the hidden white male standpoint represented in traditional scholarship. Collins and others emphasised the importance of seeing race, gender and class as 'interlocking systems of oppression'. These feminist perspectives, grounded in the diversity of women's lives, explored the interconnections between class, gender and race as they were experienced by women in specific contexts. Feminism, in particular, and critical social theory, more generally, are thus faced with the challenge to develop a theory that is able to address the complexity of how these different dimensions of women's (and men's) lives are woven together.

While class, race and gender have all been discussed in the social sciences, the intersections between them have not been developed in the ways that intersectional theorists would have hoped. There has been little attention paid to the ways in which these different dimensions of inequality overlap and, at times, contest each other.

Many authors write about the importance of exploring the interconnections between different forms of oppression, but there are no adequate theories that explain the ways in which these multiple oppressions intersect and reinforce each other. We have yet to develop an overarching theoretical framework that makes sense of how different forms of oppression interact.

A number of writers have argued against what they have called 'additive analyses' (Collins 1991; Schwartz and Milovic 1996; Razack 1998; Mullaly 2002). The effects of race, class and gender cannot simply be added on to make sense of people's lives. If, for instance, someone is a lower-income woman from a non-English-speaking background, this person is not likely to experience the single negative effects of being female, migrant and on a lower income. Rather, her experience is an outcome of the interrelationship between these different dimensions of her life as well as her individual preferences and inclinations.

While we should be careful not to suggest that any one system of domination is more important than another, we need to look at people's particular circumstances. The reality is that some forms of unearned privilege have more social consequences than others in specific contexts. Perry (2001: 49) says that 'in different contexts, in different institutional settings, one may be more visible or dramatic in its impact or different combinations might prevail'. Thus in some situations one may be more conscious of one's gender and in others more aware of one's race and so on.

At different historical moments, particular forms of dominance may assume greater or lesser significance within the wider socio-political context. Within these contexts, specific forms of privilege will become more significant than others and be more influential in relation to general life circumstances. These connections in intersectional analyses will shift as the historical conditions change.

It is also notable that most of the uses of intersectional analyses are focused on the intersections of oppression. As Acker (1999: 55) has observed, we 'know more about how gender, class and race are intertwined in the lives of members of relatively subordinate groups than we do about the lives of those in more influential positions'. Intersectional analysis needs to move beyond the study of those who are subordinate on all levels of social division to explore the experiences of those who occupy positions of both privilege and subordination, as well as those who are multi-privileged. This is important if we want to understand how those with privilege reproduce the oppression of others.

To make things more complicated, many people experience both oppression and privilege. Not all men, for example, benefit equally from patriarchy and not all white people benefit equally from racism. This means that most people cannot be categorised solely as privileged or oppressed. Many people may have access to some forms of privilege and not others. So while men may be privileged in some situations, some will be marginalised in others. While working-class men, for example, may exercise power over their female partners at home, in the context of paid work they will be dominated by foremen and bosses. In the light of this, as different dimensions of privilege and oppression can be more easily revealed through an intersectional analysis, I adopt this framework in this book.

Towards an intersectional theory of privilege: a critique of anti-oppressive theory

What an intersectional analysis makes clear is that almost everyone at some point in their life experiences both privilege and oppression. Black feminist criticisms of feminism draw attention to the fact that while white women are oppressed by their gender positioning, they also receive privileges through their whiteness. Similarly, I would add, that while working-class men are oppressed by class, they still receive some forms of gender privilege. These examples demonstrate just two of the ways in which one may be both privileged and oppressed at the same time. Collins (1991) coined the phrase 'the matrix of domination' to describe the way in which oppression operates on three levels: the personal, the cultural, and the structural. People were seen to 'experience and resist oppression' on these levels. This matrix approach can also be used to help understand how people reproduce or challenge privilege on these three levels.

Perhaps because of the pain of oppression, many people find it relatively easy to identify their experience of subordination, but find it harder to recognise how their thoughts and actions oppress others. This is because privilege is so normalised in wider society. Given that most people can be seen to exhibit some degree of both penalty and privilege, it is equally necessary for individuals to see themselves as belonging to privileged groups as well as to oppressed groups.

We have to move beyond these static categories to realise that many people who are oppressed also have access to some forms of privilege. Some people may struggle against their oppression, but, at the same time, maintain their access to various dimensions of privilege. To understand this better, Razack (1998: 159–60) suggests that we reflect upon those times 'when we are dominant and those when we are subordinate' to identify the ways in which the processes of domination and subordination interact. She gives the example of Western women reproducing their dominance when they try and save non-Western migrant women rather than organising 'against the racism that structures migration'. Such a project requires that we recognise our own involvement in the oppression of others. We can begin to do this by reflecting on what it feels like to be privileged or to be a member of a dominant group. If we have consciously enacted some form of oppression, we can also tune in to how it feels. This will be difficult but it will assist us to bring our privilege into conscious awareness.

Most writers who explore multiple forms of oppression fail to factor in forms of domination and privilege. This tension between oppression and privilege may inhibit the potential for struggles against oppression. The implication of this contradictory location is that different members of oppressed people may be pulled in different directions. On the one hand, some people will be encouraged to focus on their oppression, while, on the other hand, others will be encouraged to reproduce their privileged position. Gender, race and class consciousness is not only developed by subordinate groups. Waite (2001: 200) refers to this tension as the conflict between 'hegemonic and oppositional consciousness'. The risk is that if oppressed groups are only concerned about their oppression, they may entrench the oppression of others, as in the examples of gay men oppressing lesbians and black heterosexuals oppressing black gay men. Social movements that challenge only one form of oppression may reinforce other forms of oppression. This leads to what Waite (ibid.) calls 'one dimensional oppositional consciousness'. When people are able to define themselves in terms of one form of oppression, they may not feel the need to acknowledge themselves as benefiting from other forms of oppression.

In most people's thinking about oppression, people are either privileged or subordinated and they ignore complexities and contradictions. This can lead to the tendency to excuse abusive practices by oppressed groups because they are seen to be related to the experience of domination. Thus, for example, homophobia among black people may be seen as the product of racism and, consequently, diminish the responsibility of black people to address it. An intersectional analysis can help to deal with this complexity and assist oppressed groups to challenge exploitation and domination in their communities.

I should issue a word of caution here. As those groups who are both oppressed and privileged start to examine their privilege, care needs to be taken that they are not asked to take more than their share of the responsibility for the reproduction of privilege. Razack (1998) observes, for example, that white women's writing is judged more harshly than white men's writing. Some feminist writers, such as Mackinnon (1991), take this further to challenge the notion that white women are privileged at all. However, I think that groups who are oppressed on one dimension need to acknowledge their complicity with other relations of domination and subordination. To understand this, they need to locate themselves in the social relations of domination and oppression. If everyone were simply privileged or just subordinated then the analysis of systems of privilege would be easier. But most people live their lives with access to privilege in some areas, while being subordinate in others. Thus we are never just a man or a woman or a black person or a white person. We all experience these intersections in our lives.

At what stage does oppression on one dimension limit the access to privileges on another dimension? For example, it raises the question of whether the experience of oppression by gay men cancels out their male privilege or simply modifies it. A theory is needed that acknowledges that many people may experience both privilege and oppression in their lives, resulting from their multiple positions in the social divisions of inequality. Such a theory would need to address the complex question of whether, in some instances, some forms of oppression are so severe as to negate any benefits that one might experience from forms of privilege and not treat this as a zero-sum exercise. It is certainly clear that white middle-class women are not protected against sexism and that white middle-class gay men are not protected against homophobia. How does the class and racial privilege in this example mediate the sexism and homophobia?

Intersectional theory recognises that diversity and difference within a privileged group are complex. Therefore, challenging white privilege in a given situation cannot always be sensitive to the hierarchies within whiteness. For example, when people confront the white domination of their workplace and note that an overwhelming number of workers are white, they need to recognise that white workers also belong to subordinate groups: some are women, some are disabled, some are lesbians. Intersectional theory requires that we acknowledge hierarchies among privileged groups.

It requires that people who are oppressed not only struggle against their own oppression, but also confront their own privilege and internalised dominance. This places the onus to change on those with access to multiple levels of privilege. In advocating a greater level of responsibility by members of dominant groups for the maintenance of privilege, I also acknowledge that an understanding of privilege necessitates a structural analysis that identifies the systemic nature of privilege. In other words, privilege is not just something people can choose to ignore and reject, but can also be utilised in order to contribute to social change.

Fraser's theory of redistribution and recognition

In the last thirty years, class politics and struggles around distribution have waned and identity politics and recognition claims have escalated. Issues of mal-distribution are concerned with the unjust allocation of wealth and material resources. Misrecognition is focused on discriminatory practices towards people on the basis of their gender, sexuality, race or ability (Fraser 2003). As Fraser points out, social theorists have polarised these two forms of political struggle to the point where they are regarded as mutually exclusive. Fraser argues both forms of politics are needed if we are to attain social justice. While all oppressed groups face injustices associated with both distribution and recognition, the causes of injustice will vary from unjust economic and social arrangements for some and a lack of recognition regarding others.

Taking gender domination as an example, Fraser (ibid.) argues that theorists need to address both the structural issue of the gendered division of labour and gender divisions within paid work along with the cultural values that privilege men and masculinity and devalue women and femininity. Racial domination is similarly positioned, being based both in the economic structure of society as well as in the Eurocentric privileging of whiteness. Even in relation to the Marxist analysis of class domination, where the major cause of injustice is located within capitalist social relations, there are also forms of misrecognition associated with classism and class elitism. Discussing heterosexual domination, Fraser locates gay and lesbian oppression primarily within cultural forms of heteronormativity and heterosexism. She also acknowledges that there are resulting consequences of mal-distribution of resources, as well, that impact on the material lives of gay men and lesbians. Although Fraser does not discuss disability, Dandermark and Gellerstedt (2004) propose that disabled people constitute a bivalent group similar to gender and race.

While some forms of social division, such as class for example, will need to be completely dismantled because it cannot take an egalitarian form, other forms of difference, such as gender and sexuality, can potentially be detached from systems of privilege, although this is not without contestation. For example, there is a tension between those strategies that are aimed at democratising gender and those that challenge the existence of fixed gender categories (Cooper 2004).

While there have been many critics of Fraser's conceptual framework (Honneth 2003; I. Young 2008; Butler 2008), mainly associated with different perspectives on the nuances in the relationship between the economic and cultural spheres, I find Fraser's argument for acknowledging the importance of both forms of political struggle, without ignoring the tensions between them, is highly relevant to the project of undoing privilege.

Fraser (2008) has more recently extended her conceptual framework beyond redistribution and recognition to encompass what she calls representation. This involves changing the frame for social justice struggles from the modern territorial nation state to a globalised world. Inspired by the alternative globalisation activists of the World Social Forum, she emphasises the need for trans-border struggles against transnational sources of injustice, arguing that social justice cannot be achieved within national borders while global injustices persist and vice versa.

Fraser recognises that different axes of oppression intersect and that individuals need to be involved in struggles for redistribution and recognition in different arenas. She challenges the dominant sociological view that the economy and culture are separate spheres, arguing that social practices are both economic and cultural. While Fraser's framework embraces both the structural and the cultural and thus straddles the divide between the materialist and the post-structural, there is little consideration given to the interpersonal and psycho-social aspects of oppression in her analysis. Since oppression is also psychically imbedded, psycho-social interventions need to be examined alongside structural and cultural analyses.

The internalisation of dominance and privilege

To address the deficit in Fraser's theory, a concept that is useful to explain some of the ways in which privileged people sustain their dominant position is 'internalised domination', defined by Pheterson (1986: 147) as 'the incorporation and acceptance by individuals within a dominant group of prejudices against others'. This may explain, in part, why members of privileged groups may unwittingly or unconsciously reinforce the oppression of others. However, Tappan (2008) argues that internalised domination overemphasises the psychological aspects of dominance and obscures the institutional and structural dimensions of privilege. He proposes the notion of 'appropriated domination/privilege' as a way to combine psychological and sociological insights. It highlights the fact that psychological factors are part of the explanation of why dominant ideologies of Eurocentrism, class elitism, patriarchy, white supremacy, heterosexism and ableism are appropriated by privileged groups.

Tillner (1997: 2) usefully takes the notion of internalised domination a step further by defining dominance 'as a form of identity practice that constructs a difference which legitimises dominance and grants the agent of dominance the illusion of a superior identity'. In this process, the identities of others are invalidated. Thus dominance is socially constructed and cognitively and psychically internalised. To challenge dominant identities, an explanation of different models of identity is needed, so as to construct subjectivities that are not based on domination and subordination. In Chapter 9, I explore the extent to which this is achievable.

Social constructionism acknowledges that it is not possible for members of dominant groups to escape completely the internalisation of dominance. Negative ideas and images are deeply embedded in the culture and it is unlikely that men, whites and heterosexuals will not be affected by sexism, racism and homophobia. As noted earlier, prejudice is not necessarily always consciously enacted by members of dominant groups but more subtly woven into our consciousness.

Bourdieu's (1977) work is helpful in explaining how various forms of inequality are reproduced and internalised, that is, socially constructed. He formulated the term 'habitus' to explain how a system of stable psychological dispositions lead people to see the world from a particular perspective. Unlike Marxist and radical humanist views, which outline how people's ideas and consciousness are shaped by dominant ideologies, Bourdieu emphasises how dominant ideologies are also incorporated into the body so as to influence behaviour at an unconscious and habitual level. They are then experienced as a form of 'second nature'. He argues that dispositions are 'beyond the grip of conscious control and therefore not amenable to transformations or corrections' (Bourdieu 2001: 95). Bourdieu regards a person's habitus as a result of his or her structural location or position, whereby he or she internalises the structural context of his or her life. This concept of habitus can usefully explain the ways in which dominant groups come to internalise prejudice towards others.

The concepts of internalised domination, appropriated privilege and habitus thus help us to understand the seeming paradox that Minow (1990) identifies in relation to those who publicly criticise social inequality, while at the same time engaging in practices that perpetuate these inequalities. While she emphasises the task of examining and reformulating our assumptions about the social world, she acknowledges that this requires more than individuals learning to think differently because of the ways in which the individual's thinking is shaped by external institutional and cultural forces.

Privilege cannot thus be explained merely by internal psychological processes, where some people come to see themselves as superior to others, or solely by external sociological analyses which show how social structures and processes reproduce social differences. Privilege is socially constructed through psychological *and* social processes. So while it is important for individuals to acknowledge the privileges they have and to speak out against them, it is impossible to simply relinquish privilege. As Brod (1989: 280) notes, in relation to male privilege, it involves challenging the social divisions that perpetuate privilege which is used consciously or unconsciously to oppress others.

> We need to be clear that there is no such thing as giving up one's privilege to be 'outside the system'. One is always in the system. The only question is whether one is part of the system in a way that challenges or strengthens the status quo. Privilege is not something I take and which I therefore have the option of not taking. It is something that society gives me and unless I change the institutions which give it to me, they will continue to give it to me and I will continue to have it, however noble and egalitarian my intentions.

Given the complexity of the issues facing members of privileged groups, how might people respond when challenged about their privilege? How might they be convinced to live their lives in ways that are congruent with egalitarian values and beliefs? It is understandable to want to sidestep these hard questions. It is also easy for people to feel despair when they are constantly challenged by subordinate groups. Are there any ways of resolving these dilemmas?

Privilege and positionality: feminist standpoint theory

As suggested earlier, those in dominant groups are more likely than those in subordinate groups to argue that existing inequalities are legitimate or natural. It is often seen as understandable that privileged groups will further their own interests with little concern for the implications for others. Social psychologists Sidanius and Pratto (1999) formulate the notion of 'social dominance orientation' to explain why people value hierarchy and non-egalitarian relations between people. They argue that people develop an 'orientation towards social dominance' by virtue of the power and status of their primary group. They further maintain that dominant groups act in their own self-interests more than subordinate groups do and are encouraged to do so. In their view, human beings have a 'predisposition' to form hierarchical social relations. They argue that this social dominance orientation is largely a product of one's membership within dominant groups, although they seem to allow that some members of dominant groups may identify with subordinates.

It certainly seems to be that most members of privileged groups defend their privileged positions. In this context, government interventions aimed at addressing inequality and mobilisation by oppressed groups (important as they both are) seem unlikely to fundamentally change the social relations of dominance and subordination. So, what likelihood is there that members of privileged groups might form alliances with oppressed groups? What would encourage them to do so?

Just as oppressed groups have a range of strategies available to them to respond to their oppression, Dominelli (2002) observes three strategies that dominant groups can use to respond to concerns or questions about their privilege: demarcationalist, incorporationist, and egalitarian. Demarcationalists view the world through a hierarchical lens and endeavour to hold on to and increase their power and resources to maintain their privileged position. Incorporationalists may support incremental changes, but they also want to retain existing social divisions. Egalitarians reject the social order that grants them privileges because they recognise the injustice associated with their position. However, this is not so easy in practice and the rejection may not be wholesale.

This does not explain why privileged groups ought to develop a critical distance from their privilege. For this, it is necessary to turn to feminist standpoint theory that has its origins in Marxism. It was adapted by feminists and also embraced by gay and lesbian theorists, indigenous scholars, disability activists and postcolonialist writers. Developing knowledge grounded in the experience of oppressed groups, they sought to provide a critical stance against dominant

Eurocentric, patriarchal, class elitist, racist, heterosexist and ableist conceptual frameworks (Harding 2004).

Feminist standpoint theory posits a direct relationship between people's structural location in the world and their understanding of the nature of the world. A standpoint is seen to involve a level of awareness about an individual's social location, from which certain features of reality come into prominence and from which others are obscured. It is said that the further one is from the centre of power, the more comprehensive one's analysis will be. This is because those who are marginalised have to understand the viewpoint of the dominant groups, while those in the dominant position have no need to understand the perspective of the oppressed. A researcher's standpoint thus emerges from his or her social position and the way in which these factors interact and affect his or her everyday world (Swigonski 1993: 179).

While standpoint theory validates the experiences of the oppressed and encourages collective resistance against oppressors (Harding 2004), it is also useful for dominant groups to critically interrogate the ways in which their own world views and practices sustain the oppression of others. Harding (1995), for example, argues that standpoint theory encourages members of dominant groups to develop knowledge that serves the interests of subordinate groups. In this view, it is possible for members of dominant groups to develop the capacity to see themselves from the perspective of those in subordinated groups. However, dominant groups do not always form a homogeneous network of shared interests. It is thus possible for members of dominant groups to challenge the taken-for-granted self-interests of their own group. This is consistent with my experience of constructing a profeminist men's standpoint in researching the experiences of men (Pease 2000). I critique patriarchal dominance from within the experiences of white heterosexual profeminist men by examining how men who are supportive of feminism are responding to the feminist challenge.

Bailey's (2000) argument that members of dominant groups can develop what she calls 'traitorous identities' adds support to this position. She distinguishes between those who are unaware of their privilege and those who have a critical consciousness of their privilege. Thus traitors are those who refuse to reproduce their privilege and who challenge the world views that dominant groups are expected to adhere to. These dominant group members are able to identify with the experiences of oppressed groups. It is from this basis that white people will challenge racism and that men will challenge patriarchy. So from this premise, while it is difficult for members of privileged groups to critically appraise their own position, it is not impossible.

The process of developing a traitorous identity involves learning to see the world through the experiences of the oppressed. This may not be fully possible, but members of dominant groups can make a choice about accepting or rejecting their part in the establishment. Lakritz (1995: 7) discusses the dilemma facing the postcolonial critic 'who on the one hand declares herself to be on the side of social justice . . . but who on the other hand speaks from a position of the elite – the class against which the subaltern is defined'. What happens when one faces this dilemma? Is determination to be on the side of the oppressed enough? Lakritz suggests that rather than speaking *for* the marginalised, it is better for members of privileged groups to talk about their experiences of *engaging with* the marginalised. How are their lives transformed by their experiences of hearing their stories of oppression and exploitation?

Lugones and Spelman (1998) have articulated the challenge to 'outsiders' who speak for the privileged. Such outsiders are challenged to make their writings accountable to the marginalised and to immerse themselves in their cultures and their communities so that they may learn about their lives and about themselves. Members of dominant groups who have started to develop some awareness of their privileged position often look to oppressed groups to educate them. In doing so, however, they reproduce their dominant position and do not take responsibility for their own learning. While it is important that members of dominant groups make their practice accountable to oppressed groups, they also need to take initiative in challenging their own and others' privilege.

What does it mean when profeminist men who challenge patriarchy are listened to more than feminist women who challenge patriarchy? Alcoff (1995) has discussed at length the dangers of speaking for others. These dangers, she argues, are concerned with both the limitations on understanding arising from the structural location of the speaker and the impact that the privileged speaking position has on the already subjugated position of the marginalised. As she says: 'Persons from dominant groups who speak for others are often treated as authenticating presences that confer legitimacy and credibility on the demands of subjugated speakers . . . such speaking for others does nothing to disrupt the discursive hierarchies that operate in public spaces' (ibid.: 99). It can, in fact, reinforce those barriers that prevent the marginalised from having their own voices heard. When feminist colleagues and I have presented papers together on men's responsibility for challenging male violence, I have been concerned when my voice has been given more credibility than theirs.

These dangers ought not to lead us to the view that members of privileged groups should only speak for themselves or that they should remain silent. This has been the soft option that well-meaning liberals have articulated for many years. It is an option that lets privileged groups off the hook. Perhaps one of the most damaging aspects of privilege is the privilege of doing nothing, or of not speaking out about injustice. Privileged group members can decide to ignore the struggles of the oppressed. They have what Wildman and Davis (2000: 659) call 'the privilege of silence', which may be one of the greatest abuses of privilege.

From a social justice perspective, members of privileged groups have a responsibility to critically reflect upon their own position. From my standpoint, it is even more important for those who are privileged to challenge themselves and each other than it is to work with oppressed groups. The view that one's structural location determines absolutely the meaning of an individual's speech must be challenged. That is, the fact that people have privilege does not mean that they will inevitably reproduce that privilege when they speak. Rather, members of privileged groups need to be aware of the ways in which their speaking positions can be oppressive and dangerous and, at the same time, not retreat from political work that is contentious. After all, what could be more privileged than positioning oneself in a way that is beyond criticism? As Alcoff (1995: 110) says:

> The pursuit of an absolute means to avoid making errors comes perhaps not from a desire to advance collective goals but from a desire to establish a privileged discursive position wherein we cannot be undermined or challenged and thus become master of the situation.

A popular men's movement activist in Australia has taken to threats of legal action towards those who criticise his work and he refuses to discuss disagreements with his ideas in his workshops. From this position, we would not be required to monitor or critically reflect upon our practice and would not be subject to the scrutiny of others.

Interrogating personal privilege

While the positioning of all speakers needs to be articulated, it is even more important for members of privileged groups to critically reflect upon their own positions. Privileged academics seem to be more interested in studying subordinate groups than they are in studying the groups to which they belong. Numerous books written by radical academics seem oblivious to the privileged basis of their own position. Academics rarely focus their critical gaze upon themselves. They rarely seem reflexive about their own privileged position. Yet they are enmeshed in the social relations of dominance and subordination that they criticise. They too are likely to have internalised dominance in varying degrees. Thus, in this book, I endeavour to enact the reflexivity that I advocate. However, I am aware that in writing this book, some might say that I am suggesting that I am above reproach. I expect that in the writing, I will no doubt, at times, replicate that which I am criticising. The very act of writing a book on privilege is itself a form of privilege.

As an academic, I am part of the established order. This is not solely a question of choice. Although I teach courses and write articles and books on dominant forms of masculinity and privilege, I still benefit from gender, race, class and sexual privilege. As Currie (1993: 23) notes, 'The real challenge to self-acclaimed "radical" scholars is whether we take our own critical analyses seriously enough to help displace our privileged position – not simply in the text, but in the production of what becomes accepted as "truth" and as knowledge.' In what ways does the academic discourse exclude the voices of marginalised people? Is it enough simply to be critical of one's positioning, while doing nothing to change the material conditions that produce it? Obviously not, but if we own our positionality (where we stand in relation to class, gender and race) we at least challenge the view that the white, middle-class, male perspective represents some form of transcendent truth. To challenge this ethos, more white middle-class males need to read and reflect upon the writings by those who are marginalised and they need to learn how to listen to the experiences of marginalised people. Furthermore, the more that academics as members of privileged groups work against their own privilege, they make it harder for others to discount the experiences of subordinate groups as simply advocating their own self-interests.

Privilege as structured action: doing dominance

It is through the processes of 'accomplishing' gender, race and class and other forms of social division that dominance is reproduced. That is, people live their lives trying to attain certain valued aspirations associated with these statuses. Thus rather than seeing concepts like race, gender and class as reified categories, there is a need to understand the processes of gendering, racialising and classing as Fenstermaker and West (2002: 75) have done. They set out to analyse how race, gender and class constitute 'ongoing methodical and situated accomplishments'. They analyse how people conduct themselves in specific situations to understand how they legitimate and maintain social divisions in society.

Messerschmidt (1997: 4), similarly, in discussing crime as 'structured action', emphasises how 'the social construction of gender, race and class involves a situated, social and interactional accomplishment'. Gender, race and class are thus a series of activities done in specific situations. Messerschmidt acknowledges that these 'accomplishments' are shaped by structural constraints. However, because they involve accomplishments enacted by human agents, it is possible to resist the reproduction of social structures. Talking specifically about men, for example, Messerschmidt (2000: 81) argues that masculinity is something that has to be accomplished in specific social contexts. It is 'what men do under specific constraints and varying degrees of power'.

Perry (2001) draws upon this notion of 'structured action' to explain hate crimes. She illustrates the way in which the concept of structured action is useful in understanding how people construct dominant identities more generally. By acting in ways that live up to the normative expectations of one's race, class and gender, one is not only constructing one's gender, one is also said to be 'doing difference appropriately' and thus reproducing the boundaries that divide dominant groups from the 'other'.

When people act in the world, they are not just operating within structural constraints that are outside their control. Rather, they are also determining the nature of those structures through their actions and interactions. The structures that oppress are not only contextual, they are also constituted through human actions. While people construct their identities through their action, they also reproduce relations of power and domination. The implication is that they can challenge those arrangements by engaging in 'inappropriate' racial or gender behaviour. Herein lies the impetus for social change because individual actions can make a difference.

Various commentators have argued that structured action neglects the structural dimensions of inequality. Maldonado (2002: 85), for example, says that there is insufficient acknowledgement of 'the constraints imposed by the macro-level forces in the social environment'. O'Brien and Howard (1998: xiv) argue that this 'obscures institutional and structural power relations'. Weber (2002: 85) says that Fenstermaker and West obscure 'the mechanisms of power in the production and maintenance of racism, class and sexism' because their 'exclusive attention to face to face interaction, macro social structural processes such as institutional arrangements are rendered invisible'. In Weber's view (ibid.), the structural dimensions of social inequalities cannot be transformed by 'the attitudes and actions of a few actors in everyday interactions'.

While it is important to acknowledge the significance of locating class, gender and race relations in the context of institutional structures, it is also important to accept, as Thorne (2002: 85) does, that 'gender, and race, class and compulsory heterosexuality extend deep into the unconscious and outward into social structure and material interests'. Face-to-face interaction and social structural analyses are not necessarily in opposition to each other. It might be useful to establish a duality of micro and macro forces for analytic purposes, but structure and action need not be mutually exclusive or in opposition to each other. Because I am interested in opposition, resistance and change, social action that challenges the processes of 'differentiating persons according to sex categories, race categories and/or class categories . . . undermines the legitimacy of existing institutional arrangements' (Fenstermaker and West 2002: 99). When we challenge the dominant conceptions of manhood, whiteness and heterosexuality from within, we undermine the stability of these analytic categories.

O'Brian and Howard (1998: 25) capture the complexity well when they say that 'we are socially constituted subjects who navigate webs of opportunities and obstacles not necessarily of our own choosing'. Furthermore, the concept of interlocking oppressions must involve a recognition of both 'macro-level connections' at the level of social structures and 'micro-level processes' which describes how individuals experience their positions within the hierarchies of domination and oppression. In challenging the dichotomisation of micro and macro forces, the dynamic and reciprocal relationship between social structure and social action must be recognised. While social structure is reproduced by the widespread and continual collective actions of individuals, it also 'produces subjects'. So individuals do not simply produce gender, race and class in a vacuum. Rather, they are reproduced and constrained by institutional settings such as families, workplaces and the state. Experientially, we know that there are limits to our ability to enact different expressions of our multiple identities.

Hence I seek to move beyond the conflict between those approaches that emphasise human actions and those that emphasise structural determinants. One of the main implications of this analysis is that we must investigate privilege at interactional, cultural and structural levels at the same time that we explore the intersections of privilege with oppression. In Part Two of this book I use this framework to interrogate privilege in six intersecting sites of domination.

PART TWO

Intersecting sites of privilege

THREE

Western global dominance and Eurocentrism

Writing a chapter on Western global dominance, I need to locate myself geo-politically at the outset, as invariably my own positioning will influence the writing of the chapter and the rest of the book. I am a non-Indigenous man who grew up in the 1950s in Australia. Notwithstanding the internal social divisions of class, gender, race, sexuality and disability, many non-Indigenous Australians enjoy high standards of living, health care and education compared to most nations of the world (Habibis and Walter 2009). Thus I reside in one of the most affluent and developed countries in the West.

There are numerous theoretical explanations given to explain inequalities between countries. World systems theory, which views countries as occupying interdependent roles in a world economy, is perhaps the most enduring notion (Wallerstein 1974; 2004). In this view, the most developed nations that control most of the world's capital flows have gained their prominent place historically due to conquest, protective trade policies and economic support from the state. Less developed nations are caught in a dependency relationship with developed countries through foreign debt, import and export patterns and the practices of multinational corporations (Wallerstein 2004).

In the 1980s, the concept of imperialism was used to frame our understanding of global hierarchies in which some nations oppressed and exploited others. Neo-Marxist theories of imperialism drew attention to the domination of a small group of industrialised nations over the Third World (Sutcliff 1999). However, as Amin (1989) points out, the term 'imperialism' was seen by many as too ideological and unscientific. Thus so-called objective terms like 'transnational capital' and 'international capital' arose. From a more politicised perspective, the language of 'neo-liberalism' has recently been used by commentators to describe policies that increase the power of wealthy countries over those of the rest of the world.

A number of writers have recently argued that the current world system is significantly shaped by a form of 'new imperialism' (McLaren and Farahmandpur 2001; D. Harvey 2003; Midgley 2008). This new imperialism combines elements of the old form of military and economic interventions in the affairs of other countries with the framing of the capitalist market as the best of all possible worlds (McLaren and Farahmandpur 2001). Many books have been published in the last few years proclaiming that individualism, consumerism, capitalism and liberal democracy will foster prosperity and peace throughout the world (Midgley 2008).

The mechanisms of the World Bank and the IMF ensure that multinational corporations intensify the dependency of Third World countries through debt and foreign aid (Sutcliff 1999). To most people in the developed world, news items about the World Bank and the International Monetary Fund (IMF) mean very little. Although the anti-globalisation protest actions are reported on the news, relatively few people grasp the issues at stake. Yet, as Danaher (2001) reminds us, in his manifesto of ten reasons to abolish the IMF and the World Bank, these two organisations, which represent the wealthy nations of the world, are making policies for (and against) the whole of humanity. Thus the IMF and World Bank decide the fate of the world's poorest nations. While decisions are based upon the maximisation of profits for the minority, rather than the meeting of human needs for the majority, the root causes of global inequality are never going to be addressed.

Globalising privilege

In recent years, there have been several books on privilege published in North America (Hobgood 2000; Kimmel and Ferber 2003; A. Johnson 2006). None of these books identifies North American privilege that accrues from living in one of the most powerful, developed and affluent countries in the world. While these writers set out to heighten readers' awareness of the invisible forms of white, male and sexual privilege, for example, the privileges associated with their own geopolitical location are not named and interrogated.

Much of the recognition of privilege and oppression is framed within a taken-for-granted, geographically bordered sovereign state (Fraser 2008). Working for social justice, all too often, addresses only citizens within national borders, with little consideration given to the way in which privilege within those geographical boundaries is likely to impact on those outside of them. Just as there is growing recognition among some progressive social movements that injustice must be targeted across national borders, so, too, the recognition of privilege must be understood within an international or global frame.

Schwalbe (2002) notes that non-Western, foreign university students in North America tend to know more about the United States than most North American students. This is because non-Western students' lives are shaped by the policies of the United States government and the diffusion of North American cultural hegemony, whereas North American students do not have the same need to understand the policies of their own government or those of non-Western countries. The reality is that most Westerners are simply unaware of the impact of the West on non-Western countries (Bonnett 2004; Gray and Coates 2008). Like most of my contemporaries, I grew up in ignorance of the privileges associated with my geo-political position. In my lifestyle, my professional practice and my political work, unwittingly I perpetuated a Eurocentric vision of the world.

The idea of the West[1]

To understand global privilege, it is necessary to interrogate the concept of 'the West', which has been presented as an ideal model of progress for all countries in the world. Developments in the West are seen as flowing down to inspire traditional societies along similar routes of progress (Slater 2004).

Modernisation is a concept used to describe the growing gap between the industrialised countries of the West and the impoverishment of the non-West (R. Marks 2002). The premise is that all countries of the world should adopt the values that informed the rise of the West. This belief in the superiority of Western values and rationality is what constitutes the myth of Eurocentrism, which Marks argues is no more than an ideology that distorts the truth and

---

1. Mohanty (2004) notes that terms like West and East and North and global South focus on countries in the northern and southern hemispheres, they do not totally capture the divisions between affluence and deprivation. Jolly (2008) further argues that these geographical terms tend to dehistoricise and naturalise inequalities between nations. Kothari (in Harcourt 2007) believes that these terms have become meaningless because there is growing affluence in some parts of the South and extensive deprivation and disadvantage in parts of the North. Notwithstanding these inequalities within countries, it is still meaningful to use these terms to analyse institutionalised inequalities in wealth and power between nations.

masks Western global dominance. In fact, the greatest power that the West has is not its economic and technological supremacy, but its power to define what is progress and ultimately what it means to be human (Sardar 1999a).

While Western culture portrays itself as the only culture that is capable of engaging in a reflexive critique of it own accomplishments (Slater 2004), there is very little indication of reflections about the premises of Western superiority. On the contrary, Western dominance is sustained by what Slater refers to as 'imperial knowledge'. By this, he means a belief in the need to intervene in other 'less-advanced' societies, a belief in the legitimacy of imposing Western values on non-Western societies and a belief that non-Western cultures are inferior and consequently that their rights can be legitimately denied. Thus Western supremacy requires the silencing of non-Western cultures and demonstrates no interest in learning from these cultures.

Of course, it is understandable that the West will view history from a European perspective. This ethnocentrism would not be such a problem if the West accepted that it was simply one of many ethnocentric views of the world. However, it is the claim of the West's universal applicability of its culture to the rest of the world that constitutes it as Eurocentrism. Western countries refuse to acknowledge that their claimed superiority is based on their values and their biased perceptions of the past. Rather, they claim to base their superiority on scholarship and scientific evidence (R. Marks 2002).

A number of writers have challenged the view that the West pioneered the modern world, arguing that the West and East have been historically interconnected. In this view, the East has played an important role in the development of Western civilisation (Blaut 1993; Gran 1996; Hobson 2004). R. Marks (2002) provides an alternative historical account of the origins of the Western world and demonstrates how the West was able to present itself as progressive, while constructing Asia, Africa and Latin America as backward. Hobson (2004) also illustrates how many so-called Western concepts have Eastern origins. Similarly, Narayan (2000) challenges the view that concepts such as human rights, democracy and equality are Western. Hence, it is not simply a matter of imposing Western values on to non-Western cultures, but rather the propagation of the myth that these concepts have solely Western origins that reinforces Western supremacy.

If Western supremacy is to be challenged, it is necessary to question the rational and scientific premises of modernisation and technological development. Sardar (1999a) believes that such challenges must come from the non-West, as they formulate and advocate new concepts. This does not imply uncritical acceptance of all that comes out of the non-West. However, there will need to be a capacity on the part of the West to engage with and respect determinations that are different from their own.

If the gap between the wealthy and poorest nations of the world is to be eliminated, a move beyond Eurocentric understanding of the modern world is needed. This means endeavouring to get outside Western ways of knowing and acknowledging that such ways of knowing are Eurocentric.

Moving beyond Eurocentrism

Essentially, Eurocentrism involves the belief that Europeans are superior to non-Europeans. Blaut (1993) refers to it as 'the colonizer's model of the world' because it is premised on the view that European civilisation has superior qualities associated with race and culture compared with non-Western cultures. Western culture is also predominantly white culture. While the dimensions of white privilege are explored in Chapter 6, it is necessary to establish here that there is a direct link between Western expansion in the world and the concept of whiteness. Thus there is a close connection between Western global dominance and white cultural influences (Shorne 1999).

While all countries that constitute the West are capitalist, there is a need to mask this historical and culturally specific formation to avoid any suggestion of alternatives. Thus the West is presented as the best of all possible worlds. The economic development of the West must then be portrayed as a transhistorical social formation based upon eternal truths and instrumental rationality (Amin 1989). Dominant ideologies in the West legitimate capitalist societies as the only possible form of economic and political relations. Eurocentrism then grows out of colonial domination and provides a legitimation of inequalities between nations (Gheverghese et al. 1990).

Amin (1989) refers to Eurocentrism as a form of prejudice that distorts theoretical understanding. However, Western social sciences are so embedded within Eurocentric assumptions that most social scientists are unaware of their European bias. Eurocentrism underlies all social science disciplines, including history (Gran 1996); sociology (Connell 2007); psychology (Naidoo 1996); social work (Midgley 1983); urban theory (McGee 1995) and geography (Blaut 1993). To challenge Eurocentrism is to question the taken-for-granted assumptions that underpin all Western social science disciplines.

Blaut (1993) raises questions about the term 'Eurocentrism' because it implies a form of prejudiced attitudes. If that is so, then it can be eliminated through enlightened thought. However, Eurocentrism functions not just as a matter of attitudes, but rather is founded on beliefs informed by scholarship and science and it purports to be based on scientific and empirical evidence. If this is so, then it is validated as a form of truth about the world. Highly educated and supposedly unprejudiced Europeans are consequently not likely to critically interrogate the assumptions underpinning it.

Non-Western intellectuals have also been influenced by Eurocentrism. They are encouraged to borrow theoretical constructs and categories that have value in Western societies and relate them to their own context where their value may be questionable (Gheverghese et al. 1990). This raises difficult and complex issues when progressive Westerners encounter these developments. In 1988, I was a member of a small Australian delegation to an Asia and Pacific Social Work Conference in Beijing that was to launch the first social work course in China. As someone who was committed to local knowledge and culturally grounded social work practice, I supported efforts by Chinese academics to develop their own conceptual frameworks for social work theory and practice. However, a number of leading Chinese academics who founded the course had undertaken their PhDs in North America and adapted North American models of social work and psychology to the Chinese situation. I found myself in the uncomfortable position of promoting local knowledge that went against the views of some Chinese delegates who had cognitively adopted North American models of theory and practice.

A more inclusive form of world history requires recognition that Eurocentric world views are only appropriate to understanding the West as a historical and cultural construct. A non-Eurocentric history involves developing a more holistic understanding of global issues. Western social science understandings of the non-West requires decolonising practices and locally based scholarship (Gray and Coates 2008).

Orientalism: constructing the non-West

One of the most significant early challenges to Eurocentrism was Edward Said's *Orientalism*, first published in 1978. Orientalism is 'a body of ideas, beliefs, clichés or learning about the East' (Said 2003: 205). It forms the basis of representations of the Orient in Western consciousness. However, it is not simply a body of knowledge about non-Western societies. Rather, it involves an ideological construction of the Orient that is mythical and transhistorical. It further presents characteristics of the East as immutable and in opposition to the West (Amin 1989) and proclaims the inherent superiority of the West over the East (Hobson 2004).

Thus Orientalism goes beyond the disciplines and practices associated with the study of oriental societies. It involves an epistemological and ontological approach, which sets up a polarised division between the Orient and the West (Turner 1994). The West is portrayed as productive, hard-working, mature, honest and progressive and the East is constructed as the opposite of these values. Said (2003) demonstrates how this process of 'othering' maintains unequal power relations throughout the world and provides the legitimation for Europe to 'manage' the Orient.

Through Orientalism, the West perpetuates its dominance over the non-West by attributing essences to both the Orient and the Occident. Orientalism becomes a colonialist method of subjugation because it legitimates colonialist interventions (Sardar 1999b). Twenty-five years after the first edition of his book, Said (2003) argued that his analysis still holds true. Orientalism fuelled the anti-Islam views that were propagated under the presidential administration of George Bush in North America. While the West continues to be appropriated by neo-liberal capitalism that supports military interventions into non-Western countries, anti-Western sentiment will continue to influence the rise of radical Islamism (Bonnett 2004).

Although Said's work has been criticised by some as an anti-Western polemic, it does not set out to portray the West as evil. However, some have argued that in response to the debates about Orientalism, a form of Occidentalism arose where everything to do with the West was subjected to critique. Turner (1994) says, for example, that it is inappropriate to regard all Western analyses of the Orient as negative. Otherwise, all Indigenous and non-Western frameworks would have to be accepted as legitimate. This may, in some cases, promote political conservatism and equally distorted and prejudiced views of the West.

Said is also accused of portraying the West as monolithic and unchanging (Sardar 1999b). If all Western intellectuals are Orientalist, then does that mean that there is no progressive thought in the West? There were and are counter-hegemonic intellectuals in the West who were opposed to colonialism and who resisted imperialism and ethnocentrism (McLeod 2000). Paranjape (1993) makes the point that it is important to acknowledge that the West is a divided entity and not a monolith. It is ideologically and ethically divided in relation to the global South. Hence, it is possible to forge alliances with progressive groups within the West to promote more socially just relations.

The poverty of development

A number of development writers have noted that after more than thirty years of development programmes and foreign aid, the poorest countries of the world are worse off than they were before Western interventions (Verhelst 1990; Escobar 1995; Tucker 1999; Munck 1999). Esteva (in Harcourt 2007) has noted that in 1960, the rich countries had twenty times the wealth of the poor countries. Twenty years later, following development interventions, they were forty-six times richer. Today the gap is even wider. Given these outcomes, one must ask whether the dominant model of Western development is part of the problem. This is especially so in the context of espoused individualistic and capitalist accumulative principles rather than re-distributive and justice-based principles.

White European men wrote the history of development and established the foundations of truth that are universalised for all (Munck 1999). As early as the 1970s, critics of development were identifying the Eurocentric assumptions underpinning modernisation and Westernisation and how these interventions had increased the dependency of non-Western nations on the West. Not only had they failed to improve the living conditions of those in the non-West, they had actually intensified the poverty and hardship faced by the masses in these nations.

Peet and Hartwick (1999: 1) posit that development 'is a founding belief of the modern world'. While Western affluence was propagated as a dream for all, the reality was that it was only achievable for a few. Tucker (1999: 1) defines development as 'a process whereby other peoples are dominated and their destinies are shaped according to an essentially Western way of conceiving and perceiving the world'. Thus in this view development is connected to imperialism where developed countries impose their control over non-Western countries. This control operates not just in terms of economic processes, but also in relation to cultural meanings about the nature of the world. Tucker challenges the view of development as a natural and transcultural process, arguing that it is premised upon Western myths. Modernisation theories of development invalidate the cultures of traditional societies and impose a Western model of progress upon them whereby the imitation of the Western model of development is presented as the only solution to the growing gap between the wealthy and poorest countries of the world. Tucker points out that slavery, genocide and colonialism have all been legitimated under the guise of progress.

The challenge to those in the West to become aware of their Eurocentrism and their monocultural prejudice is not new (Verhelst 1990). However, it would appear that many NGOS that claim to be in solidarity with the people of the non-West have failed to heed this challenge. This may be due in part to the fact that development has become an industry. People are educated and credentialed at universities to work in the development sector. Thus development practitioners establish comfortable and well-paid careers. Horn (in Harcourt 2007) says that there is a tension between unpaid, mass-based social movements for social justice and the salaried end of the development sector.

In the last few years, a number of publications have documented the experiences of Western development workers who went to non-Western countries to 'help', only to discover that what they had to offer was not what was needed. Subsequently, as they developed awareness of their own assumptions and the assumptions of the programmes they were embedded within, they wrote about the failures of dominant models of development (Danaher 2001; Boulet 2003; Goudge 2003; Bolten 2008). Danaher (2001) reflects on how he was once told by a grassroots activist in Africa that, while it was appreciated that he came there because he wanted to help, if he really wanted to help, he could do more by going back to his own country and working to change government and corporate policies which supported undemocratic leaders in non-Western countries.

There is an ongoing debate about the effectiveness of foreign aid and whether it is allocated fairly. For many years, anti-development writers have been arguing that foreign aid entrenches the privilege of wealthy groups. However, at the time of writing, Peter Singer had just published a book arguing why people in affluent countries should donate money to aid agencies to fight world poverty (Singer 2009). He provides a compelling moral argument to persuade affluent people that they should not purchase luxury goods once their basic living costs have been met, but should instead donate excess money to save lives in non-Western countries. In contrast, Moyo (2009) argues that foreign aid to Africa has increased corruption and despotism and done nothing to address poverty.

Easterly (2007) has challenged the utopian agenda of trying to use aid to eliminate poverty and change political systems. He argues that the best aid can do is to improve the lives of the poor in practical and material ways. Like many development economists, Easterly seems to regard the problem of aid as having more to do with problems in social engineering rather than with corporate globalisation. Chang (2007), in contrast, argues that the rich countries, in alliance with the IMF and the World Bank, use aid to force developing countries to develop neo-liberal policies in their own countries.

Goudge (2003) argues that foreign aid not only fails to help the non-West, but also that it also falsely creates the impression that the West is doing something when it is not. An alternative to aid is to change the international trading system to benefit poorer countries. Held and Kaya (2007), for example, point out that agricultural subsidies provided in rich countries are ten times the total amount of aid given to Africa. Thus a number of writers have argued that changing the agricultural subsidies given to farmers in rich countries to supplement their income would provide more concrete benefits to poor countries (Milanovic 2007).

Furthermore, Gronemeyer (1995) asks people to reflect upon their responses if they knew someone was coming to their home with the expressed purpose of doing them some good. Citing Thoreau, she suggests that one would run for their life in case some of the good was done to them. Gronemeyer demonstrates how the concept of 'helping' the non-West has become an instrument of power with its own self-justification. Goudge (2003) distinguishes between specific forms of help that are requested and help that is imposed on others using Western theories and methodologies.

Shiva (1993) observes that whenever countries in the North intervene in the lives of people in the South, their interventions are premised upon a notion of superiority, usually legitimated on the notion of the 'white man's burden'. If the crisis in the South were to be overcome, it would require a decolonisation of the North whereby its Eurocentric assumptions and internalised dominance were critically interrogated.

The argument here is that as important as it is to be aware of the exploitative role of the IMF and the World Bank and the interventionist policies of Western governments, people must also engage in the more painful step of acknowledging their own personal Western privilege (Goudge 2003). How do the individual actions of Westerners reproduce global inequalities? Goudge argues that the more individuals in the West gain benefits from the exploitation of poorer nations, the greater their responsibility for doing something about it. The ecological argument is 'live simply so that others can simply live'.

Conspicuous consumption in the West

In recent years, numerous books have been published on over-consumption patterns in the West. Such books demonstrate the relationship between what we consume and who we are. The purchase of furniture, cosmetics, wrist watches, home entertainment systems and designer clothes are all used to highlight our status (Schor 1998). We are also encouraged to believe that having material possessions and wealth are important to improve the quality of our lives. Increasingly, research demonstrates that the pursuit of materialistic goals does not increase the levels of happiness (Kasser 2002). Rather, it sustains people's insecurities and negatively impacts on their relationships and psychological well-being. In fact, many in the West seem to be highly dependent upon their material possessions and the high consumption patterns in their lives. Hamilton and Denniss (2005) and James (2008) use the term 'affluenza' to describe the desire that people have to make more money and purchase more possessions, explaining such consumption patterns as a form of addiction.

While most of the books on over-consumption in the West focus on the consequences of materialistic values for the Western individual, few books examine the link between affluence in the West and the problems of global poverty and ecological unsustainability. There has been growing evidence for some time that the material consumption that supports average lifestyles in the West is ecologically unsustainable and grossly unfair in terms of global inequalities (Westra 1998; Rees 1998). In 1996, Wackernagel and Rees developed the 'ecological footprint' to measure human impact on the earth and to estimate the resource consumption and waste production of people within particular societies. While we are all encouraged to calculate our 'ecological footprint', it is another step, however, to measure how many times the resources of others in the South are required to support individual lifestyles in the West.

It comes as no surprise that a person's ecological footprint is directly related to his or her wealth and income. Those in rich countries have the largest ecological footprints. United Nations statistics state that 80 per cent of the goods and services produced from the resources of the earth were consumed by the wealthiest 20 per cent of the world's population (Wackernagel and Rees 1996). A baby born in the United States will consume twenty times the resources of a baby born in Africa or India during their respective life times (Sagoff 2008). While the wealthiest 20 per cent owns 87 per cent of motor vehicles in the world, the poorest 20 per cent owns less than 1 per cent of motor vehicles. The top 20 per cent of wealthiest people consume 58 per cent of the energy of the world compared to the poorest 20 per cent consuming less than 5 per cent (Hossay 2006).

There is a fundamental contradiction here between international development goals that are aiming to lift the standard of living in Southern countries towards those in the North and the reality that the global ecosystem cannot sustain current consumption patterns. This is not to argue that gross domestic product in poor countries should not be improved, but rather to suggest that current standards of consumption in industrialised countries will have to be reconsidered (Wackernagel and Rees 1996). Thus it would appear that effectively to address the destruction of the global ecosystem, we will also need to challenge the global inequalities in the distribution of wealth. At the time of writing (September 2009), there is still a standoff between the wealthy countries and poorest nations in relation to climate change. Understandably, the poor countries do not want to limit their own choices while the wealthy countries, which produce the greatest amount of greenhouse emissions, fail to develop and meet appropriate targets for greenhouse reduction.

Many of those who want to help the poor in developing countries do not want to compromise their own lifestyles and consumption patterns. It will come as a shock to some when they realise that consumption patterns in the North are undermining prospects for those in the South to improve their standard of living. Consumption in the North will have to be reduced to enable the poor to increase their share (Wackernagel and Rees 1996). Goudge (2003) challenges white

Westerners to consider the part they play in maintaining unequal power relationships. Acquisitiveness and greed in the West, she argues, are among the main causes of poverty in the non-West.

It is the unexamined belief in Western superiority that people believe gives them the right to consume a disproportionate share of the earth's resources. Those of us in the West thus need to confront the views we hold about our superiority and the rightness of our actions. We need to reconsider our role in the accumulation of material goods and to reflect upon our own consumption patterns. Our responsibility may lie more in challenging our own lifestyles than working to change the lives of others (ibid.).

No governments in the West seem prepared to put a case for modifying consumption patterns in their respective countries. In all the discussion papers on climate change and global warming published in Australia (and in other Western countries), there is no suggestion that we should challenge economic disparities between rich and poor countries. While the West continues to increase its consumption patterns by purchasing goods produced cheaply in the non-West and simply regards non-Western countries as exotic holiday destinations, global injustices will continue.

Deconstructing epistemological privilege

Dominant forms of knowledge provide the resources for colonialism and oppression. If global inequalities are to be effectively challenged, it will be important to address the epistemological underpinnings of these inequalities. As Santos et al. (2007: xiv) state, 'there is no global justice without global cognitive justice'. They contest the epistemological privilege granted to Western science and document the ways in which it suppresses Indigenous forms of knowledge.

Scientific knowledge is unable to accept diversity in knowledge systems. Santos et al. (ibid.) refer to this suppression of alternative knowledge systems as 'epistemicide'. In contrast to the monocultural form of scientific knowledge, Santos et al. propose an 'ecology of knowledges' to embrace a diversity of different systems of knowledge around the world.

To decolonise and democratise knowledge, it will mean that those in the North would need to be open to learning from the South and be open to recognising a plurality of knowledges about the world and our experience of it. To be open to a dialogue about epistemologies, one would have to accept that all knowledge systems, including Western science, are incomplete (ibid.). Postcolonial studies, Afrocentricity, Indigenous knowledge and Southern theory are four alternative discourses that have been developed to challenge the power of Western knowledge and allow alternative voices to be heard.[2]

Postcolonial studies: constructing anti-colonialist practices

Whereas imperialism is concerned with military, economic and diplomatic affairs, colonialism is at present more concerned with the transforming of local cultures and the minds of exploited people (Bar-On 1999). Postcolonialism refers to the body of work that focuses on issues arising from colonialism and its aftermath (Kirkhaum and Anderson 2002).

McClintock (1992: 87) suggests that the term postcolonial is 'prematurely celebratory' and that it may obscure the continuities of colonialism. Shohat (1992) argues that the term postcolonial implies that colonialism has been surpassed. However, McEwan (2001) emphasises that postcolonialism does not imply a shift from colonialism to after-colonialism. Rather, it involves a critique of the discursive and material legacies of colonialism. In this sense, postcolonial perspectives might be more accurately called anti-colonialism.

Subaltern studies is a good example of anti-colonialist practices arising out of critiques of colonialism in India. It was developed in the 1980s by Indian academics as a response to the top-down approach to Indian history (Bahl 1997). The term subaltern is used to signify the subordination of people in relation to caste, class, gender, language, culture and race. The focus was to provide a form of history from below and to challenge the elitism in academic work in South Asian studies (Prakesh 1994).

Over 150 million people in India, who constitute the 'untouchables', live in extreme poverty as a result of the caste system (Mendelsohn and Vicziary 1998). Caste has been the source of considerable controversy and debate. While some argue that caste is a product of colonialism and imperialism, others maintain that it is located within Indian culture (Bayley 1990). The dynamics of caste cannot be understood as a variant of class and racial hierarchies (ibid.). Although the Indian

2. There is a vast literature in all of these four areas of scholarship. I cannot do justice to the extensive debates within each field of study. My aim here is simply to provide an introduction to them as non-Western forms of knowledge development.

caste system is distinct as a form of social hierarchy, the cultural, moral and biological justifications for caste privilege are commonly used to defend various forms of hierarchy and inequality. Many of the studies of the caste system in India have been undertaken by Western writers (Dumont 1980; Bayley 1990; Mendelsohn and Vicziary 1998; Dirks 2001), some of whom have defended the system of caste. Dumont (1980) argues that caste has a basis in nature and that Western commentators who advocate equality are often unable to understand the ethical justifications for caste inequality.

Many Indians are committed to casteless egalitarianism and have been involved in campaigns against caste oppression. Such campaigns have been theorised and validated through Dalit studies, which is an integral part of subaltern studies.

The impact of subaltern studies has extended well beyond India to inform studies in Latin America, Africa and Europe. Thus subaltern studies endeavours to address the marginalisation of Indigenous and local knowledge under the conditions of colonialism. In this context, it is one of the challenges to the impact that colonialism has had upon the development of alternative forms of knowledge.

Subaltern studies draws from both Marxism and poststructuralism. This has been a source of controversy, as some have argued that the move to adopt postmodern and poststructuralist ideas have de-radicalised the transformative project (Chakrabarty 2000). In fact, in more recent years, subaltern studies has been charged with moving away from documenting the experiences of the poor and instead privileging the views of elites (Connell 2007). Bahl (1997) argues that subaltern studies ignores the material working and living conditions of people's lives, and by ignoring these material conditions, the proposed solutions are said to be individualistic.

This 'either-or' debate continues to surface in all fields of progressive politics between those who focus on material conditions (redistribution) and those who give priority to culture and dominant discourses (recognition). Furthermore, we see the same divisions between those who focus on difference and diversity and those who emphasise the commonalities of people's lives based on material conditions (ibid.).

This study is less concerned with the debate about whether strategies for resistance to colonialism are best conceived as neo-Marxist or poststructuralist (Hiddleston 2009). Rather, the focus is on the denouncing of the ethnocentric modes of thinking that underpin colonialist and imperialist ideologies.

Postcolonial studies has also been subjected to hostile criticism from various quarters. A number of commentators have suggested that postcolonial studies has given insufficient attention to class, gender and sexuality (Kirkhaum and Anderson 2002). Questions have also been raised about how postcolonial critics in the West can avoid dictating the shape of postcolonial studies, given their privileged positioning. Some have argued that postcolonial studies has become institutionalised within Western universities (McEwan 2001) and as a result, the colonised and oppressed have been excluded from having a voice.

While postcolonial studies is focused on strategies to develop anti-colonial consciousness among colonial subjects (Loomba 2005), of particular concern in this context is how one develops an oppositional consciousness among those in the West to undermine colonialism. How can the unequal relationship between Western scholars and non-Western scholars be addressed?

There are numerous appraisals of the philosophy and politics of postcolonial writers (Loomba 2005; Hiddleston 2009) and the conclusions reached about its potential to bring about radical change. While cognisant of the debates about the shortcomings and potential of postcolonial studies as a disciplinary field, nevertheless it has highlighted some of the major legacies of European imperialism and Eurocentrism.

Afrocentrism and the validation of African experience

Eurocentric theories of society and human behaviour have 'vilified people of African descent and other people of colour' (Schiele 1996: 286). Thus Western social science is a vehicle of domination that has biased knowledge about African people. African scholars have constructed an Afrocentric framework as a response to Western bias towards people of African descent.

Bakari (1997: 1) defines Afrocentrism as 'a modern way of knowing based on ancient African experience' based upon communalism, ethics, cooperation and spirituality. It aims to reconstruct the narratives, spiritualities and myths of African people's lives (Monteiro-Ferreira 2008). Unlike the Eurocentric focus on individualism and individual identity, the African sense of identity is located within a communal space (Fennell and Arnot 2009). Controversially, Afrocentricity relies more upon non-scientific knowledge, including mysticism and tradition (Pellebon 2007). In fact, spirituality is a foundational premise of Afrocentrism.

Most Afrocentric writing comes from North America where African American and African-diasporic scholars seek to make sense of the African experience of the world (Bakari 1997; Schiele 2000). There appear to be differences in the expression of Afrocentrism in North America and in Africa (Njeza 1997) and there is more popular support for Afrocentricity outside Africa.

Bar-On (1999) argues, for example, that the application of Western social work models in Africa continues the colonisation of Africa by the West that was begun with the work of Western missionaries. He is alarmed by the extent to which African social work academics have accepted Western ideas and practices and have rejected their own traditions. This has come about, in large part, because many Africans studied social work in the West and consequently 'became Western themselves' when they returned to Africa (Bar-On 1999: 17). Thus Western social work has unconsciously become part of the Eurocentric hegemony.[3] In response to the Eurocentric bias of social work and human services practice in North America, Schiele (1997) proposes the development of an Afrocentric approach to human services based upon the philosophical concepts, traditions and experiences of African Americans (Schiele 2000).

Afrocentrism has been criticised from many quarters. Some critics challenge the notion of cultural unity in Africa. Connell (2007) critiques the African philosophical tradition for its assumptions about static culture and nationalist thought. She emphasises the danger of founding contemporary knowledge on traditional cultural beliefs. However, the critical question is whether an acknowledgement of heterogeneity and diversity in Africa necessarily invalidates an Afrocentric perspective (Njeza 1997; Schiele 2000).

Afrocentricity is also criticised for being homophobic and sexist. Akbar (1992) and Asante (2007), for example, argue that homosexuality is against the values of Afrocentricity. Mutua (2006a) is also concerned that some expressions of Afrocentricity focus on the issues facing black men at the expense of the plight of black women. In fact, some suggested strategies of male empowerment rely upon the subordination of women (Mutua 2006b).

---

3. See also Osei-Hwedie (1993) on to the impact of Western knowledge on social work in Africa.

Some critics charge Afrocentricity with ignoring class analysis and class domination. Williams (2005) notes that in rejecting Marxism, Afrocentrists also reject a realist epistemology. In doing so, they are unable to address structural arrangements and institutionalised inequalities that shape the life chances of Africans. By focusing solely on culture as the primary source of racial oppression, they end up focusing on attitudes and consciousness as the major basis of change. Dick (1995) maintains that Afrocentrism is unable effectively to address Eurocentrism because it does not acknowledge the political and economic determinants inherent within capitalism. Rather, it focuses solely on the cultural manifestations of Eurocentrism. Akinyela (1995) also argues that Afrocentricity focuses too much on racial domination and does not address political and economic power differences and other forms of oppression such as sexism and heterosexism. For many of these critics, Afrocentrism is not able to address intersectionalities in the construction of African identity.

Defenders of Afrocentricity argue that critics are simply imposing Eurocentric Western concepts on to a perspective that has different philosophical assumptions (Schiele 2000). Certainly, some of the critiques of the Afrocentric perspective are predicated upon Eurocentric premises and seek to defend Eurocentric hegemonic thought (Conyers 1996; Schiele 1997). Further, many critics fail to acknowledge the Eurocentric and colonialist context which gave rise to Afrocentrism in the first place.

Some Afrocentric writers have responded to the critiques by expanding the Afrocentric perspective to include other conceptual frameworks. Oyebade (1990), for example, believes that Marxism can be incorporated with Afrocentrism to analyse how Africa's economy is dominated by the global economy of the capitalist West. Akinyela (1995) argues for the development of 'critical Afrocentricity' that develops strategies against the multiple forms of oppression that African people experience.

Making space for indigenous knowledge

Fennell and Arnot (2009) note that the universalising agenda of modern knowledge is up against Indigenous knowledge. Indigenous knowledge relies upon a spiritual as opposed to a scientific understanding of the world. Tuhiwai Smith (1999) emphasises how Indigenous knowledge involves a different understanding of subjectivity, time and space, which is at odds with the scientific approach to understanding the world.

While there are differences between Indigenous people around the globe, there appear to be common understandings about a holistic approach to the world that embraces spirituality and harmony with the land (Briskman 2007). Tuhiwai Smith (1999) identifies the relationship with the land as the distinguishing feature of the clash between Western and Indigenous belief systems. Attitudes to the land are fundamental to Indigenous knowledge systems, whereas in Western culture, disconnection from the land is the norm (Hawthorn 2002).

Many forms of Indigenous knowledge are not recognised within a Western science paradigm. Rather they are regarded as forms of superstition and expressions of irrationality. Hence, Western international agencies operate on the premise that they have 'good' knowledge that will address the problems that people in the non-West experience.

Western social work, for example, has been increasingly challenged by Indigenous and anti-colonialist writers for reproducing Western imperialism. More than twenty-five years ago, Midgley (1983) wrote about what he called professional imperialism in social work. The widely held belief that social work was based on universal values and was applicable to all societies was rarely challenged. He echoed the views of many Indigenous activists that such an approach constituted a Western liberal framework that was incompatible with Indigenous cultures. While the world has changed dramatically since then, and there has been substantial writing about these issues over the years, Midgley (2008) argues that professional imperialism in social work (and one could argue in other Western professions as well) has not been adequately addressed.

In the context of increasing awareness of globalisation, many universities in the West were encouraged to indigenise their curricula to acknowledge the diversity of cultural experiences. However, Gray and Coates (2008) point out the difference between indigenisation of the curriculum in professional education courses and supporting Indigenous practice. The former involves finding ways to import Western knowledge to the cultural particulars of a specific country or population group, as opposed to affirming the knowledge of Indigenous cultures.

Traditional research epistemologies constructed within the West have also come under criticism by Indigenous and postcolonial scholars. Rigney (1999) says that research epistemologies should be critiqued in the context of colonialism and racism. Mutua and Swadener (2004) argue that research itself can be considered to be a colonising construct. Clearly, as a result of different histories, experiences, values and cultures, Indigenous people are likely to interpret reality and the world differently (Rigney 1999). Thus they should explore the implications of anti-colonial epistemologies and methodologies to validate their local knowledge and experiences.

A number of writers have identified the significance of Indigenous knowledge as an important resource for developing strategies of social change (Rigney 1999; Yang 2000; Foley 2002; Kincheloe and McLaren 2005). Tuhiwai Smith (1999) provides an extensive critique of Western paradigms of research and knowledge from the position of a Maori woman. She challenges traditional Western ways of knowing and calls for a 'decolonisation of methodologies' by developing new non-Western epistemologies and methods of inquiry. Writing in the Australian context, Foley (2002) documents how the British system of knowledge eliminated Indigenous knowledge, traditions and cultural practices. He puts the case for the acceptance of Indigenous knowledge and Indigenous standpoint theory.

The writings of Indigenous people validate alternative ways of knowing and provide a basis for oppositional practices against Western imperialism (L. T. Smith 1999). Thus to challenge Eurocentrism we will need to recognise the struggle of Indigenous people to affirm and validate their knowledge.

Southern theory and Northern dominance

Connell (2007) demonstrates how the social sciences, which represent ideas as universally valid, reflect the views of the global North. When the privileged North claims that its knowledge and values are universal, it becomes part of a hegemonic project. Northern theory builds on the work of a privileged minority of people in the world and then assumes that it is valid for the majority of the world's population. In Connell's view, this entails a perspective shaped by privilege and affluence that is then extended to include marginalised and subordinated peoples across the globe. This process of producing and circulating knowledge further reinforces Northern dominance and Southern marginalisation.

Connell (ibid.) demonstrates that a close reading of mainstream social theory reveals its ethnocentricity, as it pertains specifically to the issues facing Northern societies. Theories arising from the colonised world are rarely cited in general social science texts published in the North. Thus important ideas about the world in the South are neglected in mainstream social science. Furthermore, colonial experience and its associated social processes are usually erased from Northern social theories.

Although Connell's book is focused on sociology, similar books have been written on other social and behavioural sciences and professional disciplines as well. Connell (2006) acknowledges that her own earlier work shares most of the dimensions of Northern theory. I would say that this is also true of my own major work (Pease 1997a; 2000; 2002a). It is only in recent years that I have acknowledged the global dimensions of masculinities and endeavoured to address the white Western bias in masculinity studies (Pease and Pringle 2001; Flood et al. 2007).

To address this issue, Connell argues that it is important to reconstruct the relations between the North and the South to allow for shared learning. Therefore, it is important to circulate knowledge and experiences that come out of non-Northern geo-political contexts. If social science is going to live up to its function of social critique, it will need to produce knowledge that informs democratic social movements and challenges the control of knowledge by the privileged.

Five years before Connell, Canagarajah (2002) wrote a book from a Southern perspective addressing the concrete practicalities of trying to get ideas from the South published in the North. He documents his own attempts, and those of his colleagues in India, to get scholarly work published in mainstream academic journals. He similarly argues that knowledge produced in 'third world communities' is marginalised and appropriated by the West. Many of Connell's arguments are rehearsed in Canagarajah's work. He writes about how the mainstream publishing domain reproduces the intellectual hegemony of the West. Furthermore, he documents how Western interventions in marginalised nations often get it wrong because they are informed by Western paradigms. Ironically and significantly, it is Connell's book rather than Canagarajah's that will be most widely read.

Conclusion

The struggle of oppressed groups is as much about validating their world views as it is about empowerment and equal rights (Schiele 2000). If we are to avoid the imposition of the Western world view on to non-Western nations, the West will need to interrogate the historical basis of its own discourse and be open to other ways of organising social relations (Tucker 1999). The challenge is how Western academics such as myself can decentre ourselves and our knowledge systems in ways that challenge existing unequal power relationships. Young (1990) alerts us to dangers of developing an awareness of Eurocentrism without disrupting Western privilege and the dominant power base.

Most commentators agree that it is essential to establish a dialogue between the West and the non-West. But the challenge is how to engage in this dialogue in the context of Western hegemony and unequal power relations. The West must find a way to avoid assuming an a priori normative high ground and be prepared to submit the premises underpinning its own social sciences to reappraisal (Tucker 1999).

The aim of this chapter has been to find ways to decolonise the minds of those of us from the North. To do this requires learning to see ourselves through the lives of others (Bulbeck 1998). As most of the readers of this book are likely to be Western,[4] the challenge is to engage in what Bulbeck calls 'world travelling': understanding the lives of others to question the dominant practices of Western culture. Boulet (2003) reminds us that there is much to learn from Indigenous knowledge systems and cultures 'less developed' than our own.

Esteva and Suri (1998) argue for the development of an 'epistemological humilty' that is able to recognise and accept limits to scientific knowledge. This means challenging the notion that only Western knowledge is legitimate knowledge. In a similar vein, Hawthorn (2002) emphasises the importance of an 'epistemological multiversity' where the context and real-life experiences of people are valued.

This work on recognising Eurocentrism and Western privilege must be located within the wider alternative globalisation movement. Anti-globalisation struggles have been framed as a confrontation between the global South and the global North (Santos 2007). Such struggles are not against globalisation per se. Rather, the focus is on challenging neo-liberal globalisation from alternative, counter-hegemonic forms of globalisation from below (ibid.) or what Danaher (2001) calls 'people's globalisation'.

---

4. As I stated in the preface, because the book is targeted at those with privilege, in this case Western privilege, I address readers in the West. However, I also hope that the book might invoke interest in the non-West as well.

Danaher identifies the many dimensions of the work of the global justice movement, including downsizing Western materialism, fair trade, eco labelling, socially responsible investment, shareholder activism, alternative models of ownership, micro-enterprise lending groups and the corporate accountability movement. Many writers have encouraged local initiatives and small grassroots activism. Simple living based upon spiritual and ecological principles is encouraged.

These counter-hegemonic forces came together at the global level in the World Social Forum of Porto Alegre and have now spread throughout the world. The World Social Forum provides the basis for conceiving of alternative worlds that can coexist alongside each other. In a context where many people are endeavouring to protect and defend their privileges, others are trying to create a new world order.

The view from the South will experience the North as a homogeneous bloc (Connell 2006). Wealth and poverty are not defined by national boundaries. Just as pockets of wealth can be found alongside the wider impoverishment of the population in most countries of the global South, in the West, class-based and racially oppressed populations reside within the wider affluence and wealth of the general population.

Notwithstanding the need to globalise privilege and oppression, it is still, nevertheless, important to challenge forms of privilege within national borders as well. Wilkinson and Pickett (2009) suggest that egalitarian societies are more responsive to global injustices. Whereas, those societies that condone privilege within their borders will be less likely to recognise their Eurocentrism in the international arena. As we shall see in subsequent chapters, the North also contains many social divisions and complex inequalities based upon privileges within the nation state and country borders.

FOUR

Political economy and class elitism

Most discussions of class within critical theory focus on the possibilities and limitations of the proletariat as a force for progressive change in capitalist societies. While some argue that the working class has ceased to have any capacity to be an agent of social change, others maintain that it continues to be the only potentially revolutionary force in modern capitalist societies. How one answers this question depends in part on how one understands the changing composition of the working class. Given that more people work in community services and universities than in transport and construction (Donaldson 2008), does this mean that a new class of professionals and intellectual workers has emerged or do we need to broaden the definition of the working class to encompass the increase in professional occupations? The focus of this chapter is on the class identification and class politics of these professionals, many of whom consider themselves to be middle class because of their job, their education, their relative wealth and where they live.

While a few members of the owning class have become allies to the working class in class struggles, because of what they have to lose, many of them will be unlikely to be responsive to the arguments advanced here. This chapter is thus directed more to those who possess relative class privilege and questions how class privilege operates among those who are positioned between labour and capital. It asks how those who have some class privileges engage with their class positioning and classed subjectivity to act in a progressive way on class issues.

A personal narrative of class

At the outset, I should locate myself in relation to class. I am a university academic and a professional social work educator who grew up in a working-class household in inner Sydney in Australia. My father worked as a timber worker in factories throughout his working life, as did my older brother. When I turned fourteen, I was expected to leave school to work with my father in the timber yard. For the first five years of my working life, I engaged in physical labour amid the whirring machinery, noise and sawdust of the timber yard. A chance encounter with a woman from another class opened up an alternative pathway for me. So at the age of nineteen, I went to night school to complete the last four years of high school to enable me to go to university. I was the first in my extended family to gain a tertiary education and notwithstanding the completion of four degrees, including a doctorate, I always felt that I did not quite belong in the middle class.

My analysis of class is grounded in my own experience of upward social mobility. My foray into the middle class was an uncomfortable one for me. I remember when I first read Richard Sennett and Jonathon Cobb's *The Hidden Injuries of Class* (1972) how strongly I related to the experience of not feeling comfortable in any class situation. I mixed in middle-class circles with people who always assumed that university would follow the completion of my secondary schooling. However, while I read widely in the social sciences at university, my general vocabulary was more limited and this would become evident in relation to the use and pronunciation of certain words. When I spoke, my class markers were often evident. Some of these experiences of working-class discomfort in middle-class milieu are movingly described in anthologies of the experiences of university academics from working-class backgrounds (Tokarczyk and Fay 1993; Dews and Laws 1995; Ryan and Sackrey 1996).

What then is my class location? While I grew up in a poor working-class family, I am now a university academic. Am I working class or middle class? Given the qualifications I have attained, the control over my work and where I live, I would be regarded as middle class. However, I do not identify with that class positioning in terms of my interests and my political involvements. The irony for me was that as I studied critical social theory, I became more closely identified with my working-class positioning, just as I was moving away from traditional working-class labour.

My father thought that I betrayed my class by going to university, just as I was becoming politically active for the first time on class issues associated with homelessness and unemployment. I could relate to the views of the working-class young people in Paul Willis's (1981) study who had the talent to break away from their class, but chose not to because of what it would mean for their relationships with their family, their friends and their community. So my journey towards critical class consciousness coincided with my move from low-paid factory work to university education and later on to professional work. I entered a world of relative class privilege at the same time that I was developing a politically conscious working-class sensibility and coming to feel a strong allegiance to the struggles of working people.

Those of us who have experienced a degree of upward class mobility experience both privilege and oppression. By representing myself as middle class, I receive many unearned privileges. However, like Loomis (2005) in his account of growing up working class and moving into the middle class, I was also subjected to classist discrimination and I continue to carry some elements of internalised oppression associated with my previous class positioning.

Theorising class

There is a rich sociological literature on class, most of it published during the 1970s and 1980s. Thus there are numerous theories of class, including Marxist approaches (Westergaard 1995; Wright 1998); Weberian models (Goldthorpe 1980; Parkin 1983), stratification theories (Kerbo 2003) and cultural studies approaches (Bourdieu 1987b; Jameson 1991; Hall 1997).

Determining class membership is a matter of some debate, depending upon whether the focus is on income, educational qualifications, origins or workforce status (Brantley et al. 2003). In stratification theories, there are numerous levels of class distinction based on income levels and occupational status. In non-Marxist writings about class, relations of ownership and control disappear to be replaced by occupational categories and the working class is replaced by the language of 'the lower class' (Aronowitz 2004).

In a Marxist analysis, class location is determined by the relationship to the means of production. In this view, there are two main classes: the capitalist class and the working class. The capitalist class has control and ownership of significant amounts of capital and productive resources and the working class, which provides the labour, is dependent upon wages to survive. There are also intermediate classes that stand between these two classes, but they are not seen to be of historical significance or revolutionary consequence. Some Marxists argue that anyone who works for wages is a member of the working class, while others would argue that managers and professionals should be excluded because they have too much of a stake in the system. This is a question to which I will return.

At the time of writing (September 2009), there is a deep recession in the United Kingdom, North America and Australia, brought about in large part by the reckless actions of the chief executive officers of big banks. While there is understandable anger directed at the bankers, the economic crisis is generally presented as reflecting the individual weaknesses of the bankers and politicians rather than framed as a problem endemic to capitalism itself. There is little sense that these bankers and leaders of government constitute part of a ruling class (Connell 1977) that were engaged in socially structured economic exploitation.

While I adopt a structural Marxist understanding of class in terms of its relation to the means of production, I also believe that we need to understand the way in which class is subjectively experienced and reproduced in our lives. This means understanding the ways in which class is culturally constructed as well as structurally determined. Bourdieu's (1987b) analysis of class is useful here because he differentiates between economic and cultural forms of capital. He identifies the cultural capital accruing to people from their attainment of educational qualifications. He also outlines the importance of social capital based on group membership and connections. Those who hold these various forms of capital have access to legitimised power. Some forms of Marxism have under-emphasised the role that cultural capital plays in reproducing class-based oppression. However, cultural understandings of class are not necessarily in conflict with viewing classes as locations in social structure.

The most salient meaning of class is that which arises from specific class struggles, as it is choices and actions in relation to specific class interests that determine whether individuals are allies or not (Walkowitz 1999). This study is thus more concerned with whose class interests are served by our practices in the world than how we might fit into particular class schemas, even though our identities are constructed in terms of class-based experiences.

Whither class?

It is difficult to write about class in 2009. In the 1970s and 1980s, class was at the centre of analyses of social and economic inequalities. In the last twenty years or more, the debates about class have declined dramatically. Numerous academics have noted the marginalisation of class in social theory across a range of academic disciplines (Skeggs 1997; I. Ferguson 2002; Aronowitz 2004; Hollier 2004; Acker 2006b).

Some writers claim that class does not exist any more or that 'class is dead' (Pakulski and Waters 1996). I. Ferguson (2002) also observes that class is used more often than not in the Weberian terms of different levels of economic and bureaucratic power and prestige.

In the field of social work education where I work, there has been a lack of class analysis and a neglect of the impact of class on the lives of people. Searling (2008) has noted that class-conscious social workers are likely to feel some ambivalence about the social control practices in the profession and that such discomfort cannot be easily resolved. Perhaps this explains in part why class has been neglected in social work. Even much of the critical and anti-oppressive social work literature (Thompson 2006; Nzira and Williams 2007) does not address class and when it does, it tends to focus only on class as a source of discrimination and prejudice.

It is not only in social theory and professional education that class has been marginalised. Mantsios (2003) has noted in the United States how the majority of people do not talk about class oppression or the class-based nature of North American society. Most people do not experience their identity in class terms. Rather, the discussion is about the wealthy and the poor and such statuses are seen as immutable and natural rather than socially constructed. Between the wealthy and the poor are the middle class, where class differences are muted and class conflict and exploitation are avoided. The United States, the United Kingdom and Australia are regarded by many as classless societies.

Whither socialism?

The decline of class in social analysis can be understood in part as a response to the fall of the Soviet Republic and the dismantling of the socialist block in Eastern Europe. There has been considerable analysis in the last twenty years of the collapse of communism in Eastern Europe (Habermas 1990; Auerbach 1992; N. Robinson 1995; Kennedy and Galtz 1996; White 2001). Much of this analysis has focused on the consequences of the collapse of socialist regimes for Marxism and critical theory in the West (Habermas 1990; Kennedy and Galtz 1996). Does the end of state socialism mean that Marxism holds no inspiration for radicals who envisage a world beyond capitalism and neoliberalism? The collapse of communist regimes is used to argue that another world beyond capitalism is not possible (George 2004). If socialism is not a viable alternative to capitalism, what is the value of class analysis of capitalist societies?

Marxism has always had a fraught relationship with communist regimes. Western Marxists were critical of these regimes well before their collapse in the late 1980s because they sacrificed democratic ideals in the pursuit of centralised state power. The collapse of communist regimes should not be equated with the failure of Marxism as social theory. While communist states used Marxism as a form of legitimation, Western Marxists never regarded highly centralised political and economic power within an authoritarian state as an embodiment of the socialist alternative (Wright 1993). Thus the collapse of these regimes is not evidence of the failure of Marxism as a normative and theoretical framework.

In spite of the lack of logic in equating the demise of state socialism with the refutation of Marxism as a social theory, nevertheless, these events inevitably raised questions about the utility of class analysis and Marxist social theory. Many contemporary Marxists recognise that if Marxism is to continue to be useful in analysing capitalism, it will need to be reconstructed (Habermas 1990; Wright 1993).

It is thus important that Western Marxists engage with the relationship between the rise and fall of Communist regimes in Eastern Europe and Marxism as an explanatory social theory. This will mean confronting the reality that Marxism has been both neglected and rejected in Eastern Europe. This will be important if Marxism is to continue to provide inspiration for radical politics.

The myth of meritocracy and upward social mobility

Most people identify as middle class now, as everyone is purportedly getting richer through social mobility. The concept of the middle class allegedly embraces everyone with the exception of a few rich people at the top and a small number of poor people at the bottom (Aronowitz 2004). Over thirty-five years ago, Parker (1972) made the point that positing the notion of a homogeneous middle class ignored the differences between the upper and lower strata of that class. He could be writing today when he discusses the persistence of the 'myth of the middle class'. Such a notion of homogeneity serves both blue-collar workers, because it takes the 'sting' out of the reality of the class structure for them, while easing the conscience of the upper-middle-class professionals, because it posits that their privileges are available to everyone. The view that everyone is middle class is a myth that continues in spite of the fact that class differences seem so obvious.

In the view of many people, the term middle class has lost any connection to a notion of economic class. This lack of class identity limits the potential for professional workers to develop politically progressive responses to widening inequalities. Thus a middle-class identity that is devoid of class meaning is likely to be an obstacle to practices that promote social justice (Walkowitz 1999). Also, the problem with the language of the middle class is that it is just as likely to be the class of choice by manual workers as non-manual workers (Scott 2000). The majority of working-class people believe that hard work can enable them to achieve economic security and wealth. With the election of an African-America president in the United States, the rhetoric of anyone (whatever their class or race background) being able to succeed is further confirmed.

Burgmann et al. (2004) has noted that although the Australian Labor Party was traditionally the party of the working class, they do not use the language of class any more. During the Labor Party election campaign of 2004, the then Labor Party opposition leader Mark Latham promoted the notion of a ladder of opportunity whereby people could move up the ladder from their current position to improve their economic situation. The capacity of the Australian labour movement, both in terms of the Labor Party and the trade union movement, to mobilise working-class opposition has declined significantly over the last twenty years.

The same comment about the retreat from class has been made of British Labour's 'third way', where the language of 'social exclusion' has replaced class analysis and an acknowledgement of class divisions (I. Ferguson 2002). In New Labour's third way, it is clear that there is little room for recognition of class divisions or the undermining of inequality by class relations. The priority has been to combat social exclusion, a discourse that denies the validity of class analysis and the very existence of class divisions.

Various explanations have been offered as to why working-class opposition to capitalism has declined. Some have maintained that many workers have become stakeholders in the system that exploits them. Many working-class people have the resources to purchase their own home, late model cars and consumer goods (Aronowitz 2004). Some even have market shares in companies. Thus it is argued that working-class people will come to defend the system that protects their investments. Connell (2004) has noted that while many people own company shares, very few derive a significant income from such ownership. Yet the claim by some is that anyone can achieve wealth in Australia and that most of the wealthy are self-made millionaires (Gilding 2004).

In spite of this marginalisation of class as a sociological concept and as a subjective source of identity, the reality of living in a class-based society is all too central in the lives of many people, whether they frame their experience in terms of class or not. Research in the United States (Mantsios 2003), the United Kingdom (Cannadine 1999) and Australia (McGregor 1997) reveals immense variations in economic well-being. One's class status continues to have a significant impact on one's level of economic prosperity and vice versa.

From a structural point of view, one's location in the class structure shapes access to material resources, including material comforts, the physical demands of one's work and one's diet and health. Numerous studies demonstrate the impact of class upon our health and life chances (Wilkinson 2005). Working-class people die younger and experience more ill health than those from more privileged classes. The reality of a class-dominated society is that individuals cannot impact on these structural class forces.

Thus there is considerable evidence that class divisions are alive and well. Illusions of upward mobility fail to match economic realities. The best predictor of a person's class position continues to be the class position of one's parents (Holvino 2002). I. Ferguson (2002) also notes that it is still the case that if a person is born and brought up in a working-class family, the likelihood is that he or she will end up in a working-class occupation. In spite of the belief in social mobility and meritocracy, Aronowitz (2004) demonstrates that less than one-third of people move even one step beyond their social origins to reach technical and professional occupations.

In Australia, studies show that very few working-class boys and girls go to university (McGregor in Burgmann et al. 2004). While in Britain, a government-sponsored White Paper demonstrated that the class positions of parents continued to have a significant impact on whether or not an individual went to university and if they did, which university they attended (Mortimer 2009). The school system thus continues to reproduce and legitimise class inequality.

There is no denying that there is some class fluidity, and some individuals will change their class status. I am sure that everyone can think of someone who has significantly changed their class location. However, class is not as fluid as most people believe. The belief in social mobility leads people to blame themselves if they do not succeed. Leondar-Wright and Yeskel (2007) reflect upon the particular cruelty of people believing they can succeed when the class forces in place make it less likely that they will be able to do so.

Almost forty years ago, Sennett and Cobb (1972) described the impact of meritocracy on people as 'the badge of ability', whereby people evaluate their human worth in terms of what they have achieved or not achieved. Since financial rewards are not always directly correlated with what people do, most economically disadvantaged people experience their lives in terms of personal failure. Those who do blame themselves for not succeeding have internalised class oppression into their psyches (Barone 1998).

Aronowitz (2004) believes that class is deeply buried in the unconscious. Lack of attention to class creates a major difficulty in being able to highlight class inequalities in capitalist societies (Holvino 2002). If one lives in a classless society, then class differences do not exist. Challenging exploitative class relations is often difficult because of the reluctance to acknowledge a class identity. Given this context, it is not surprising that there is so little anger and opposition to unearned class privilege.

One must raise the question about whose class interests are served by arguing that class no longer exists. Milner (1999) suggests that the denial of class can itself be seen as a consequence of class forces. In particular, he raises the question of whether the lack of attention to class by middle-class professionals and academics may serve the class interests of these groups, as most university academics come from middle-class backgrounds. Skeggs (1997) notes that those with class privilege have promoted the retreat from class, which coincidentally has taken the attention off their own privilege. Erasing economic class is a strategy that ensures the identity of the middle class. Theorists of mobility, individualisation and identity who are displacing class are in effect reproducing their own middle-class power and they avoid having to name it or accept responsibility for it. Hooks (2000) says that class-privileged people who remain silent about economic inequality do not want to open up the issue of 'where they stand' because of what they have to lose.

From redistribution to recognition

With the decline of traditional working-class radicalism, new sources of opposition to the existing social order have surfaced.

There has been a move away from struggles in relation to poverty and economic deprivation towards those focused on identity and difference (I. Ferguson 2008). A number of post-Marxists have argued that the new social movements represent the most likely basis for social transformation (Laclau and Mouffe 1985). Even Connell (2004), who is not antithetical to class theory, has noted in the Australian context that the main opposition to the system has come from alternative health movements, Greenpeace, queer politics and refugee support groups. She acknowledges that these groups have little connection to working-class people, let alone the labour movement.

The move away from class in new social movements can be seen in part as a criticism of the tendency for class analysis either to ignore or marginalise the oppression of women, disabled people and people of colour (I. Ferguson 2008). In making these forms of oppression a central focus, class was often ignored completely. Oppression was understood in terms of the actions of individuals and groups rather than arising from the structures of the state and the social relations of capitalism.

Aronowitz (2004) believes that such social movements are premised upon a pluralist analysis of societal power that disassociates class relations from sex and race. He argues that whatever their radical potential may have been, many social movements have now been absorbed into the establishment. Milner (1999) also argues that the new social movements are often antithetical to class politics because they focus on individualistic rather than structural solutions to problems. He attributes this to the fact that most of the activists come from class-privileged backgrounds and they have no interest in challenging class divisions in society. It is possible to be concerned about gender inequalities and inequalities associated with race and sexuality, but not challenge the inequalities based on class (Hollier 2004).

While it is true that race and gender studies may ignore structural analyses of class, it is also the case that some neo-Marxist analyses have not engaged with the personal and social dynamics of oppression outlined by feminists and critical race theorists (Barone 1998). It is important to challenge the view that the labour movement is just a fading enterprise. However, reasserting the importance of class analysis over, rather than in conjunction with, analyses of race, gender and sexuality is not the way forward. To reaffirm the importance of class-analytic frameworks, some revision of class analysis is needed (Grusky and Sorensen 1998). As discussed in Chapter 2, focus on both redistribution (class) and recognition (status) is crucial in the struggle for social justice (Fraser 1995; Young 1997).[1]

The politics of the professional-managerial class

When middle-class people get involved in activist politics, they tend to take the form of identity politics, new social movements or community politics associated with such issues as education, housing, health care and the environment. Given the charges levelled against middle-class social movement activists, what potential is there for them to engage in more class-conscious progressive politics? If most professionals do not experience themselves as part of the working class, how are they to act in relation to class issues and class struggles? Thirty years ago, A. Ferguson (1979) argued that parts of the professional-managerial class had as much potential as the traditional working class to be revolutionary. The ongoing question relates to how progressive alliances can be formed across local struggles.

Professionals organise themselves primarily through professional associations rather than trade unions. During the 1970s and onwards, there have been various attempts to articulate a radical professionalism. Ehrenreich and Ehrenreich (1979a) believe that many of the practices of radicals in professions were aimed at protecting the interests of their class against challenges from the working class. At the same time, they noted that many radical professionals developed a 'negative class consciousness' that interrogated their own claims to special knowledge and expertise. Radical doctors, teachers, social workers and lawyers became actively involved in challenging professional elitism.

Class consciousness requires an understanding of tensions and contradictions inherent in professional–working-class relationships. If professionals were unaware of their own class location, they would unwittingly undermine the class consciousness of working-class people. In turn, working-class people may be antagonistic towards professionals who uncritically subject them to surveillance and control, especially since most were employed in public services.

So, how can professionals and working-class people form alliances

---

1. This discussion of class is confined to Western societies. As discussed in Chapter 3, caste systems in India persist despite economic growth and development. Caste and tribal allegiances also complicate class in Africa and other non-Western countries.

for social change that move beyond this antagonism? According to the Ehrenreichs (1979a), this can happen only when professionals identify and challenge their attitudes of elitism and condescension that reproduce class oppression. It requires professionals to theorise and interrogate their own class location without ongoing defensiveness.

In the meantime, how are salaried managerial and professional workers to be theorised? Scott (2000) uses the language of intermediate classes to designate the class position of those between subordinate and advantaged classes. He locates those employed in managerial, professional and technical occupations in this class. Giddens (1973) refers to them as 'the new middle class'. Bourdieu (1987a) considers them to be a dominated fraction of the dominant economic class, whereas in neo-Weberian theory, they constitute a separate service class (Milner 1999).

For many Marxists they form part of the new working class. Donaldson (2006), for example, argues that conflict and hostility between professionals and manually based occupations does not constitute class division and does not place these occupational categories in different classes. He believes that it is simply part of the changing composition of the working class. Attempts to synthesise Marx and Weber lead to designating them as 'privileged strata within the working class' (Milner 1999: 155).

Over thirty years ago Barbara and John Ehrenreich (1979a) explored this issue in a seminal paper that was the subject of extensive and heated debate. At the time they noted that the left in the United States was comprised predominantly of activists who identified themselves as middle class. They argued that professional, technical and managerial workers comprised a distinct class in capitalist society, what they termed the 'professional-managerial class'. While such workers are not part of the owning class, they are actively involved in the reproduction of capitalist class relations and capitalist culture. This places them in an antagonistic relationship to the working class.

There were many Marxist challenges to this argument. Carter (1979) argued that professionals would not willingly relinquish the power that kept the working class in their position. Because of their contradictory position in relation to capital and the working class, she believed that professionals were dubious allies in class struggles. They are dubious allies because to some extent they would lose out as the working class made gains. These contradictory pressures upon them can make them waver.

Noble (1979) believed that the notion of the professional-managerial class was another example itself of middle-class elitism. Aronowitz (1979) challenged the conflation of professionals and managers, believing that managers should be separated from technical and professional employees. Later, Aronowitz (2004) argued that such workers should be located as part of a new working class rather than as part of the middle class.

Perhaps the most theoretically elaborate critique, however, came from Erik Olin Wright (1979). He argued that professionals and intellectuals occupied contradictory class locations. Rather than occupying clear class positions, they were torn between the major classes in that they shared interests simultaneously with both the working class and the petty bourgeois. For Wright, they were both working class because they had to work for wages and had limited control over their labour process and middle class because they have control over the work of others. What Wright captured in his notion of contradictory class locations was that salaried professionals were both exploited and exploiters. In his view, it was necessary to grasp the contradictory character of professionals' class location to understand their relationship to class struggles.

Ehrenreich and Ehrenreich (1979b) criticised Wright's notion of contradictory class locations for being too economically determinist because it defined class solely in terms of production and ignored the cultural sphere. They argued that a person's political consciousness was shaped by other experiences outside of occupational categories, including, family, friendships and experiences of consumerism. For them, the class issues outside the labour force needed to be considered too.

Ehrenreich revisited this issue in 1989 in *Fear of Falling: The Inner Life of the Middle Class*. In this book, she outlined how professionals and managers came to see themselves as constituting a distinct class and how that was connected to class elitism. She explained how professional elitism reproduces structural barriers that inhibit cross-class alliances. One strategy, she proposed, was to remove the barriers preventing access to the professions and to expand opportunities for all to blur the boundaries between the professional elite and those who they serve.

Walkowitz (1999) suggests that social workers, as representative of professional workers, can be considered as part of a 'working middle class' in that, like many salaried professionals, they have limited control over their work processes. In spite of this proletarianisation of their work, many professionals continue to identify themselves as middle class. Walkowitz explains that the professional-managerial class has fractured into two quite different groups, with some professionals identifying themselves as part of a new middle class, while others frame their allegiances to the working class.

Professionals in the service occupations such as teaching, social work, community development, law, social policy, health sciences and international development are more likely to be open to developing a consciousness of the class positioning than middle-level managers in the corporate sector. Professionals in these fields will also come into contact with working-class people as clients, consumers, patients and students, where they will have authority and power to make judgements about their lives (Ehrenreich 1989). To the extent that professional workers regard themselves as middle class, however, they will distance themselves from those whom they serve (Walkowitz 1999).

It is clear that professionals have a range of privileges connected to their relative job security and control over their labour process and the work of others (A. Ferguson 1979). So, their material interests are connected to the status quo. For this reason, many commentators have argued that middle-class radicalism is unlikely to challenge class inequality (Milner 1999). This is the case even though many state sector workers and professionals have found that these privileges are also being eroded and their work proletarianised (Walkowitz 1999). Over the last thirty years, a number of writers have observed an increasing proletarianisation of professional work in general and social work in particular. Many have observed increasing bureaucratic controls, decreasing work autonomy and increasing paper work (Braverman 1975; Wright 1979; C. Jones 1983; Walkowitz 1999; I. Ferguson 2002).

I. Ferguson (2002) locates professional workers as part of the working class rather than as a separate service class because they have to sell their labour power. He does, however, acknowledge that some members of the salaried classes are in positions where they are involved in the social production of capital. They perform social control functions for capital by keeping the working class in their place and they receive special privileges and rewards for doing so.

Within Marxism, the question of the class position of professionals continues. There is a tension between professionals being representatives of the dominant economic class, while still being salaried employees of the state. Many members of the professional-managerial class support the ideological apparatuses of the state. They reproduce the dominant ideology of the social order while also facing the increasing proletarianisation of their own work processes (Corrigan and Leonard 1978; Walkowitz 1999). This tension is often reflected in the competing pressures of professionalism and unionism as alternative sources of occupational identification and mobilisation. In general, professionalising processes tend to encourage the construction of middle-class identities, while unionisation fosters working-class consciousness.

There is a middle element between the major classes. This is well accepted. There is disagreement, however, about whether this middle section is a stratum, a class or whether it occupies a contradictory position. However classified, there has been a substantial growth of white middle-class employees in occupations that have different class locations than manual and trade workers (Milner 1999). Professionals are not part of the traditional working class, yet they are not part of the petty bourgeoisie or the capitalist class.

Professionals occupy a hybrid or double-class identity that encompasses both middle- and working-class dimensions (Walkowitz 1999). This is why those in the professional-managerial class need to develop a critical consciousness of their contradictory class positioning and be cognisant of that positioning if and when they engage in social activism. They need to come to terms with what will be lost as well as gained as they work towards a more egalitarian social order (Ehrenreich 1989).

Middle-class privilege and internalised dominance

Gilbert (2008) asks what it means to be a person of class privilege. Many meanings are possible, yet one set of meanings is key. Dominant group members come to believe that they are more deserving, more intelligent and more articulate than working-class people. For the most part, children of middle-class and owning-class families grow up to believe that they are more intelligent and superior and are born to be in control (Leondar-Wright and Yeskel 2007). Most are socialised into oppressor patterns of behaviour that will enable them to take on middle- and owning-class occupations and world views (Barone 1998).

As with other forms of privilege, middle-class experience is presented as universal. The white, heterosexual, gentile middle class is presented as the normative standard that others are expected to aspire to. Skeggs (1997) talks about 'respectability' as one of the key signifiers of this class positioning, as it is the basis upon which people pathologise others. Respectability is a normative standard. Skeggs (ibid.: 2) says that it 'embodies moral authority', as distinct from those who need to be controlled. It is the basis upon which middle-class people position themselves against 'the masses'. Most middle-class people construct their identity by distancing themselves from the working class. It can be difficult for middle-class people to recognise their own class conditioning because they are led to believe that they represent the ideal towards which working-class people aspire (Leondar-Wright 2005).

Class Acts (2007), a women's collective at the Women's Theological Center in Boston, USA, adopted Peggy McIntosh's list of white privileges to develop a comparable list of class privileges. They identified seventy-one forms of class privilege, including the following:

- I can manage to know only people of similar background by exclusively frequenting places where such people gather.
- I can avoid people of other classes and races if I choose.
- I buy what I need/want without worry.
- I do not fear being hungry or homeless.
- I am free of the burden of debt.
- I am in control of how I spend my time.
- I have the time, education and opportunity to enhance my inner life and my personal growth.
- I can live where I choose and can move when and where I choose.
- When I am in the company of people of my class in any situation I have little discomfort.
- In my community I am trusted and not perceived as a threat.
- I can buy things for my comfort or my luxury.
- I can buy items that imply wealth and status.
- I have the time and financial resources to care for my body.
- I can employ people to help with the tasks of daily living.
- I can employ people to care for my children.
- I can see myself as being above doing housework.
- I can take vacations when and where I want.
- I can afford medical and hospital care.
- I can anticipate my retirement years without financial anxiety.
- I can have a seat at the table to make, influence, have an impact on decisions, rules, policy.
- I have the freedom to be unaware of the living conditions of others.

- I have the freedom to be unaware of the working conditions of others.
- I can dismiss viewpoints that differ from my own.

To talk about class privilege itself threatens the myth of equal opportunity and social mobility (Gilbert 2008). It is necessary to remember that while the professional-managerial class have privileges compared to the traditional working class, they are also subjected to the power and privilege of the owning class. Thus in developing a consciousness of their relative privilege, they need to contextualise this in relation to the corporate power of the dominant class (Ehrenreich 1989).

Towards cross-class alliances

Leondar-Wright (2005) notices the disjuncture between middle-class movements for change that are not connected to working-class people's experiences. She underlines the limited support that middle-class people have given to working-class movements. Sennett (2003) believes that this class divide is overcome by developing mutual respect. In his view, real compassion about the experiences of others can only come through solidarity with their struggles. This entails people challenging their assumptions about class superiority. To develop solidarity with working-class people, middle-class professionals will need to challenge their socialisation into dominating class positions. Skeggs (1997) challenges middle-class academics to develop a more dialogical approach to the working class, where they listen to their experience rather than simply make judgements about them and their arguments. She argues that academics need to take greater responsibility for the judgements they make about others and how such judgements reproduce power relations.

To progress class analysis, we must find ways to develop class alliances and, in particular, to encourage professional and managerial workers to explore alliances with the traditional working class against the interests of the dominant class. At this historical moment, it is time to challenge middle-class entitlements as a key step towards such alliances. Middle-class social activists need to understand how they may be perceived by working-class people. When working-class people express feelings of deference and hostility towards professional workers, it may be due to feelings of paternalism and contempt the workers have towards them (Ehrenreich and Ehrenreich 1979a).

Leondar-Wright (2005) stresses that it is important for middle-class people to demonstrate greater humility and to challenge their inclinations towards superiority.

Class and the intersections with other forms of oppression

Experience of class is shaped by gender, sexuality, race, region and ability/disability, among other sources of identity (ibid.). Class also plays an important role in perpetuating other forms of oppression. At the simplest level, class intersects with other forms of oppression by determining access to other forms of privilege. For example, in the West most wealthy people are white and most poor people are black or Indigenous (Leondar-Wright and Yeskel 2007). Wright (1997) also argues that non-class forms of oppression are manifested in forms of class oppression in the sense, for example, of women being much more proletarianised than men.

Middle-class lives are also shaped by race and gender. Some middle-class people may experience oppression on the basis of gender, sexuality, race or disability. Even so, they still need to face their privileged class position. Bell hooks (2003) examines this issue in relation to middle-class black men and women. The social mobility of small numbers of black people into the middle class was held up as an example for all black people. Meanwhile, many middle-class blacks looked down upon less privileged black people who were used to measure how far they have moved. Thus class privilege mediates some of the oppression caused by racial supremacy. This privilege is not available to others who are on the receiving end of racism. In this way, class privilege undermines struggles against racism because it creates a 'safe house' from the worst forms of racial discrimination. Their allegiance to their class interests overrides their commitment to their race. While they will still face the issue of racial discrimination, they will not acknowledge their class power. The challenge hooks identifies is how black people can have access to class power without undermining their solidarity with those less privileged.

Gendering and racialising class

Perhaps the most significant challenge to class analysis has come from feminists who have contested the view of Marxists that class was more important than gender. Many feminists argue that class analysis was unable to account for women's experience of oppression and exploitation. Acker (2006b) argues that class analysis focused on the experiences of white men and ignored the experience of women and people of colour because it was developed from a privileged white male perspective. Acker (2006b) addresses the neglect in class analysis of male and white privilege and demonstrates how both hegemonic masculinities and white supremacy supported class domination and oppression. She argues that gendering and racialising processes and practices are essential to the reproduction of class inequalities.

In recent years, some Marxists have responded to the feminist critique of class. Aronowitz (2004) argues that the women's movement has been more concerned with assisting women to break into the echelons of top management than addressing the demands of working-class women who are relegated to subordinate positions in the class structure. Hooks (2000) has also observed that many white middle-class women were campaigning for equality with men of their class rather than being engaged in challenging class inequality which impacted on working-class women of colour. Only the more radical forms of feminism challenged racism and class domination.

Acker (2006b) acknowledges that conceptualisations of class are embedded with feminist assumptions about gender and that they do not always address the realities of many women's lives. Relations of gender may not be able to explain the full range of women's experiences under capitalism, as I. Ferguson (2002) notes however, it is equally distorted to dismiss them completely. It is rather a matter of understanding how class and gender (as well as other forms of oppression) interconnect in specific situations (Wright 1997).

Although I. Ferguson (2002) acknowledged that men act as agents of women's oppression, he rejects the view that men benefit from the oppression of women more generally. Since men are also constrained by family relationships, he is unable to see how families benefit men. Furthermore, he argues that women's oppression is not a product of male power when it comes to the working class because they are in positions of powerlessness. It is true that white working-class men will not feel very privileged, given their class subordination, and they are likely to reject claims of being powerful and privileged. The argument is that if working-class men are oppressed by class, this cancels out any access they might have to privilege (A. Johnson 2006). Certainly it is true that white working-class men may not be able to claim all of the benefits and privileges associated with being white and male.

What is more problematic in I. Ferguson's (2002: 100) analysis is the claim that 'no section of the working class benefits from the oppression of any other'. He rejects the view that men benefit from the oppression of women or that white people benefit from the oppression of black people and so on. Notwithstanding their class oppression, straight, white working-class men still have some access to male privileges in a patriarchal society as well as privileges associated with their whiteness and their heterosexuality.

Furthermore, some white working-class men have come to accept their subordination to wage labour by constructing their subjectivities as superior to women and black men (Acker 2006b). A. Johnson (2006) also notes that working-class men often emphasise their assumed racial and/or gender superiority over people of colour and women so as not to be at the bottom of the heap. Acker (2006b) believes that many white working-class men have been able to adjust to their subordination as workers by viewing themselves positively as heads of households and breadwinners. These identities have ensured the subordination of women and the exploitation of their unpaid domestic labour. At the same time, working-class men's dominance in the home may have inhibited their involvement in class struggles against their powerlessness in the workplace. Hence, different sources of oppression and privilege create tensions and divisions between and among members of oppressed groups that make progressive alliances difficult to achieve. These tensions and divisions are addressed in Chapter 9.

Class-based oppression and classism

Most class analysis is more concerned with the effects of class structures on societies as a whole and less concerned with the impact on individuals. Barone (1998) argues that class oppression needs to be extended to include an understanding of classism. This involves an understanding of both social structures and human subjectivity and agency. Thus it is important to remember that class is not only about economics. It is internalised in our psyches and it shapes our subjectivity and identity. Class affects people on an emotional as well as an economic level (Brantley et al. 2003).

Barone (1998: 4–5) defines classism as 'the systematic oppression of one group by another based on economic distinctions, or more accurately one's position within the system of production and distribution'. Unlike some writers who use the language of classism, he locates the primary cause of class-based oppression as the capitalist mode of production. Barone argues that classism plays a key role in the reproduction of class divisions and economic exploitation. In his view, class struggles also occur at the cultural level.

Classism seems to have two meanings in the literature. Some writers use it to refer to a class-based system of exploitation and oppression, while others use it to describe class-based prejudice and discrimination (Pincus and Sokoloff 2008). Pincus and Sokoloff are critical of the term because most of those who use the concept ignore class conflict and capitalism. They argue that the theory of class implicit in the concept of classism is the stratification view of economic inequality, whereby classism has come simply to mean prejudice towards working-class people. Pincus and Sokoloff (ibid.) point out that not all forms of class-based oppression can be captured by prejudice and discrimination. The social relations of capitalism that frame the economic exploitation of workers cannot be addressed as a form of discrimination. While the sources of class-based oppression are located within capitalism, however, discrimination and prejudice against working-class people still constitute significant harm and are important to address in their own right, as long as the structural underpinnings are acknowledged.

In addition to the material consequences of class oppression, there are also psychological consequences. Leondar-Wright and Yeskel (2007) identify the harms caused by classism in terms of low expectations and self-doubt about one's intelligence. There are many emotional and psychological costs associated with people's class locations. Yet, most people seem unable to relate the causes of their suffering with their locations in social structure (Hollier 2004) and to the extent that people internalise oppression, the class system is perpetuated, as I argued in Chapter 2.

Even those who do not feel impeded by class or do not recognise it, are shaped by it. Skeggs (1997) discusses the experiences of working-class women who denied their class positioning. Even though these women did not have sufficient capital to define themselves as middle class, they did.

At the subjective level, passing as middle class has its costs. It is not easy to hide one's class background (Barone 1998). This uncertainty does not plague those born with class privilege. Passing as middle class reproduces the class system and delegitimates the working class, rather than challenges it (Skeggs 1997). Those who have class privilege have cultural capital. It comes down to entitlements. Most working-class people do not believe that they have the same entitlements as most middle-class people (ibid.).

Skeggs argues that to reinvigorate class analysis, it is important to focus on class entitlements and the effects these entitlements have on others. Because class entitlement is produced and institutionalised, it can be challenged and reconstructed. This class struggle is at the cultural level where class subjectivities are contested. While class and class divisions must be understood in the context of objective structures, they are also legitimated at a subjective and cultural level by classist attitudes and beliefs. Class is internalised within the psyches of individuals who slot themselves, and are slotted, into positions of subordination and domination.

Oppression functions on institutional, cultural, intergroup and personal levels. Beyond the structures of class oppression, working-class people experience prejudice and negative attitudes directed towards them due to stereotypes of working-class people. These individual beliefs are based on cultural norms that legitimate class oppression through notions of meritocracy (Barone 1998). As we have seen, middle-class professionals occupy a precarious position between the owning class and the working class. They are both oppressors and oppressed. They are socialised into a position of dominance over those below them. In this sense, classism is another form of systematic oppression that 'is held in place by systems of beliefs that rank people according to economic status, family lineage, job and level of education' (Brantley et al. 2003: 3).

Conclusion

There is a tension in critical theories of oppression and privilege between how much to focus on the face-to-face interactions of individuals and groups and how much to focus on the institutional and structural dimensions. Class is not just performed and one cannot simply change one's class by an act of will or choice. The social capital associated with class is structural and institutionalised (Skeggs 1997). Sayers (2005) makes the point that professionals treating working-class people equally and avoiding class-based prejudice will not challenge the economic foundations of class inequality. Because of the sources of class domination in social structure, challenging class-based privilege will be more difficult than changing some other forms of social inequality where recognition of difference is more important than distribution. Working-class people do not need recognition of their difference. However, while addressing the symbolic domination of class prejudice will not in itself challenge the objective social structures of class domination, it will encourage people to position themselves as part of a counter-hegemonic force against class domination.

While I accept the notion that much of the experience of class-based oppression is a product of unequal social structures, I also believe that those who occupy positions of class dominance act in ways that are either complicit with those structures or stand in opposition to them. So, while anger is an appropriate response to class-based forms of exploitation (Sayers 2005), those of us in the middle class must also address the complex feelings associated with our complicity in reproducing those structures. We also need to recognise that while class is a reflection of objective social conditions, it is also reproduced and reformulated through our actions and practices. Thus middle-class subjectivities are constructed in ways that reproduce the oppression of working-class people.

Marxists are right to argue against the view that the politics of recognition should replace the politics of distribution. This does not mean that the politics of recognition should be abandoned. We need to construct a class politics that addresses the subjective experiences of class and the cultural construction of class-based identities at the same time as we challenge the structural bases of economic inequality. One cannot be done without the other.

Weber (in Collins et al. 2002) argues that this is not an either/or proposition. Systems of oppression operate at both macro-structural and micro-psychological levels, as I argue throughout this book. While oppression is socially constructed, it is also re-created through ideological and psychological dimensions. In Marxist formulations also, there is a subjective dimension, as a class only becomes true to itself through a critical consciousness of itself (Milner 1999).

Acker (2006b) argues that social structures are embedded with social relations that are constantly constructed and reconstructed. Thus she frames race, class and gender as racialised and gendered class practices rather than as structures. In this view, individuals are 'enmeshed in complex webs of racialised and gendered practices that change over the course of the lifetime' (ibid.: 67). This is because identities are both fluid and contradictory.

My approach to class in this book avoids what I see as the false dichotomy between objectivism and subjectivism that plagues many writings about class. What is missing in relation to sociological debates on class is how class constructs subjectivities and identities. My argument is that the identities and subjectivities of individuals are significant in either reproducing or challenging structures of privilege and oppression. Those of us who are professional workers need to understand how we have internalised class into our psyches and address the role that we play in reproducing class-based oppression.

FIVE
Gender order and the patriarchal dividend

I first engaged with the issue of privilege in response to being challenged by women about my entitlement as a man. As a straight white man, reading feminist theory and being in a relationship with a feminist woman, I was forced to confront some of my experiences of male privilege. My partner would come home from women's consciousness-raising meetings and challenge my limited participation in housework and my over-commitment to paid work at the expense of our relationship. I had to work out what these challenges would mean not only for my personal relationship, but also for my chosen career of social work and my political activism on issues of social justice.

I have written elsewhere about my experiences in the 1970s of living with a woman who was discovering feminism and about my involvement in anti-sexist men's groups and campaigns about men's violence (Pease 1997a). This engagement with gender privilege would take me into theorising and research with men about the pathways by which some men become profeminist and how to analyse men's power and resistance to change (Pease 2000). I have also written about my experiences of teaching university courses on critical studies of men and masculinities (Pease 1997b; Pease 1998) and running patriarchy awareness workshops for men (1997a). This chapter draws upon that earlier work. As I began the process of writing this chapter, I found myself approaching the subject anew in light of the wider theorising about privilege that is the focus of this book.

During the 1970s and the 1980s, as the second wave of feminism swept the Western world, the study of gender understandably focused on women's experience of oppression under patriarchy. Although there were early responses by men to feminism during the 1970s and 1980s (from feminist supportive to anti-feminist hostility), it was not until the 1990s that the issue of masculinity would became a popular topic both in non-academic books about men and in the scholarship of men's studies and critical studies of men and masculinities. In university courses about gender, there was a shift from solely focusing on the experiences of being oppressed to the issues faced by those who were the oppressors (Schacht 2003). With the development of new courses on men, these courses and women's studies became subsumed into a single field of gender studies.

Many feminists criticised the notion of gender studies for fear that it might once again marginalise women's experience under generic labels (Yea 1997). It might also imply parity between women's and men's studies, premised on a belief that the study of men is worth equal time. There were further concerns that men would focus more on the hazards of men's lives than the privileges that men enjoy. It was certainly observed that many men's studies courses gave insufficient attention to a critique of men's power and privilege (Hearn 1996).

In addition, Canaan and Griffin (1990) were concerned that men's studies might deny women's experiences of men and masculinity. They pondered the genuineness of men's motives, suggesting that it might be yet another source of research and publishing jobs for the boys. Thus many feminists within universities were very cautious about the development of men's studies. They were mindful of Hearn's (1987) warning over twenty years ago that such programmes might attract male social scientists who had no commitment to feminism or, worse still, a commitment to some form of anti-feminist position. The important issue here is the theoretical and political orientation of this work to ensure that it challenges male domination.

From gender difference to the social construction of masculinity

There is an enormous volume of literature on men and masculinities. Theoretical approaches have ranged from socio-biological, psychoanalytical, Jungian and sex role theories through to materialist and discursive approaches. The aim in this chapter is not to provide an overview of the different theories (see Pease 2002a), but rather to theorise men's gender privileges and situated dominance in relation to women.

In spite of the vast scholarship on men and masculinities published in the last twenty years, and the developing awareness that challenges traditional thinking about male dominance, the common-sense approach to understanding men continues to invoke a language of biological differences. Claimed biological differences between men and women continue to legitimate male dominance and gender inequality.

Stephen Goldberg's (1973) *The Inevitability of Patriarchy* is perhaps the best historical example of this argument. Goldberg argues that differences in concentrations of particular hormones give men an 'aggression advantage' over women. He believes that it is rational for women to accept a subordinate position because they do not have the same competitive edge: 'Men must always have the high status roles because women are not for psychological reasons as strongly motivated to obtain them' (Goldberg 1973: 47). Apparently, this 'aggression advantage' means that men will inevitably dominate women, as 'the hormonal makes the social inevitable' (ibid.: 49).

The central argument here is that if inequality is based upon some natural order, opposition is futile. In this view, there is no point in trying to equalise the genders because patriarchy is regarded as an inevitable product of biology. Nor is there any point in trying to change the basis of gender relations because it will only upset the natural order. Consequently, in this view, the feminist vision of a gender-equal society is doomed to failure. Goldberg updated his book in 1993 and reaffirmed his analysis in spite of considerable anthropological and sociological criticism of his thesis (see, for example, Connell 1987; Clatterbaugh 1990; Messner 1992). This socio-biological analysis is still alive and well in much contemporary popular writing about men (Moir and Moir 2003; Biddulph 2008).

As I have written elsewhere (Pease 2000; 2002a), I maintain that there is no convincing evidence to sustain an argument that biological differences constitute a foundation for male dominance and gender-segregated work. Instead, I argue that gender and masculinity are socially constructed throughout life. Following Connell (2000a), I believe that it is most useful to understand men and masculinities as involving six key dimensions:

1. Multiple masculinities that arise from different cultures, different historical periods and different social divisions between men.
2. Different positions reflected in these multiple masculinities in relation to power, with some forms of masculinity hegemonic and dominant while other masculinities are marginalised and subordinated.
3. Institutionalised masculinities embedded in organisational structures and in the wider culture, as well as being located within individual men.

4. Embodied masculinities that are represented physically in how men engage with the world.
5. Masculinities produced through the actions of individual men.
6. Fluid masculinities that change in relation to the reconstructive efforts of progressive men and in response to changes in the wider society.

Within this theoretical context, Connell (1995) identifies four forms of masculinity: hegemonic, complicit, marginalised and subordinate.

Hegemonic masculinity is the culturally dominant form of masculinity that is manifested in a range of different settings (Connell 2001). Such masculinity is idealised and promoted as a desirable attainment for boys and young men to strive towards. It is presented as heterosexual, aggressive, authoritative and courageous (Connell 2000a). The manliness of men and boys is judged by their ability to measure up to this normative notion. Sporting prowess, work status and power over women are the key signifiers of this form of masculinity, especially in Australia.

Hegemonic masculinity is also associated with violence. Some have suggested that hegemonic masculinity establishes the foundations for men's violence against women (O'Toole and Schiffman 1997). Many writers have noted the close links between exalted masculinity and the legitimation of violence, especially in response to perceived threat (Messerschmidt 2000).

The concept of hegemonic masculinity has been criticised from various quarters (Donaldson 1991; Petersen 1998; Demetriou 2001; Jefferson 2002). These criticisms range from the charge of essentialising and psychologising men on the one hand to claims about structural determinism on the other. However, the concept still captures the social divisions between men and the hegemonic influence of dominant forms of masculinity.

Although the majority of men do not adhere to hegemonic masculinity, it nevertheless represents the most valued form of masculinity and all men are positioned in relation to it (Connell and Messerschmidt 2005). It does not have to correspond to all or even the majority of men to hold power over men's experiences of being a man.

The majority of men engage in what Connell (1995) refers to as complicit masculinity, whereby those men who do not meet the normative standard of hegemonic masculinity, nevertheless benefit from it in various ways. The concept of complicit masculinity is useful in understanding how men who do not regard themselves as oppressors nevertheless act in ways that reproduce men's dominance and male privilege.

Complicit masculinities also maintain the structures and ideologies that reproduce men's violence (M. Mills 1998). One might refer to these men as 'perpetuators of violence' (Pease 2008). While the majority of men may not engage in excessive forms of hegemonic masculinity, they do not challenge patriarchy and male privilege that supports this form of dominance (M. Mills 1998) because they adhere to the dominant discourse.

Marginalised and subordinate masculinities are useful in understanding the relationship between gender and its intersections with other dimensions of stratification such as class, race and sexuality. Connell (2000a) uses these concepts to illustrate how the diversity of masculinities is marked by hierarchy and exclusion. This hierarchy of masculinities means that men do not benefit equally from male privilege.

Theorising male dominance and men's privilege

As outlined in the theoretical framework presented in Chapter 2, gender is manifested at structural and cultural levels of social organisation, as well as at the level of interpersonal interactions and in the identities and subjectivities of individuals. This suggests that masculinities and male dominance are best understood through the levels of the material world, discourse and the psyche. Rather than positing a single theoretical frame, it is most useful to straddle the tensions in these multiple levels of analysis. Consequently, feminist-informed materialist, discursive and psychoanalytic perspectives together offer the most promising insights in my opinion.

Materialist perspectives locate men in the context of social institutions. Masculinities are constructed in schools, workplaces, families and the state through both cultural and structural processes (Haywood and Mac an Ghaill 2003). Tolson (1977) was an early writer to focus on the way in which masculinities are reproduced by working conditions and class divisions. He argued that the social organisation of paid work shaped the various forms of masculinity and that these forms were differentiated by class divisions leading to particular working-class and middle-class masculinities.

In this view, male dominance is explained in socio-economic and structural terms.

In contrast to those perspectives that emphasise workplace cultures, feminist materialist analyses point out that the sexual division of labour within the home is as important in understanding men's power and privilege as class divisions in paid work (Edley and Wetherell 1995). Hearn (1987), for example, stresses the importance of sexuality, child-rearing, nurturing and care for others as significant practices in the production of masculinity. McMahon (1999) has developed a materialist analysis of men's labour in relation to the domestic sphere and has examined how men's participation or non-participation in household work shaped their experience of masculinity.

Discursive theorists argue that materialist approaches are structurally determinist and neglect the potential for individual agency and the possibility for resistance and change (Whitehead 2002). Discursive approaches emphasise the role of culture, ideology and discourse in constructing masculinities (Beynon 2002). In particular, they examine the way in which masculine norms are constructed by dominant discourses, which motivate men to take up particular subject positions (Edley and Wetherell 1995; Pease 2000).

It is within discourses that we are offered subject positions, which convey notions of what it is to be a man (Pease 2000). Men are invited to take up or turn down different subject positions and the sense of masculine identity that goes with them. In this view, one brings about social change through producing alternative discourses that lead to new subject positions (Ramazanoglu 1993). The progressive potential of this analysis is to reveal alternative possibilities for the construction of masculinities not yet realised (Saco 1992).

However, discourses are not autonomous from social relations and material oppression. On their own, they do not engage with the structural dimensions of gender associated with the state and political economy and with materialist practices in the family. As we have seen, gender relations are not only shaped by cultural norms, but are also influenced by paid work, domestic labour, childcare, sexuality and violence.

Men's dominance is both discursive and material and thus it is necessary to attend simultaneously to both diversity and difference in men's lives resulting from multiple subjectivities and the wider structural dimensions of power and privilege (Pease 2000). Whitehead (2002) maintains that such a position is 'untenable' and that one cannot hold both a structural and poststructural position. I flatly reject this view, as I believe that we need to straddle the modernist/

postmodern divide to develop a more complex understanding of the relationship between the material and symbolic structures.

What is not included in the materialist and discursive perspectives is the process by which male entitlement is internalised by men and how men might come to work for change. Also missing in these perspectives are the mechanisms through which men's masculinity comes to reflect the socio-economic structure of capitalism and the gender relations of patriarchy. We need to understand the ways in which the dominant ideology is internalised in the psyches of men and how this ideology interacts with material conditions to shape men's experience. Thus we also need to examine the relationship between subjectivity and the unconscious (Pease 2003).

Psychoanalytic perspectives focus on the mind and the psyche in relation to the production of desire, fantasy and emotions (Edley and Wetherell 1995). Orthodox psychoanalytic theory has much to answer for in relation to the reinforcement of women's subordination.[1] However, in 1975 Mitchell wrote a qualified defence of psychoanalytic theory, arguing that it was important for feminist struggle. For Mitchell (1975), dominant ideologies were deeply buried in women's unconscious and psychoanalytic theory was essential for understanding the ways in which these ideologies were internalised.

The feminist engagement with psychoanalytic theory coincided with a series of Marxist–psychoanalytic dialogues that attempted to explain capitalist alienation not only in terms of political and economic oppression, but also in terms of emotional impoverishment and psychic oppression. Leonard (1984) argues that an understanding of the nature of the unconscious at particular periods in history enables us to unmask important aspects of dominant ideology. What is required, then, is not only a change in the external world and a change in consciousness, but also a transformation of the inner structure of people's unconsciousness. These analyses have implications for understanding internalised dominance as well as internalised oppression.

From a feminist psychoanalytic perspective, hegemonic masculinity and male domination are reproduced by denying the feminine (Frosh 1994). Such repression leads men to feel antagonism and hostility towards women, which in turn, reproduces men's dominance. In this

1. In the 1970s, psychoanalytic theory was subjected to numerous feminist critiques. See, for example: Firestone 1971; Figes 1972; Millet 1972.

view, it is men's hatred and fear of women that fuels their need to dominate and control them (Jukes 1993).

Rowan (1997; 2007) argues consequently that the process of transforming the male psyche will need to involve 'unconsciousness raising' as well as consciousness raising because some elements of hegemonic masculinity are deeply buried in the unconscious. He uses the term 'patripsyche' to describe the formation of patriarchal patterns in the psyche. These internal patterns mirror the external oppressive structures, which Rowan believes are kept in place by an oppressive male ego.

Segal (1987) contends that violence and discrimination against women result from inequalities of power between men and women rather than from internal psychic dynamics in men. I do not see these sources of men's dominance as necessarily 'either-or' and I believe that a feminist-informed psychoanalytic theory has an important (if insufficient) contribution to make to understanding the ways in which male privilege and men's sense of entitlement is reproduced within men's psyche.

Over twenty years ago, Grosz (1988) developed a conceptual framework for understanding the various forms of knowledge underpinning misogyny and discrimination against women. She distinguishes between sexist, patriarchal and phallocentric forms of knowledge that underpin women's oppression. Sexism refers to observable discriminatory practices that privilege men and disadvantage women. These can include hostile, suspicious and excluding practices whereby women are treated differently because they are women. Patriarchy encompasses more systemic forms of domination that go beyond individual practices of gender discrimination. This includes the underpinning structures of gender oppression that positions men and women differentially in the gender order and legitimates the sexist discriminatory practices. Phallocentrism operates at the discursive or symbolic level whereby women are represented in terms that are consistent with masculinist norms. This multi-level framework is useful for interrogating the various levels of male privilege.

Patriarchy and systemic domination

Feminists from the 1970s onwards used the concept of patriarchy to articulate the overarching framework of the various forms of male domination and men's systemic exploitation of women. A. Johnson (1997) identifies three dimensions of patriarchy: male-dominated, male-identified and male-centred. Male-dominated refers to men's authority and control over the major social, political, economic, religious, legal and military institutions. Male-identified refers to the cultural ideals about good, normal and desirable forms of masculinity and the various ways in which women are devalued in our society. Male-centred refers to the way in which men's experiences come to represent human experience more generally.

Some feminist writers have critiqued patriarchy for being ahistorical. Rowbotham (1981), for example, rejected it because of its biological connotations and the suggestion that male dominance was unitary and unchanging. Barrett (1980) also criticised it for being apparently fixed and unchanging and suggesting a transhistorical and universal oppression. Whitehead (2007) similarly expresses reservations about the concept because he says that it implies a static and fixed state of women's oppression rather than recognising the extent to which male dominance is fluid and changing. He believes that patriarchy does not acknowledge feminist achievements and advances towards gender equality and does not capture the complexity of men's dominance over women.

Some early feminist versions of patriarchy did not seem to allow a place for intervention and seemed to offer no position from which women and men could challenge the gender order. Implicit in some theories of patriarchy was the notion that male dominance and masculinity were reflections of each other, where all men are seen as a coherent gender class with the same vested interests in controlling women. Such analyses are biologically or structurally determinist and the political prognosis is pessimistic. If all men were the enemy, then it would be difficult to envisage the possibility of men and women working together against patriarchy (Edley and Wetherell 1995).

Notwithstanding these criticisms, patriarchy is still useful to describe men's systemic dominance over women across a wide range of social institutions and gendered sites. The benefit in continuing to use the term patriarchy is that it focuses attention on the systemic and global nature of women's subordination and it provides a framework for identifying the privileges and advantages accruing to men as a result of their dominance.

Many feminist writers acknowledge that patriarchy is not monolithic and that it contains contradictions (Rahman 2007). Patriarchy is not fixed, as its form changes over time and different aspects of it have greater or lesser significance in different contexts (Walby

1990). Patriarchy is best understood as an historical structure with changing dynamics and it needs to be seen as involving the intersection of numerous factors and multiple levels of experience (Dragiewicz 2009). It may be more useful to refer to patriarchies in the plural to acknowledge the culturally specific forms that arise from different regions of the world and in relation to different forms of oppression.

Phallocentrism and symbolic order

The origins of the term phallocentrism are located in Lacanian psychoanalyis (Lacan 1987), which emphasises the importance of language in reproducing power relations. Derived from the Greek word *phallos*, the representation of the penis comes to embody patriarchal authority and hegemonic masculinity. Phallocentrism was first used by Derrida (1976) to describe the privileges associated with the male phallus. It operates at the discursive or symbolic level of male privilege and is generally used to refer to the assumed dominance of masculinity and male-centredness across multiple sites of cultural and social relations (Davison 2007).

Since phallocentric discourses are so commonly shared and pervasive and are often internalised unconsciously, their oppressive dimensions are rarely recognised. As most men's beliefs about male superiority are experienced as being natural and normal and are institutionalised and culturally exalted, they generally do not notice their advantages. They may even express opposition to blatant forms of sexist discrimination but not see the relationship between sexism and male privilege.

French feminists, such as Kristeva (1980), locate privilege and oppression within the structure of language. Adams et al. (1995), for example, identify the ways in which men use language to reinforce their assumptions about male dominance. Men construct what Adams et al. call a 'discourse of entitlement' that enables them to believe that they are designed to dominate women. Hatty (2000) argues that discourses such as these legitimate men's violence against women. From a discursive perspective, one challenges phallocentric discourses by replacing the male phallus with alternative forms of symbolic power.

Sexism and coercive control

Mederos (1987) differentiates between the institutionalised systems of patriarchy or the structural advantages and privileges that men enjoy, and the personal patriarchal system, which involves men's face-to-face interactions with women both at home and in the public sphere. He makes the point that because all men are socialised within patriarchy, they will all believe to some extent that they have a right to make normative claims upon women. Men will differ in relation to what claims they believe they make and how they may enforce them. These claims include deferential treatment, unpaid domestic labour and childcare, sexual services and emotional support. Most men come to believe that they deserve something from women which they then experience as an entitlement. The totality of these entitlements and claims are what constitute male privilege. This sense of entitlement may not necessarily be conscious and it may only come into their awareness when they are deprived of this unreciprocated service.

While some men have learnt to see the oppression of women, far fewer men have learned to see male privilege. Belief in male superiority and male authority are deeply embedded in most men. Brittan and Maynard (1984) argue that all men are exposed to socialisation experiences that turn many of them into 'male supremacists'. In this view, men are under pressure to internalise beliefs and feelings that naturalise their commitment to the subordination of women.

One of the key features of patriarchy is control. Mederos (1987) argues that all men are controlling to some extent and that there are no substantial differences between men who are violent to women and men who are not. Some men engage in control over women in response to their own experience of being controlled by other men at work. Given that men judge their manhood by how much control they have, A. Johnson (1997) argues that these men's control of women serves as a form of compensation for their lack of control at work.

Stark (2007) believes that the entrapment of women in personal life cannot be adequately understood by violence, not even by extending the definition of violence to include a range of abusive and controlling behaviours. He argues that we need to use the language of coercive control to best capture the multitude of ways that men dominate women through intimidation, economic oppression, limitations of movement and speech. Defining men's violence as abuse of their authority and power implies that men's power over women is legitimate.

For many men, being in control is an essential part of what it is to be a man. To challenge men's coercive control of women will be even more difficult than preventing men's violence because it involves challenging the normative foundations of men's privilege and their sense of entitlement to make claims upon women (ibid.). Challenging the legitimacy of men's power over women leads to the heart of men's sense of entitlement.

Gender regimes and the gender order

In 1987 Connell set out to develop a comprehensive theoretical overview of gender relations. Drawing upon important feminist work at the time, she formulated the concept of 'gender order' to describe the socially constructed pattern of gender relations between men and women. While patriarchal power and unequal gender relations constitute the basis of most forms of gendered social organisation, she emphasised that there was no inevitability that the patterning of gender should be patriarchal. Within the context of this wider gender order, Connell used the notion of 'gender regimes' to describe the current pattern of gender relations within specific institutions such as workplaces, schools, government and other apparatuses of the state (Connell 1987).

It was in her book *Gender and Power* that Connell first formulated her then three-fold model of gender as a structure of social practice: labour, power and cathexis (emotional attachment). Connell (2005) later added the fourth dimension of symbolism because she realised that she had previously underestimated the significance of culture in constructing masculinities. These four dimensions of gendered power can be used to disaggregate various forms of male privilege.

At the level of power relations, Connell documents the various forms of subordination of women to men. This is manifested in men's control over most of the senior positions in power in both the corporate and government sectors, including the military, the police and other sectors of government (Connell 1995). Male privilege is normalised through cultural understandings of men's monopoly of the upper echelons of these private corporations and public sector institutions. Powerful interrelationships between hegemonic constructions of masculinity and hegemonic constructions of management and leadership produce a taken-for-granted association between maleness and organisational power (Collinson and Hearn 2005). Male managers often find that management offers a powerful validation of masculine identity in expressing many of the qualities of successful manhood (Whitehead 2002).[2]

Men's violence against women can be located within this framework. Connell (1995) regards men's violence against women as providing a general benefit to men's dominance because it provides a threat to women, even if it is not overt or actualised. Many writers have connected men's privilege and sense of male entitlement to violence against women, arguing that we live in a culture that legitimises and sanctions violence. Most men believe that they have the inherent right to control decision-making and the division of labour in the family. Since women's domestic work is seen as an affirmation of a patriarchal masculinity, these men are easily disappointed and frustrated when women do not do what they expect of them.

Historically, feminist analyses have argued that violence against women is a reflection of patriarchal structures that subordinate and oppress women. O'Toole and Schiffman (1997) understand violence against women as flowing logically from inequalities in power between women and men. Here, men's violence against women is conceptualised in terms of gendered and unequal power relations (Itzin 2000). There is a considerable body of empirical evidence to support this feminist view. Kimmel (2000) surveyed cross-cultural and anthropological research that demonstrates that gender inequality is the most significant cause of men's violence against women. Websdale and Chesney-Lind (1998) point out that numerous studies link power relations in families to the extent of men's violence against women. They show a significant relationship between economic dependence of a woman on a man and greater likelihood of her experiencing acts of violence.

At the level of the gendered division of labour and production relations, Connell (1995) examines the dividends men derive from their status and position in patriarchal authority relations in terms of higher wages and other material benefits. Men have higher levels of workforce participation, earn twice the average income of women and control most of the wealth in society. Men earn consistently more than women in comparable jobs and women are more likely to be working part-time and have less access to superannuation (R. Smith 2001). On the global scale, while women undertake approximately

2. See Flood and Pease (2005) for an analysis of how male privilege is manifested in public sector institutions.

two-thirds of the economically productive work in the world and provide almost half of the food, they receive only 10 per cent of all income and only 1 per cent of all property (A. Johnson 1997). These gendered inequalities persist in spite of legislative changes and challenges by the women's movement.

Patterns of gender inequality are also evident in domestic work in heterosexual living arrangements. Men's lack of involvement in family work is documented in numerous studies. Many surveys demonstrate men's proportional involvement in childcare and housework has increased only marginally in spite of women's increased participation in the paid labour force (Dienhart 1998). Studies carried out in Australia in the last fifteen years consistently demonstrate that the sexual division of labour in the home is very rigid. Only 1–2 per cent of fathers share equally in the physical care of children and 5–10 per cent are significantly involved in day-to-day care of children. Women undertake approximately 90 per cent of all childcare tasks and 70 per cent of all domestic work. A study of dual-income families reported that 82 per cent of mothers had overall responsibility for children (Russell and Barclay 1999). Thus, even when men's and women's work outside the home is equal, women still do significantly more housework than men (Bryson 2007). Another Australian study published in 1997 showed that women completed more than 65 per cent of all unpaid household labour and this did not include the invisible work of thinking about and planning meals, and so on (Dempsey 1997).

At the level of cathexis and emotional attachment Connell interrogates the expression of sexual desire. Heterosexuality for men embodies specific privileges in relation to women's subservience to men's sexual pleasure and men's receipt of emotional support from women partners that they do not have to reciprocate (Connell 1995).[3]

At the level of symbolism, Connell notes that men are culturally exalted over and above women in part because they control cultural institutions, such as the media, universities and religion, where men's and women's statuses are defined and promoted. Women are defined as subordinate to men and consequently receive lower levels of recognition for their contributions to society (Connell 2000a).[4]

---

3. See Chapter 7 of this book for an analysis of the privileges associated with heterosexual desire.

4. Connell's level of symbolism can be equated with the concept of phallocentrism previously discussed.

Connell's four dimensions of gender practice collectively form what she calls 'the patriarchal dividend'. This patriarchal dividend constitutes the advantages that men gain from their maintenance of gender inequality (ibid.). For Connell, men have interests in actively defending these benefits that they receive.

Understanding male privilege

Sexism and patriarchal arrangements can only be overcome if we acknowledge and address male privilege. When gender inequalities are acknowledged, they tend to be discussed more in terms of women's disadvantage than male advantage and privilege. Even many profeminist writers who recognise gender inequality do not theorise male privilege (Carbado 2001). So rather than talking in terms of women's lack of resources, we should talk about men's surplus of resources (Connell 2002). Eveline (1994; 1998) has drawn attention to 'male advantage' in contrast to 'women's disadvantage', pointing out that focusing solely on women's disadvantages and ignoring male privilege normalises and legitimises masculinist standards.

If men do not recognise the unearned privileges they receive as men, they will be unable to acknowledge the impact of these privileges upon the women in their lives. Schacht (2003) adapted McIntosh's (1992) list of white privileges to identify the various ways in which he benefited from male privilege.[5] Some of the main unearned benefits he identified are listed below.

- I can be reasonably sure that most of the jobs I might apply for I will not only have a better chance of getting them than a comparably qualified woman, but I will be paid more than a woman doing the same job.
- When I read a newspaper or watch the nightly news, I can largely assume that the vast majority of the stories will be about the accomplishments of men.
- Should I enjoy watching sports, I am virtually guaranteed that all the important most skilled participants will be men.
- If I am married or cohabitating, I can count on my 'wife' doing most of the housework and being responsible for most of the childcare should we have children, regardless of whether she works or not.

---

5. See Chapter 6 of this book for an analysis of the privileges associated with whiteness.

- Should I feel the need to physically assault my 'wife', I can be reasonably assured that I will largely not be held accountable for my actions.
- When venturing out in public, I can be reasonably assured that I will not be sexually harassed or sexually assaulted.
- Should I feel the desire to search for positive role models in positions of authority, nearly everywhere I look I can easily find a male to fill this need.
- When attending school, I can often count on the teacher (he or she) to perceive my presence and enquiries as more important than those of the females who are in attendance.
- When undertaking conversations with women, I can largely count on my voice being heard more often and my comments being more validated.
- Should I choose not to partake in any of the above conditions, the mere fact that I can make this choice is in itself indicative and quite telling of the privilege upon which it is predicated.

Men gain these benefits whether they actively support male domination or not. Even those proactive against men's privileges will continue to reap the benefits of them. Men must examine their lives to become more aware of the privileges they experience every day simply because they are men, as a precursor to changing what they do. Towards this end, privilege lists such as these are important in bringing these issues into the foreground.

Intersections and the social divisions among men

The list of privileges by Schacht also reveals him to be a middle-class white man. His relationship to patriarchy is different from a working-class black man. As previously noted, Connell (1995) acknowledged that men's interests are divided by class, race and sexuality and consequently that men do not have equal access to the patriarchal dividend. Indigenous men, immigrant men from non-English-speaking backgrounds, working-class men, disabled men and gay men do not benefit from patriarchy in the same way as middle-class white straight men. Differences are also found across cultures and through historical time. Connell (1993) has pointed out that the discourse about 'masculinity' is constructed out of 5 per cent of the world's population of men, in one region of the world, at one moment in history. We know from ethnographic work in different cultures, how non-Western masculinities can be very different from the Western norm.

Furthermore, although most of the early work on men and masculinities was based in North America, the UK and Australia, in the last ten years there has been an internationalisation of masculinities research and theorising that has resulted in major anthologies and research monographs from many countries and regions of the world along with global comparative studies.[6] Our geo-political positioning will influence our theorising and our understanding of the relationship between gender and other social divisions. It must be acknowledged then that this examination of male privilege is undertaken in a Western context and that the literature reviewed is biased by Western knowledge.[7]

The question is whether the recognition of differences between men means that we lose sight of men as a gender. In acknowledging men's differences, we have to also ensure that we do not lose an understanding of the institutional power of men (Messner 2003). However, to critique a homogenised category of men is not to deny the reality of gender inequality. That men are divided among themselves along ethnic and class lines only makes the task of analysis more difficult (Brittan 1989).

Many men deny that they have any privileges because they are subordinated by class, race or sexuality and so on. Even if they are marginalised by other social divisions, they still maintain gendered advantages over women within their marginalised communities. Furthermore, Messner (2003) has identified that some of the strategies marginalised and subordinated men use to resist their class, sexuality and race-based oppression can often reproduce men's domination

---

6. See Pease and Pringle (2001), A. Jones (2006), and Flood et al. (2007) for introductions to these global perspectives on men and masculinities.

7. In the early 1990s, Mohanty (1991) challenged Western feminism for portraying 'Third World' women as an undifferentiated 'Other' and as being victims of timeless systems of patriarchy. She argued that Western feminism was itself embedded with unexamined assumptions of ethnocentrism and privilege, which led it to universalise the experiences of women. Many Western feminists have responded to this challenge, recognising that women globally do not face the same universal forms of oppression. Rather, it is understood that divisions between women in relation to race, nationality, religion, class, language and sexuality both within and across nations are more significant than was previously recognised (McEwan 2001).

over women. It is thus important to maintain the tension between an analysis of systemic gendered oppression and differentiated forms of male power flowing from other social divisions (Haywood and Mac an Ghaill 2003).

The unintended consequences of men's power and privilege

Although men are privileged, it does not mean that men do not experience pain in their lives. Men can be both privileged and miserable at the same time. Kaufman (1994) argues that men's lives involve both power and pain and that much of men's pain arises from men's power and privilege to constitute what he calls 'the contradictory experiences of men's power'. Thus the patriarchal dividend is not totally successful in advantaging men because men experience emotional and physical costs associated with their dominant position (Whitehead 2007). Connell (1995) acknowledges that there are disadvantages for men associated with their gendered privilege. For Connell many of the costs for men are by-products of the advantages they gain from the patriarchal dividend.

When the costs of masculinity are documented in popular books about men, however, they are rarely framed in terms of the unintended consequences of men's advantages. Populist writers of books about men talk about a 'crisis in masculinity' as men find their traditional privileges and symbolic power being eroded (Horrocks 1994; Biddulph 2008).

A number of writers have expressed concern about the ways in which men's physical and mental health issues have been used to position men as the 'new disadvantaged' (Connell 2000a; Whitehead 2002; Pease 2006; Riska 2006) Whitehead (2002) argues that 'the male crisis discourse' distorts the connections between hegemonic masculinity and men's health. The idea of masculinity in crisis may itself be a strategy enacted by men to reinforce their power (Allen 2002). Connell (2005) also makes the point that most of the costs associated with patriarchy for men are not necessarily experienced by the men who gain most of the benefits. Many current men's health policies and programmes fail to recognise the social and economic context of men's lives and the impact of class and race divisions on their health (Connell 2000a; Pease 2006; Bentley 2007; Pease 2009).

The current focus on what men have to gain from gender equality does not sufficiently acknowledge what men have to lose. Men need to be encouraged to see their involvement in campaigns for gender equality as attaining a more ethical sense of self as opposed to the benefits they might get out of gender equality (Pease 2008).

In contrast to the crisis of masculinity discourse, Connell (1995) prefers to talk about 'crisis tendencies' that arise from structural tensions and inequalities in the gender order. These crises are generated in the structures of gender by women's advances towards greater equality in public policies, women's increased participation in the paid labour force and women's challenges to men's sexual prerogatives. Men's responses to these crises range from anti-feminist backlashes to profeminist support for gender equality.

Men's resistance to change

Attempts to articulate the benefits for men in gender equality and non-violence must acknowledge the reasons for men's resistance. Connell (2003a) identifies four areas:

1. The material benefits, including the care and domestic services men receive from women.
2. The identity problems about change involving men's internalisation of hegemonic notions of masculinity about strength and toughness.
3. The resentment felt against gender equality programmes by men who get very little of the patriarchal dividend.
4. The ideological defence of male supremacy by men who have deeply internalised a sense of male entitlement.

There are also major cultural and political infrastructures reproduced by men that maintain patriarchal power relations.

To involve men in changing unequal gender arrangements, they must be persuaded that the costs associated with the current system outweigh the benefits (Connell 2003b). So how do the health disadvantages and the work pressures add up against the services of domestic and emotional support that men receive from women? While many of the arguments about men's involvement focus on how men will gain from gender equality, the reality is that most men do not see the gains as benefits. In the prevailing view, much of men's opposition to gender equality is based on their ignorance of what is in it for them. Too often gender equality is conceptualised in terms of attitudes, as if the real issue were in men's minds. In this instance, we think that if we construct a good enough argument, most men would change their minds. However, focusing on what men will gain by gender equality and non-violence has not seemed to work very well for practical policies and programmes targeted at men. Gendered power and privilege are often ignored in this approach (Magnusson 2000).

As previously mentioned, if we move towards greater gender equality, men will lose some of the domestic services performed by women. They will have less power over women and there will be an erosion of cultural traditions that prioritise men (Connell 2003b). It will not necessarily be a 'win-win situation' (Lang 2002). While there may be long-term gains for men in terms of improved relationships with women, greater capacity for emotional intimacy and better psychological and physical health, there are certainly short-term losses. As a result, the reality is that many men will not be willing partners in the change process. It would appear that most men believe that, on the whole, the existing gender relationships serve them very well. Connell (2002) maintains that most discussions of changing men tend to underestimate the extent to which men have material interests in maintaining the current hierarchical gender arrangements.

While men will often refer to critiques of patriarchy as 'male bashing', it is in part because they are unable to separate out patriarchal arrangements from their own experience. Many men have difficulty untangling a critique of patriarchy as a particular form of gender order from a general critique of men. Many men think that a critique of patriarchy implies that all men are oppressive in their behaviours towards women. Some men will act defensively, however, because they identify with the values of patriarchy and they do not want to relinquish the male privileges associated with it (A. Johnson 1997).

It is often difficult for men to acknowledge the oppression of women because they are implicated in it. Gender is differentiated from many of the other social divisions because it is experienced in the context of intimate relationships at home (Rideway and Correll 2004). When it comes to men's wives, mothers, sisters and daughters, it is likely that they have participated in the subordination of these women who are a part of their life. Many men are reluctant to acknowledge that male privilege exists because they fear they will have to face guilt and shame for their part in maintaining their privileges (A. Johnson 1997).

Conclusion

Connell (2000a: 205) articulates a vision of an egalitarian society by advocating changes in the four major structures of gender: the relations of power, the relations of production, patterns of emotional attachment and symbolic systems. Changing power relations involves usurping men's political dominance in the state, the professions and management and by ending violence against women. Changing production relations means equalising incomes from paid work, valuing and respecting previously defined 'women's work' and ensuring an equitable division of household work. Changing emotional relations involves 'reconstructing heterosexual relations on the basis of reciprocity not hierarchy and disconnecting masculinity from pressures towards violence'. Changing the symbolism of gender means 'formulating different gender meanings for men and images of different ways of living' (Connell 2000a: 205).[8]

Men have to be involved in the process of challenging patriarchy. While many have been resistant to the challenges to their privilege, there have always been small counter-hegemonic groups of men who are opposed to patriarchy. Their ability to reconstruct their subjectivities and challenge the cultural and structural foundations of their privilege is the subject of extensive debate within feminism and profeminist masculinity politics. In my view, it is possible for men to develop a cognisance of their gender privilege and to act in ways that challenge the reproduction of gender inequality (Pease 2000, Pease 2002a).

The concept of doing gender (first introduced by West and Zimmerman 1987), focuses our attention on the interactional dynamics that men engage in to reproduce our privileges. This idea challenged the structural determinist approaches to gender that seemed to leave little room for resistance and change. Undoing gender, which describes interactions that challenge gender inequality (Deutsch 2007), allows us to identify how we can challenge the reproduction of male privilege.

Although feminism offers men the promise of a socially just and gender-equal world, most men have developed a defensive reaction to feminism. As men, we remain threatened by the autonomy of women. Having to meet women in their autonomy and independence is a challenge to the superiority men have assumed. Whatever our rationalisation, it is difficult for us not to feel that women are

8. See Pease (2002a) for my elaboration of a slightly different framework encompassing the revisioning of family life, the redistribution of economic power, the transformation of the culture that supports men's violence against women and re-creation of the masculine self.

'ours'. Possessiveness is so deeply embedded within our culture and so internalised in our identities that it is hard to work it through. Even to acknowledge the depth at which feminism threatens us as men would be a first step (Seidler 1991).

In Connell's (2000a) view, the primary motivating factor for men to support gender equality will come from their 'relational interests' winning out over their egotistic interests. It is men's relationships with partners, daughters, mothers and sisters that will provide the basis upon which men will come to support change (Connell 2000a: 204). Such a stance requires the development of what Kimmel (2000: 335) calls 'democratic manhood', where men will take a stand against gender injustice on the basis of moral and ethical commitments. We must not underestimate, however, how difficult it is to challenge unequal gender regimes. This is due in part to the fact that the powers of those who are defending these regimes often overpower those who are challenging them (Acker 2006a).

Nevertheless, there have always been practical things that men can do every day if they have the moral courage to challenge the reproduction of patriarchy and male privilege: men can read feminist and profeminist literature; they can join an existing profeminist men's group or they can get together with some other men and start one themselves; they can ensure that they do their fair share of household work; they can stop interrupting women when they speak; they can stop sexualising women's bodies; they can speak out against men's violence; they can listen to women, and so on.[9] For this to happen, men have to acknowledge that patriarchy and unearned male privileges exist, that they are reproduced by the practices of men and that men will have to develop the moral courage to act in concert with women to live lives based on reciprocity rather than unearned entitlement.

9. Numerous lists of what men can do to challenge sexism and violence against women have been developed over the years and are available on feminist and profeminist sites on the Internet. There is no shortage of practical and concrete actions that men can take if they want to.

SIX
Racial formations and white supremacy

Race has been used historically to categorise and value people on the basis of their physical characteristics. Essentialists attribute psychic and biological differences to people of different races. Biologically based theorists of race have thus legitimated racial inequality because within a biological framework racial difference is regarded in a hierarchical way. Those who continue to defend racial categorisation make the distinction between racialism, which they claim does not make value judgements on the basis of categorised physical features, and racism, which does make such judgements (Machery and Faucher 2005). Yet, the scientific claims of racialism have been the basis for the belief in the superiority of white people over people of colour. Those who believe in racial supremacy do not necessarily see themselves as making political and ethical decisions. Many believe that they are simply defining reality 'as it is'. Challenging racial inequality can therefore be interpreted as trying to upset the natural order.

There is considerable evidence to demonstrate that race does not have a genetic basis and that it is socially constructed (Kendall 2006). As a result, the meaning of race changes from place to place and over time; it is not a static or fixed category. Notwithstanding the socially constructed nature of racial difference, because it continues to be used to rationalise and legitimate unequal treatment, it constitutes a material force that shapes people's lives. For this reason, it is important to continue to use the concept of race in analysing racism and white privilege.

Growing up white

What does it mean to be white and why should those who are white think about it? I was thirteen years old when my older brother formed a relationship with an Aboriginal woman in Australia. When my parents became aware of this relationship, they were outraged and disowned him as a son. It took some years before they were able grudgingly to accept my brother's partner as a part of the family. Even then, they needed to exceptionalise her. They needed to see her as somehow different than other Aboriginal people so that their racist views were not disrupted. Encountering my parents' racism as a child shocked me. No less shocking was the connection it gave me to Aboriginal city slums and rural reserves, where many Indigenous people lived. The more I connected with some aspects of urban and rural Aboriginal culture in Australia, the more I developed a consciousness of being white. In my teens I did not have an awareness of how this experience of whiteness represented privilege. While I was very critical of what I saw as the racist attitudes of my parents, the experience did not in itself lead me to a consciousness of my own internalised racism. All of this would come much later.

People's perceptions of the world are influenced by their personal biographies and their social locations. Some writers refer to this notion as 'positionality'. This means that how people think and what they see in the world is limited and constrained by the positions they occupy. Once they recognise this positionality they can also see how they can 'reposition' themselves. Those in dominant positions are not locked into a position of dominance and have room to move. Through understanding how their position is reproduced, they can choose to act in ways that challenge their privileged position.

I am white. I am conscious that when I write or talk about white privilege as a white male academic it is likely to carry more credibility than if a person of colour raises these issues. This is one of the consequences of privilege; the views of the privileged are more likely to be listened to. There is power in speaking from the dominant positioning in part because I benefit from the privileges that I critique. While there are tensions here, I have a responsibility to use that power to name and speak out against white privilege.

Racism as prejudice

Studies of race relations and racism tend to focus on racial prejudice. Like most people, I came to think about racism as a form of prejudice – bigoted views that one group of people hold about another. Not surprisingly, racism is also something that one is unlikely to identify with or own as a part of oneself. How many people have begun to talk about non-white people with the following statement: 'I'm not racist, but …'? Even white supremacists are not likely to see themselves as racist.

As I challenged racism, it became clear to me that it was more than simply prejudice or bigotry. Racism is more pervasive than that and it involves everyday beliefs that whites carry around that defend our/their advantageous position. As one participant in a study carried out by Lawrence and Tatum (1997: 336) said, 'I had been taught that racism was an individual act of meanness perpetrated against some minority group. I never suspected that it was an intricate system of advantages of which I was a part.'

Seeing racism simply as a form of prejudice places all forms of racial prejudice on the same level. In this view, non-white people can be racist in relation to white people and other people of colour. However, in critical perspectives on race relations, racism is understood as 'prejudice plus power' (Rothenberg 2000). Within this definition, only white people can be racist in a white supremacist society because only they have the institutionalised power to convert their prejudiced attitudes into legislative policies and organisational practices. Understanding racism solely as a form of prejudiced attitudes does not allow us to name and interrogate the institutionalisation of racial hierarchy in white-dominated societies. Also, because racism is more than prejudice, one does not have to be racist in order to reproduce racial inequality.

Race relations and colour blindness[1]

Colour blindness has become a strategy for challenging racism. In this view, people do not see colour, as in the statements: 'I see only people,' or 'Why do we look at people by the colour of their skin? It shouldn't matter.' This notion encourages people to ignore ethnicity and race when they form impressions of others (Hitchcock 2002). In the eyes of some, consciousness of colour is seen as being racist. In this instance, seeing racial difference equates with being prejudiced. That is why we are encouraged to see everyone 'as individuals'.

Frankenberg (1993) talks about white people believing that they can see 'the real person' beneath the skin. People's humanness is emphasised and the race of a person is ignored. Racism, in this view, is something connected to individual acts of discrimination. Being 'colour blind' means that we do not see racialised structures of

---

1. The use of the word 'blindness' as a metaphor for lack of awareness has been criticised by disability theorists for trivialising sight deprivation. See, for example, Schor (1999).

inequality and unconscious racism. We may recognise how people of colour face discrimination without understanding how white people are privileged. Colour blindness also does not recognise the pride that people may associate with their colour. For some racialised groups, their experience of a racialised identity provides them with a sense of empowerment and solidarity that acts as a buffer against some of the negative effects of racism.

This colour-blind approach can also be used to charge those on the receiving end of racism with racism, when they seek special treatment to counteract the disadvantages they suffer. For the argument goes that if we are all just individuals, then special treatment would not be justified. Disavowing institutional racism, the colour-blind approach reinforces white privilege while enabling white people to consider themselves non-racist. However, Dei et al. (2004) challenge the idea of white people being 'non-racist'. In their view, we are all either anti-racist or racist. That is, not actively challenging racism implies complicity in condoning it. They use the notion of 'aversive racists' to describe those who think of themselves as free of prejudice while enjoying the privileges accruing to their white skin. Grimes (2002) believes that between 80 and 90 per cent of white people who regard themselves as non-prejudiced are likely to express aversive racism. It is this kind of attitude that enables white people to support egalitarian values and tolerance for difference, while benefiting from structures that continue unchallenged.

Diversity awareness: race as the 'other'

Another problematic approach to race relations is diversity awareness. There are many books and courses on understanding how various cultural groups differ from white people. Race is something that white people tend to attribute to other people. Many white people are now trying to appear to be more conscious of difference. Diversity is a buzz word at the moment, in the classroom and the workplace. Versions of diversity awareness have even become 'corporatised' in education and business. Whites are trained in 'cultural competence', defined as 'the capacity to work effectively with cultural others' (O'Hagen 2001: 83). Frankenberg (1997) has observed that such training focuses attention on cultural difference at the expense of examining white dominance. Once again whites re-emerge as the normal standard bearer, with whites magnanimously wanting to become 'competent' in relation to members of 'marked' cultural groups.

The diversity approach seems to assume that it is only non-white people who have a culture and a race. A few years ago, the Australian Association of Social Workers engaged in a review of its code of ethics for social workers. One significant development in the new code was the prescription of social workers to ensure that they were responsive to cultural difference. This was ironical, given the unstated assumption in the new code that all of the social workers were white. This is an instance of how unexamined whiteness unconsciously informs professional thinking.

Racism and race relations are also often taught in universities as an issue facing people of colour. Moreton-Robinson (2000) has written about how white feminist academic women in Australia have incorporated cultural difference into their curricula, but have failed to acknowledge or challenge their own middle-class white positioning. They have not racialised themselves, and Moreton-Robinson charges them with complicity in racial oppression of other women.

Lasch-Quinn (2001) also notes that diversity training has burgeoned to the point of creating a 'diversity industry'. DeRosa (1999: 190) has called this 'racism as tourism': 'Stopping along the road of life to learn bits and pieces of other cultures but not understanding the political implications of misappropriation, cultural intrusion and seeing "the other" as "exotic".' Certainly, many white people have used the cultures and traditions of Indigenous people and people of colour for their own purposes.

The racial diversity approach often assumes that racial differences are inherent and it tends to ignore the relations of power that reinforce these differences. The focus is often on cultural and ethnic differences at the expense of structural and political issues. People seldom see the ideologies and structures of white supremacy named and interrogated within diversity awareness training (Jensen 2005).

Making whiteness visible

Most white people have very little awareness about their own racial identity.[2] Whiteness is a concept that has meaning for white supremacists, but it is ignored by the majority of white people, who

2. Throughout this chapter I explore the complex layering of whiteness. It should be acknowledged, of course, if one is talking about African-Americans or Aboriginal Australians, that non-whiteness has complex layers as well.

do not think of themselves as white even though they benefit from white privilege.

If you are a white reader, you might say 'I don't see myself as white.' This is a statement that I have encountered many times when I have asked students what it means to be white. The most common response is that they haven't really thought about it. White male students have often commented to me that they see themselves as 'persons' or as 'individuals'. White people, like members of all dominant groups, are more easily able to think of themselves as individuals rather than as racialised persons because they locate their behaviour as part of their personal characteristics rather than framing it by the colour of their skin.

When white people speak, they claim to speak on behalf of humanity as a whole. People who are raced, however, are only able to speak for their race (Dyer 2002). This is an example of what Anderson (2003) means when he says that whiteness is 'the invisible norm'. Since whiteness is unexamined, it is seen as what is normal and natural. White people are encouraged not to think of themselves in racial terms. Whiteness represents normality and humanness. It is the universal standard against which judgements are made about moral worth. Of course, while whiteness is often invisible to those who have it, it has always been highly visible to those who are not white.

In recent years, a new field of scholarship has emerged called 'whiteness studies' or 'critical studies of whiteness' (Roediger 2006). Unlike the usual focus of race studies on the problems facing culturally diverse groups, this field of study involves an investigation of the experiences and behaviours of white groups.

The most widely cited premise of critical studies of whiteness is that white people do not recognise their unearned white privileges (Rasmussen et al. 2001). The task identified by many anti-racist activists and scholars is to make whiteness more visible. Just as feminism has challenged men to reflect critically upon their masculinity, so anti-racism challenges white people to reflect upon what it means to be white. Just as men have been challenged to not take 'male' for granted, so white people have been challenged to not take 'white' for granted. For white men, of course, this involves a double challenge.

Frankenberg (1993) describes this as 'race cognisance', whereby racial inequality is understood as being related to social structure. This latter approach involves white people explicitly naming themselves as white because of the understanding that one of the ways in which white privilege is maintained is through white people not naming themselves in racial terms.

Referring to this developing awareness of whiteness as 'critical whiteness' Knowles (2003: 199) defines it as 'challenging the privileges accruing to whiteness and seeing it as a set of racially located positions among others and not as a norm'. This means that we need to understand what has happened in the past if we are to take responsibility for acting in the present. Critics label this as the 'black armband' view of history and tell us that what happened in the past has nothing to do with us (McIntyre and Clark 2003). For example, in Australia there has been an extended public discussion of the idea of Aboriginal reconciliation. A question rarely asked, however, is whether reconciliation between white people and Aboriginal people can be achieved without interrogating whiteness. As Dom, a participant in a study by Wadham (2001: 289) put it: 'whiteness must become a problem for Australians if reconciliation is to be achieved'. If we do not see ourselves as white, it is easy to deny that we have anything to do with maintaining white privilege.

One of the strategies of interrogating whiteness is to encourage white people to recognise the racialised nature of their experience and to see themselves in the context of their particularity (Garner 2007). The aim is 'to induce self-consciousness or awareness of one's racial privilege and racial embodiment' (Seshadri-Crocks 2000: 161). As a tactic for raising this awareness, Thandeka (2000) suggests that white people play the race game that invites white people to experiment for a week using the word 'white' whenever they refer to a white person. The exercise upsets the norm of whiteness among white people and has a consequence of making them more conscious of being white. Thus, when I speak, I speak as a white person.

White people often feel most white or conscious of their whiteness when they find themselves in a minority among an otherwise non-white gathering. When I was attending a conference in Washington DC, I inadvertently wandered into a predominantly African-American neighbourhood in search of a restaurant. As I walked in to the restaurant, I not only became conscious of being the only white person there, but also that my presence was clearly taken as being out of the ordinary for the other diners. Since this experience happens so rarely for me, and because I can easily go elsewhere and avoid the situation in the future, this is not the same as experiencing the racialised gaze felt by people who are not white. Nevertheless, for just a moment, I felt what it means to be the object of a racialised gaze.

Most of the scholarly writing on whiteness is published in North America, although there is a developing literature in the United Kingdom (Bonnett 2000; Garner 2007) and Australia (McKay 1999; Moreton-Robinson 2004). We need to be careful not to overgeneralise the culturally specific knowledge developed.

In Australia, discussions of whiteness need to be located in the context of the ongoing colonisation of Indigenous people and particular government policies on migrants, refugees and asylum seekers. Historically, Australia has not been willing to acknowledge its occupation of Indigenous people's land and, although there is a growing awareness of past injustices against Indigenous people (Briskman 2007), Australian governments have failed to recognise Indigenous sovereignty. There is ongoing public debate about the need for white and Indigenous reconciliation, and what form it should take. In 2008, Prime Minister Kevin Rudd made a formal apology to Indigenous people affected by the removal of Aboriginal and Torres Strait Islander children from their families, but the failure to confront land rights and sovereignty indicates that there is a long way to go in addressing colonising relations in Australia and elsewhere.[3]

Recognising white privilege

One of the reasons for studying whiteness is to make more visible the privileges and entitlements white people receive so as not to cast all non-whites inadvertently as the 'other'. For Levine-Rasky (2002) this means understanding the following: the historical dimensions of whiteness, how white dominance gains legitimacy, how it is socially constructed and practised, and how it is modified or reinforced by other social divisions.

Addressing privilege requires recognition of it. The problem is that because most people are rarely challenged about their privilege, they are not likely to be reflective about the benefits they receive. They have to learn to see those processes that reproduce their privileged identity (Sacks and Lindholm 2002).

---

3. Although I draw upon the international literature about whiteness in this chapter, and my argument about white privilege applies to all white-dominated societies, invariably my experiences of white privilege are shaped by the particular experiences of Aboriginal Australia.

Peggy McIntosh, in a frequently reprinted article referred to in Chapter 1, identified fifty privileges that she benefited from as a white person. She turned the tables to examine the other side of racial disadvantage (McIntosh 1992). This list provides an excellent illustration of how white privilege is reflected in the everyday lifestyles of white people. Below are some of the privileges McIntosh identifies:

- I can if I wish arrange to be in the company of people of my race most of the time.
- If I should need to move, I can be pretty sure of renting or purchasing housing in an area which I can afford and in which I would want to live.
- I can be pretty sure that my neighbours in such a location will be neutral or pleasant to me.
- I can go shopping alone most of the time, pretty well assured that I will not be followed or harassed.
- I can turn on the television or open the front page of the newspaper and see people of my race widely represented.
- I can be sure that my children will be given curricular materials that testify to the existence of their race.
- I can speak in public to a powerful male group without putting my race on trial.
- I can do well in a challenging situation without being called a credit to my race.
- I am never asked to speak for all people in my racial group.
- I can be pretty sure that if I ask to speak to 'the person in charge', I will be facing a person of my race.
- I can take a job with an affirmative action employer without having co-workers on the job suspect that I got it because of my race.
- I can be sure if I need legal or medical help, my race will not work against me.

When I use this article in my teaching, I ask the white students to identify the privileges they have and to consider what their lives might be like if they were not white. I also ask them to reflect upon which of these privileges, if any, they could discard and which, if any, they believe should not be extended to all people irrespective of the colour of their skin.

If you believe that race is not a significant factor affecting life chances, then you are unlikely to see your own advantages and privileges. If you do believe that race is a significant factor, you are likely to be using individualistic explanations for achievement in the world. White people are inclined to maintain that the achievements in their life are a result of their hard work, not the privileges of their skin colour. Those who have less than them are cast as lazy and incompetent (Dei et al. 2004).

As a white person, I benefit from whiteness as a system of privilege every day whether I want to or not. We all tend to think that we have earned the privileges we enjoy. After all, we have worked hard and made sacrifices along the way. While I am not denying the reality of hard work and sacrifice, many of the privileges we have as white people are unearned.

Even many of those who acknowledge the reality of racist oppression blame it on historical circumstances and systemic structures outside people's control and thus ignore their own complicity in those systems of injustice. Many white people who see themselves as progressive do not acknowledge their complicity in reproducing the structures of racial stratification. If they do not recognise the privileges that accrue to them because they are white, their actions against racial dominance are unlikely to be effective.

Whiteness and intersectionality

McIntosh's list of white privileges is limited in so far as it does not acknowledge how class and other forms of oppression intersect with the advantages of having white privilege. Some critical race theorists have regarded race as the central organising dynamic of oppression and have ignored the roles played by class and gender dynamics. Critics have pointed out that there is a tendency in much of the critical whiteness literature to overlook the differences and social divisions that exist within whiteness. O'Grady (1999: 132), for example, argues that we have to be careful not to 'essentialise race or see everything in terms of race alone'. Some of the discussions of whiteness rest upon notions of a fixed or natural essence. As Frankenberg (2001: 76) argues, 'whiteness as a site of privilege is not absolute but rather is cross-cut by a range of other axes of relative advantage or subordination; these do not erase or render irrelevant race privileges, but rather inflect or modify it'. Just as all men do not have the same access to what Connell (1987) calls 'the patriarchal dividend', not all white people are able to take the same degree of advantage from white privilege. Whiteness intersects with gender, class, sexuality, ethnicity, age and able-bodiedness (Alcoff 2000), and the relationships to these attributes impact on the degree of white privilege people are able to access.

White people are never only white. They also have a gender and a class location, are aged and express themselves sexually and so on. All of these aspects comprise people's identity. Some of these aspects of identity are more important at some times than at others. Whiteness may fade into the background when faced with discrimination based on gender, sexuality or class. White privilege is thus likely to be mediated by these other aspects of identity.

Marxists have emphasised the role that capitalism and class divisions play in promoting racial hierarchy. They have also drawn attention to the differences in class privilege among white people (Philip 2004). In North America, poor working-class white people are represented as 'white trash' (Wray 2006). Some authors see this group's oppression as comparable to that of racial minorities, while others emphasise the importance of raising awareness among this group of their racism and white privilege.

While both men and women are implicated in white privilege, there are significant differences in the ways in which men and women embody these privileges.

Yet, when I attended a whiteness studies conference, where most of the white participants were women, there were no papers and no discussion of how whiteness is mediated by gender. We should be careful in talking about white women as being privileged in an absolutist way (Levine-Rasky 2002).

Kim (2004) also raises the concern that whiteness studies constructs a binary white/non-white framework that does not acknowledge the differences in the experiences of non-white groups. There is a tendency to locate all non-black people as white. Some racial minorities who may not be as disadvantaged as black people may be regarded as white, even though they are relatively disadvantaged compared to white people.

The question is whether recognising diversity within whiteness takes the focus off white dominance (Philip 2004). Although white people do not all have the same degree of access to white privilege, the notion of white privilege per se is not negated, just complicated. That some whites also experience some form of oppression does not let them off the hook from addressing their white privileges. All white people are capable of being racially prejudiced and unaware of their white privilege, irrespective of their gender, sexuality or class. However, many debates about how differences among white people influence their racism and/or their privilege tend to be quite polarised. Either, it is said that working-class white people are more racist than middle-class white people, or working-class white people are presented as a marginalised group who have no responsibility for racism.

Whiteness accrues most privilege when it is associated with upper-class men who are dominant in most institutions (O'Brien and Feagin 2004). There is a problem when explanations of white privilege fail to acknowledge how class, gender and other social divisions influence white identities and the privileges associated with them. Strategies that challenge institutionalised racism must take account of these structural differences and differences in consciousness among white people (Dei et al. 2004).

Transforming or disowning whiteness

Once those of us who are white acknowledge our whiteness and the privileges that flow from it, we then have to decide what to do about it. The strategies are often framed as either transforming or disowning whiteness. Can whiteness be reconstructed or does it have to be repudiated? One argument is that we can construct a positive version of whiteness; that whiteness can be more than a form of domination. Flagg (1997: 629) argues that white people can develop 'a positive white racial identity' that is 'neither founded on the implicit acceptance of white racial domination nor productive of distributive effects that systematically advantage whites'. In this view, whiteness as domination can be unlearned, just as men can unlearn hegemonic masculinity. Helms (1995) developed a six-stage process that white people can move through to develop an 'autonomous white identity'. The final stage represents the internalisation of a positive anti-racist white identity that is not hampered by racism.

Should white people try to create positive white identities? Such work lends itself to understanding racism as arising from individual personality disorders that leave the cultural and structural bases of white privilege unexamined (McKinney 2005). It also raises the question of whether whiteness is capable of being reconstructed towards a more inclusive form of subjectivity and whether it can be separated from the exercise of oppression (Kim 2004).

Some writers have argued that any attempt to find goodness or acceptance in whiteness is problematic (Lopez 1996). These writers talk about disowning whiteness by becoming a 'race traitor'. The journal *Race Traitor*, founded by Noel Ignatiev, takes the position that: 'It is not merely that whiteness is oppressive and false; it is that whiteness is nothing but oppressive and false' (Roediger 1991: 13). In this view, whiteness is only about domination. The motto of *Race Traitor* is: 'Treason to whiteness is loyalty to humanity' (Garvey and Ignatiev 1997: 346). Ignatiev (1996: 292) argues that white people should 'forget that they are white and promote their interests as workers or women'. In this view, the project of repudiating white privilege also means repudiating white identities.

Critics of this strategy argue that whiteness cannot simply be rejected or abandoned by an act of will (Rodriguez 1998; Seshadri-Crocks 2000; Garner 2007).

While whites may develop a traitorous identity in relation to white privilege, it does not mean ignoring that they are white. To think of oneself as raceless raises the danger of ignoring the implications of race for one's life and the lives of others. Those of us who are white will continue to receive privileges for being so while white dominance persists (Sullivan 2006).

I am not so sure that we should be aiming to create a positive white identity. In a context where racial domination continues to exist, I do not believe that we can simply construct individual non-oppressive white subjectivities. While whiteness may be able to be reformed at the level of identity, I do not believe that this means it is able to be completely disassociated from white privilege. This aim could only ever be achieved when white domination ends.

Doing and undoing whiteliness

Whiteness is a process. It is one of the ways in which we 'do' social dominance. So it is not just an identity that comes out of having a white body; it is also something that is performed or practised (Levine-Rasky 2002). Knowles (2003: 25) refers to this process as 'race making'. What this means is that people reproduce racial inequality through 'a myriad of ordinary everyday social processes'. It is thus the activities of people in their everyday lives that sustain white dominance. For those of us who are white, we make ourselves through our habitual practices. It follows that there is potential for us to 'undo' some elements of the maintenance of white privilege. Perhaps, through changing what we do in the world, we can influence both who we are and what we gain from being white.

There is debate about whether we can 'do' race in ways that do not reproduce racial hierarchy. Critics suggest that seeing whiteness as something that is simply performed fails to make connections with institutionalised dominance (Ahmed 2004). The maintenance of whiteness involves group loyalty and material interests, as well as individual performance (Anderson 2003). However, to suggest that whiteness is socially constructed through everyday activities challenges the conception of whiteness as a fixed social category. White privilege is not something that can be simply rejected and denounced. White people cannot give up their whiteness, but developing an awareness of one's whiteness and one's racial prejudice can be a part of challenging racial inequality.

Sullivan (2006) argues that while the structural concept of white supremacy captures deliberate forms of white domination, it is unable to articulate the habitual practices that sustain white privilege. Sullivan acknowledges that racism operates on conscious and unconscious levels. This means white supremacy must be resisted through transformation of the self as well as through restructuring structures and institutions. Whiteness is internalised in individual white people as 'an unconscious habit' and as such it is often outside people's experience or knowledge. White domination is located both in the world and in the individual white person (ibid.). While racism is embedded within global political and economic structures, it is people's commitment to these structures that reproduces them. To explore how racism takes root in people's lives, changes in institutional structures need to be complemented by psychic changes in individuals. One cannot fully shirk racist habits, however, while conducive political and social structures are in place. Thus one needs to be working on personal, cultural and structural fronts at the same time.

Sullivan (ibid.) makes the distinction between being white and being whitely. Being white simply refers to white skin colour, whereas being whitely embraces habits and dispositions that reproduce racial hierarchy and white privilege. In her view, one can be white without being whitely. So in this view, one can detach oneself from whiteliness that reproduces racism by challenging all racist habits and dispositions. The process of unlearning whiteliness is not one of transcending white privilege but rather of acknowledging it and using it to struggle against racial domination.

Bush (2004) also argues that there is an important relationship between prejudiced attitudes and racialised social structures. She believes that systemic racial inequality is reproduced through individuals' complicity with ideologies that support those structures. If you are white and you believe that you are not part of racially unequal structures then you can enjoy the benefits of being white without having to do anything about them. Whites may even express anger at the injustice of those structures as long as they are not implicated in them or held personally responsible for them. By demonstrating how the everyday consciousness of people sustains those structures, spaces open up for individuals to eliminate white domination.

Facing whiteness: emotions and the catalysts for change

If I have managed to convince white readers that they have privileges that non-white people do not have, the next question is: why you should you relinquish these privileges. Why should you not enjoy them and if necessary defend them? What motivation for change would prompt you to challenge your own privileges?

Wanting to create a better world is one motivation. Justice and fairness should motivate at least some people to let go of privileges (Rothenberg 2002). For others (for example, Wise 2005), challenging racism is motivated by a desire to live their life ethically and morally. The issue of motivation is captured in a vignette that he describes when he was challenged by a black woman's expressed lack of trust towards him despite his anti-racist work. His response was to say that he was not challenging racism for her, but was doing so for his own humanity. Hopgood (2000) argues that white privilege damages and impoverishes the lives of white people as well as non-whites. When it comes to motivation to change, Wise (2005) also believes that it is only when whites realise how it damages their own lives that they will then be prepared to do something about it.

Recognising the privileges accruing to whiteness is likely to engender anxiety for many white people. Jensen (2005) says that the continuance of racism should cause discomfort. If white people are serious about challenging white dominance, then some discomfort will ensue. Rodriguez (1998) believes that some degree of confusion and destabilisation and even trauma is likely to be experienced by people when they start to engage with their own whiteness. For Jensen (2005), the overwhelming feeling of acknowledging white privilege is sadness. Such an emotion is inevitable when we consider the level of racial injustice in our society.

In Australia, the formal apology given by Prime Minister Kevin

Rudd to those Indigenous people affected by the widespread removal of children from their families marked a significant change in Australian race relations (Rudd 2008). The apology was only a small step towards reconciliation, yet symbolically it encouraged white Australians to acknowledge and confront the stolen generations as an aspect of the colonial legacy. I was among many white Australians who, on the day the speech was delivered, found myself emotionally overwhelmed by the public acknowledgement of these injustices.

Guilt is the emotion that often arises when white people start to engage with privilege. White people often respond defensively to the suggestion that they have white privilege because they do not want to feel guilty. Views are divided about whether guilt is positive in anti-racist work. Some people believe that there is no place for guilt and shame in addressing racism because it is a waste of time and energy. Many white people do not believe that they should feel any guilt at all (Hitchcock 2002). They charge those who talk about white privilege with demonising white people. It must be remembered that they do this within a culture that refuses to acknowledge anything negative about whiteness.

Some people regard guilt and shame as a 'wake-up call' and as a catalyst to change. For them, the refusal to feel any guilt can lead to a refusal to acknowledge any complicity in the suffering of others. Ryde (2009) believes that guilt and shame can play an important role in addressing white people's complicity in white privilege.

Defending whiteness: resistance to change

Defences to acknowledging white privilege take a number of forms. They range from the view that white privilege does not exist to defences of white privilege on the basis that it is a good thing because of the contribution of white Europeans to civilization, or because white people are morally superior (Jensen 2001). Wellman (1993) identifies the various ways in which white people defend their white advantages. The key strategy is to explain racial inequality in ways that do not implicate them. Even those who acknowledge that white privilege may not be morally defended argue that it cannot be changed because it is part of human nature for one group to dominate the other. Still others retreat into cynical despair.

Challenges to unjust systems of privilege are often experienced by members of the privileged group as a threat to their identity. As noted at the outset, because white identity is founded on a belief in the natural superiority of white people, challenges to the 'natural order of things' will unsettle an identity that is founded on superiority (Sacks and Lindholm 2002).

Others have used the meritocracy argument, noted earlier, that they have worked hard and thus deserve the rewards they receive. Some white people believe that if they accept the reality of white privilege it will negate their achievements. It is easy for me to construct a narrative about the hard work I did and the class barriers I had to overcome to attain the class privilege of being a university academic. It is much more difficult for me to acknowledge that being a white man opened many doors for me along the way.

Some white people believe that they are a disadvantaged group because of affirmative action policies that favour non-white people. Many white men believe that they are missing out on key positions because of the advances made by women and people of colour. They often feel that they are discriminated against for being white because they are victims of anti-discrimination policies (O'Brien and Feagin 2004). Some even construct being white as an obstacle to life opportunities, and in so doing, deny that whiteness is a privileged social location (Garner 2007).

The politics of whiteness

There is a possibility that whiteness studies may reproduce white dominance rather than unsettle it. Ahmed (2004) cautions that using the term 'critical' in relation to whiteness studies does not offer protection from the dangers of appropriation. How do you study whiteness without recentring white privilege? Whiteness and dominant white identities are privileged daily to the detriment of other racial identities. While Cuomo and Hall (1999: 3) argue that the process of 'critically interrogating whiteness seeks to decentre rather than recentre whiteness by making performances of whiteness visible', does this eventuate? How are we to discuss whiteness without once again putting it in the centre?

Some critics have argued that whiteness scholarship creates new forms of white privilege because it opens up new opportunities for white academics (Anderson 2003). Hill (2004) is sceptical about what has been achieved by the whiteness scholars since the emergence of the field, beyond the creation of new, privileged academic positions.

In North America, Omi (2001: 226) has reported that many African-Americans are concerned that whiteness studies may be 'a sneaky form of narcissism' and that it may shift 'the focus and the resources back to white people and their perspective'. Clarke and O'Donnell (1999: 4) talk about 'white fetishism' and discuss how 'even critical white studies can recentre dialogue around whiteness'. They report that in some multi-cultural conferences in North America, discussions about whiteness dominate the discourse about race. Gillborn (2006: 319) regards it as a move to bring the voice of white people back to the centre in terms such as: 'But enough about you, let me tell you about me.' Hooks (1992) also points out that in some discussions of whiteness there has been an overemphasis on how racism is victimising to whites. She argues that even though this strategy is aimed at encouraging whites to act against racism in their own interests, it is misguided.

One of the other dangers of critical whiteness studies is that whites may only read what other whites have to say about whiteness, just as many masculinity scholars do not read feminism. Subordinate groups 'have done most of the work of figuring out how privilege and oppression operate', so we need to read what they have written (A. Johnson 2001: 156). It is important to remember that people who are not white have written the most important work on whiteness and it was non-white academics who first brought the issue of whiteness to prominent attention (Hill-Collins 1990; hooks 1992; Morrison 1993).

Some critics have charged whiteness studies with overemphasising the cultural dimensions of whiteness at the expense of the structural determinants of racial inequality (Garner 2007). McLaren (1998) argues that we need to focus anti-racist struggles on the redistribution of resources rather than on white identities. We must remember, however, that racism is an ideological reality as well as having a material base. Whiteness functions as cultural capital in the form of values and norms (Garner 2007).

It is worth distinguishing between whiteness as identity, as ideology and as institution. Frankenberg (1993: 1) says that we need to separate out whiteness as a form of structural privilege from whiteness as a standpoint from which we view ourselves and others, and again from whiteness as 'a set of cultural practices that are visibly unmarked and unnamed'.

It is true that some forms of white studies analyse the impact of whiteness on particular white people without examining the links whiteness has to privilege and racial inequality (Bush 2004). Attitudinal change among whites will not in itself dismantle white privilege.

It is important to move beyond studies of prejudiced attitudes of white people to understand the ideologies and structures of white dominance. The danger is that studies explore white identities without locating them in the context of unequal racial formations. This is a danger that must be faced because white people's roles in challenging racism must be addressed. Any focus on whiteness should always connect racism with white privilege.

To struggle against racism is not to transcend it, but is rather to acknowledge one's relationship to it. Ahmed (2004) challenges white anti-racist activists to consider ways in which the recognition of white privilege itself may also potentially intensify it. As white people, we always remain implicated in whiteness and white privilege. Sometimes out of our desire to take action we are unable to listen fully and hear from non-white people about the effects of racism on their lives. To stay accountable, there needs to be ongoing engagement with non-white anti-racist activists.

Listening to those who experience racism

An important part of this process of undoing privilege from within is learning to see ourselves through the eyes of others. Kincheloe and Steinberg (2000) argue that if white men see themselves through the eyes of Indigenous people and people of colour, they may be more able confront their inclination to negate the impact of racism. The question is: how can whites be encouraged to be more open to seeing themselves as others see them?

If whiteness is to become something other than privilege and racial dominance, whites must listen to what non-whites have to say about us. A key aspect of challenging white subjectivities involves encouraging whites to listen to non-white people. We must take the perspective of those whom we define as the 'other' seriously. Learning to listen responsively to the experiences of non-white people is often a challenge for white people. Studying the insights of Indigenous peoples and others from non-white cultures is important not only to understand their experience of oppression, but also to learn about their ways of perceiving the world and whites within it.

Sacks and Lindholm (2002) suggest that those of us who are privileged need to overcome what they describe as 'social distance' between ourselves and those who are marginalised. In effect, this means that we need to spend time with people who are different from us rather than always associating with 'our own kind'. However, there are also times when white people's presence in the worlds of non-white people will not be appreciated. Knowing when to engage with non-white people and when not to is a complex matter and we need to develop an awareness about when our presence is not wanted.

Conclusion

The starting point for any form of anti-racism by white people must be an acknowledgement that they are white. We must also recognise that we live in a white supremacist society, that white people have privileges accruing to their whiteness and that they are personally implicated in the reproduction of the ideologies and structures of white dominance (Jensen 2005). White people must come to understand that what we do in the world reproduces our privileges.

It is difficult for all white people to comprehend the complexity of our connections to white privilege, how we collude with the system that perpetuates it and what to do about it. Our opposition to it does not necessarily negate it. White anti-racist activists need to acknowledge that developing an oppositional stance against white privilege does not stop them accruing privilege by virtue of their white bodies. It does not guarantee that their anti-racist practice will be free of complicity with racial domination (Philip 2004). Those of us who rebel against injustice need to recognise that it is more than likely that we will also be contributing in some ways to that injustice as well, in spite of our opposition to it. It is not possible to be completely detached from the system that grants us privileges. We need to transform the system, while being open to recognising when we get it wrong.

The concept of whiteness is useful as part of the critique of white supremacy because it is important to challenge the invisibility of whiteness as normative. It is possible to construct an oppositional white identity as long as we do not lose sight of institutionalised racism and structural inequality between people categorised as white and non-white.

SEVEN

Institutionalised heterosexuality and heteroprivilege

Few heterosexually identified men have written about heterosexuality. Most writings in the emerging field of critical heterosexual studies have come from heterosexual and lesbian feminists and gay and queer theorists. Writing about heterosexuality from within the dominant position poses a number of difficulties because when heterosexual men have written about sexuality, they have done so as a form of objective truth. Our ways of knowing and seeing the world have inscribed a particular form of epistemological dominance over contemporary debates, what Ryder (2004) calls 'epistemological imperialism'. This is particularly so when we define the experiences of others rather than talking about ourselves and our experiences of privilege. This chapter problematises heterosexuality as a given.

I know that I am in a contradictory position writing this chapter because while I attempt to challenge heterosexist practice, I continue to benefit from heterosexual privilege. I proceed because many lesbian and gay writers have challenged heterosexuals to talk about and problematise our heterosexuality rather than just assuming it (Humphries 1987; Jeffreys 1993). In short, we should not leave it to gay men and lesbians alone to deconstruct heterosexuality.

While I am conscious that there are problems in talking from within the dominant position, there are equal problems with silence. I hope that by writing from within the dominant heterosexual position, my comments may provide some basis for dialogue with feminist, lesbian, gay and queer theorists on heterosexuality. I know that I continue to learn from my gay and lesbian colleagues and friends. My 'taken-for-granted' privilege as a straight man has been pointed out to me on many occasions. Also, it is my own experience of homophobia and heterosexism that has contributed to my consciousness of it in others.

Theorising (hetero)sexuality

Perhaps the most significant division in sexuality studies is between the essentialists and the constructivists. Essentialists regard sexuality as a biological force, whereas constructivists regard sexuality as being socially constructed. Many gay theorists have argued that being gay or lesbian is grounded in a fixed and stable sexual identity (Appleby 2006). Gay essentialists argue that there is an 'essence' within homosexuals that makes them homosexual. There is considered to be some gay core of their being or their psyche or their genetic make-up. Arguing that gay and lesbians were born that way is an attractive idea to many gay men and lesbians (Jackson 1999). Essentialism has greatly influenced some sections of the gay liberation movement and the formation of a positive homosexual identity. This movement has attained greater recognition of the legitimacy of gay and lesbian lifestyles and challenged much of the prejudice and discrimination that non-heterosexual persons have faced.

In contrast, gay constructivists argue that homosexuality is culturally and historically constructed and they are critical of the idea of a fixed homosexual nature. Rather than asserting a gay identity, they believe we should engage in struggles to dissolve sexual identity and break down the division between heterosexual and homosexual. They point out the tension of attacking a naturalised system of sexual hierarchy, while at the same time affirming an essential homosexuality.

Katz (1995) argues against the biologically determinist view of homosexuality and sexual orientation that has underpinned some gay rights strategies, believing that sexual desire is not embedded in people's bodies outside the social context of their lives. He is critical of gay activists who want to naturalise homosexuality to demand its legitimacy. While he acknowledges that the affirmation of a 'natural' homosexuality has been important in the struggle for homosexual rights, he believes that this approach cannot address the sources of homosexual oppression because it cannot challenge the dominant assumption that heterosexuality is normal. Scott and Jackson (2000) similarly believe that the essentialist approach is unable to address the social inequalities that arise from sexuality. I, too, accept that when we posit heterosexuality as immutable, we maintain a hierarchical relationship between heterosexuality and homosexuality whereby homosexuality is constructed as deviant.

In raising this debate within gay scholarship, my purpose is not to take a position about the construction of gay subjectivities and identities. Rather, my focus is on the construction of 'heterosexuality'. There has been a tendency for social construction theories of sexuality to be confined to gay studies. As yet, it has not been widely discussed in relation to the dominant form of sexuality. This is an issue because there are very real dangers in examining gay, lesbian and queer identities without at the same time interrogating heterosexual subjectivities (Sumara and Davis 1999). Many critics fear that constructivism will be applied only to homosexuality and leave the construct of heterosexuality unchallenged. Why should lesbians and gay men develop a consciousness of a socially constructed sexual identity when heterosexuals do not?

The construction of heterosexuality as natural and normative

One of the ways in which heterosexuality is sustained is through silence. Unless we are otherwise informed, most of us will assume that everyone we meet is heterosexual. People generally 'do' heterosexuality without thinking critically about it (Jackson 2005). The only time that heterosexuals name it is when it is experienced as being under threat or challenge (Jackson 1999). Yet it is through the naming of heterosexuality that the taken-for-granted identity is made visible.

Those who are heterosexual do not usually think of themselves as having a sexual identity in the same way that gay men and lesbians do. They simply regard themselves as 'normal'. Research shows that most heterosexual people accept their heterosexuality without question and do not recognise the social forces that influence and shape it (Evans and Broido 2005). Because it is normative and assumed, the privileges associated with it are also taken for granted. This is even the case with many queer-friendly heterosexuals who recognise the disadvantages associated with homosexual desire but do not acknowledge the advantages flowing from their own heterosexual orientation (Carbado 2004).

When heterosexuality is accepted as normative, it becomes the standard for all legitimate sexual behaviour (Ingraham 2005). Other sexualities are then judged against it and found wanting because they do not conform to the established norm. For heterosexuals to see themselves as normal, gay men and lesbians must remain abnormal (Katz 1995). Hence the normalisation of heterosexuality provides a regulatory function (Carabine 1996). Jackson (1999) observes that homosexuality has long been regulated and consequently stigmatised and oppressed, while heterosexuality remains institutionalised and unquestioned. We also need to analyse the ways in which heterosexuality is institutionalised through gender hierarchy. We need to recognise how heterosexuality has become an oppressive political institution that privileges some at the expense of others and is rationalised in heterosexist legal discourses (Ryder 2004).

Since sexuality is understood as a natural biological drive, heterosexuality is legitimated through its assumed naturalness. The naturalisation of heterosexuality prohibits critical analysis (Katz 1995). Biology and nature are used to rationalise heterosexuality and its assumed superiority in ways similar to the naturalistic discourses that legitimate racism and sexism. To the extent that we see heterosexuality as an outcome of natural drives, it is unlikely that we will be able to overcome resistance to its dominance (V. Robinson 2007). If being a heterosexual is natural, then homosexuality is unnatural and abnormal. Homosexuals have somehow been failed by or transgressed from nature (Ryder 2004). For Hanscombe (1987), however, heterosexuality is no more natural than feudalism. For heterosexuality to have an egalitarian future, we have to rescue it from nature. We need to interrogate the assumed naturalness of heterosexuality and to see it as constructed and organised in very detailed ways rather than assuming it just to be the way we are.

It is important to debunk the key myths about heterosexuality to expose the assumptions upon which its hegemonic power is maintained (Yep 2003). In contrast to the view that heterosexuality is natural, universal, transhistorical, fixed and monolithic, Yep argues that it is has a history and constantly needs to reproduce itself.[1]

To challenge the naturalisation of heterosexuality, we need to historicise it. Katz (1995) demonstrates how the concept of heterosexuality is a relatively recent invention that arose in the late nineteenth century. By studying the history of heterosexuality, Katz hopes to challenge its hegemonic power. He demonstrates how heterosexuality is simply one particular form of sexual pleasure that signifies one historical arrangement of the sexes and their pleasures.

As I have indicated, the first step in denaturalising heterosexuality

1. This discussion of heterosexuality is largely confined to Western cultures. Heterosexuality is likely to be worked out differently in different cultures where homophobia, heterosexism and heteronormativity may be more or less prevalent.

is to name it and to make it visible. Richardson (1996) suggests that those of us who are heterosexual ask ourselves why we consider ourselves to be heterosexual. Because heterosexuality is taken to be the norm, heterosexuals are rarely asked to name their sexuality (Logan et al. 1996). In response to this avoidance, Martin Rochlin (2003) developed a heterosexuality questionnaire to turn the tables on the multiple interrogations of the lives of gay and lesbian people. Heterosexuals are asked to consider the following questions:

1 What do you think caused your heterosexuality?
2 When and how did you first decide that you were a heterosexual?
3 Is it possible that your heterosexuality is just a phase you may grow out of?
4 Is it possible that your heterosexuality stems from a neurotic fear of others of the same sex?
5 If you have never slept with a person of the same sex, is it possible that all you need is a good same-sex lover?
6 To whom have you disclosed your heterosexual tendencies?
7 Why do you heterosexuals feel compelled to seduce others into your lifestyle?
8 Why do you insist on flaunting your heterosexuality? Can't you just be who you are and keep it quiet?
9 Would you want your children to be heterosexual, knowing the problems they'd face?
10 A disproportionate majority of child molesters are heterosexuals. Do you consider it safe to expose your children to heterosexual teachers?
11 Even with all the societal support marriage receives, the divorce rate is spiralling. Why are there so few stable relationships among heterosexuals?
12 Why do heterosexuals place so much emphasis on sex?
13 Considering the menace of overpopulation, how could the human race survive if everyone were heterosexual like you?
14 Could you trust a heterosexual therapist to be objective? Don't you fear that the therapist might be inclined to influence you in the direction of his/her own leanings?
15 How can you become a whole person if you limit yourself to compulsive, exclusive heterosexuality and fail to develop your natural, healthy homosexual potential?
16 There seem to be very few happy heterosexuals. Techniques have

been developed that might enable you to change if you really want. Have you considered trying aversion therapy?

Turning the tables on heterosexuality challenges it as a 'default position' (P. Johnson 2005). If heterosexual people began to reflect upon why they think they are heterosexual, they might start to challenge its normative status and hence its privilege and domination. While heterosexuals continue to be naive about their sexuality, little progress will be made. Jeyasingham (2008) reminds us that all sexual identities are performed through practices and behaviours.

Throughout this book, I have argued that to understand privilege we need to give attention to experience, structure and discourse. These psycho-social, structural and cultural realms are interconnected and it is important to explore these interconnections to understand how oppressive practices and beliefs are sustained (Rocco and Gallagher 2006). This same framework can be used to analyse three layers of anti-homosexual prejudice: homophobia, heterosexism and heteronormativity. There is a tendency in the literature to focus on one of these dimensions to the exclusion of the others. Homophobia focuses on prejudiced individual practices and ignores the wider structural factors. Heterosexism is based on the institutionalisation of heterosexual privilege. Heteronormativity addresses dominant discourses and explores the 'taken for granted' assumptions about the normalcy of heterosexuality (Crowhurst 2002).

Homophobia and anti-gay prejudice

The term homophobia is attributed to George Weinberg, who in 1972 wrote *Society and the Healthy Homosexual*. Homophobia is usually used to refer to fear and/or hatred of homosexuals and also to anti-homosexual prejudices and beliefs. The latter includes the perception of homosexuals as being perverted, sick and unnatural in comparison with heterosexuals, who are seen as normal and natural (Flood and Hamilton 2008). Weinberg used the concept of homophobia to pathologise those who regarded homosexuality as sick or deviant.

Many writers have argued that the concept of homophobia alone is too psychological and individualistic (Fish 2007; Bryant and Vidal-Ortiz 2008). Some are concerned that the terminology of 'phobia' locates anti-gay prejudice within a psychiatric discourse outside political and moral critique (Hopkins 2004). Given its origins in psychology and individual pathology, it has limited usefulness for challenging cultural and institutional forms of discrimination against lesbians and gay men (Griffin et al. 2007). As Hicks and Watson (2003) argue, one of the limitations of homophobia is its concern with 'bad attitudes' rather than social practices, ruling relations and official discourses. Challenging homophobic attitudes might help at one level, but it leaves the systems which privilege heterosexuality in place.

Nevertheless, the concept of homophobia is still used to describe anti-homosexual prejudice (Plummer 1999; Flood and Hamilton 2008; V. Robinson 2007). Beneke (2004) believes that it is important to differentiate between heterosexual men's anxiety about any homosexual desire they may feel within themselves and the prejudice underlying oppressive practices against gay men and lesbians. He argues that by conflating homophobic anxiety with homophobic oppression, opportunities to work with straight men's discomfort with their homoerotic feelings are lost. Given that most straight men will feel some level of homophobic anxiety, a less hostile environment is necessary because straight men need to be willing to explore their homophobic feelings if they are to become allies with gay men.

I was only able to acknowledge my own homophobic feelings in a context where I shared a house with a gay male academic during a period of study leave in Canada. At home in Australia, I prided myself on my gay affirmative attitudes both among my friendship group and among my social activist colleagues. However, it was only in a context where I was immersed in gay-majority spaces and where my heterosexuality was not assumed, that my homophobic feelings began to surface. This led me to critically interrogate more substantially the 'taken for granted' aspects of my sexual identity.

Sedgewick (1985) believes that homophobia can best be understood in the context of homosociality, whereby the non-sexual social bonds between men reproduce their dominance over women. Recently, there have been moves to develop concepts to acknowledge the wider structural and institutional dimensions of the problem that go beyond the prejudicial attitudes of individuals (Peel 2001; Bryant and Vidal-Ortiz 2008).

Heterosexism and institutional heterosexuality

Heterosexism is a more explicitly political concept than homophobia in that it focuses on the privileges associated with heterosexuality and the legitimating discourses that naturalise those privileges (Hopkins 2004). Bella (2002: 2) defines heterosexism as 'the assumption that heterosexuality is the only natural, normal and moral sexuality'. This ideology or taken-for-granted belief constructs heterosexual as superior and entitling one to privileges. Nelson (cited in Cashwell 2005: 25) defines it as 'the continued promotion by the major institutions of society of a heterosexual lifestyle while simultaneously subordinating any other lifestyle'. Herek (2004: 497–8) defines heterosexism as 'an ideological system that denies denigrates and stigmatises any non-heterosexual form of behaviour, identity, relationship or community'.

Heterosexism refocuses the problem away from individual attitudes to consider the role played by social customs and institutions. It puts the focus on the institutional and structural advantages of heterosexuality and how they are manifested through customs, institutions and legal frameworks and embodied in language, organisational practices and everyday encounters (Flood and Hamilton 2008). Heterosexism plays a key role in reproducing heterosexuality because it naturalises it, penalises homosexuality (Ryder 2004;) and obscures the system of privileges and advantages attached to its institutionalised practices (Griffin et al. 2007).

Simoni and Walters (2001) state that heterosexism encompasses both homophobic attitudes and institutionalised heterosexual dominance, while some writers argue that heterosexism should be used as an alternative concept to homophobia. Plummer (1999) points out that they are not the same. There are, however, clear links between them. Heterosexism is regarded by some scholars as the foundation upon which homophobia rests (Hopkins 2004) and Flood and Hamilton (2008) regard homophobia as a part of heterosexism. Certainly, if you believe that heterosexuality is the only natural expression of sexuality, you are likely to believe that discrimination against gay men and lesbians is legitimate (Whitley and Aegistottir 2000).

Some activists prefer to use the language of homophobia because it carries more emotional and rhetorical weight (Hopkins 2004). Beneke (2004) argues that while heterosexism challenges structural privilege accruing from heterosexuality, it is unable to address the hatred that some heterosexual individuals feel towards homosexuals. This has led some scholars and activists to use the language of homo-hatred and to describe anti-homosexual practices as hate crimes (Alden and Parker 2005).

Heteronormativity and compulsory heterosexuality

Heteronormativity refers to 'the institutions, structures of understanding, and practical orientations that make heterosexuality seem not only coherent ... but also privileged' (Berlant and Warner 1998: 548). Warner (in Sumara and Davis 1999: 294) defines it as the complex ways in which 'heterosexual culture thinks of itself as the elemental form of human association'. This means that heterosexuals learn to 'see straight, to read straight and think straight' (ibid.).

The concept of heteronormativity provides a way of understanding how many men and women do not consider any alternative other than being heterosexual. It establishes a hegemonic and normalising discourse in relation to heterosexuality (Yep 2003). One of the consequences of heteronormativity is that gay men and lesbians are under pressure to pass as heterosexuals in the workplace and other public places. This 'passing' further reinforces heterosexual privilege and creates a form of heterosexual identity among lesbians and gay men (C. Johnson 2002). When gay men and lesbians 'come out' and when they display affection in public places they challenge the power of heteronormativity (ibid.). To do so in many public contexts, however, may be dangerous and may invoke homophobic and anti-homosexual practices by heterosexuals who are threatened by this behaviour.

Many heterosexual people believe that they are not homophobic or heterosexist because they 'tolerate' non-heterosexual lifestyles. They may repeat the old chestnut: 'Some of my best friends may be gay.' However, such tolerance exists only in a context where lesbians and gay men pose no challenge to heterosexual privilege (Scott and Jackson 2000). Brickell (2005) locates the concept of tolerance within the philosophy of liberalism and argues that it underpins heteronormativity. Inequality still exists when those who tolerate are heterosexual and those who are tolerated are gay or lesbian. Liberalism obscures both the impact of social structures on individuals and the ways in which we are always enmeshed in power relations. Liberalism also reinforces the subordination of homosexuality and the dominance of heterosexuality through the tolerance of homosexuality. Consequently, heterosexuals are often unable to identify the privileges that flow from unequal power relationships.

Heterosexual privilege: the other side of sexual oppression

The other side of the costs of homophobia, heterosexism and heteronormativity for gay men and lesbians is the privilege associated with those who are heterosexual. Heterosexual privilege is legislated through laws that confer a variety of benefits and rights on heterosexual spouses that are not available to homosexual partnerships (Ryder 2004). Heterosexuals are not subjected to the discrimination and marginalisation that face lesbians and gay men (Flood and Hamilton 2008). By conforming to the dominant construction of heterosexuality, they receive various incentives and perks. Heterosexuals have greater economic security and family and social acceptance of their sexuality. They are able to marry, have custody and adoption rights, along with tax benefits, inheritance, immigration and pension entitlements (Simoni and Walters 2001). A. Johnson (2006: 29–30) identifies some of the main privileges accruing to heterosexuality:

- I am free to reveal and live my intimate relationships openly – by referring to my partner by name, and displaying pictures on my desk at work without being accused of 'flaunting' my sexuality or risking discrimination.
- I can rest assured that if I am hired, promoted or fired from a job it will have nothing to do with my sexual orientation.
- I can move about in public without fear of being harassed or physically attacked because of my sexual orientation.
- I don't run the risk of being reduced to a single aspect of my life, as if being heterosexual summed up the kind of person I am.
- I can usually assume that national heroes, success models and other figures held up for general admiration will be assumed to be heterosexual.
- I can assume that my sexual orientation won't be used to determine whether I'll fit in at work or whether teammates will be comfortable working with me.
- I don't have to worry that my sexual orientation will be used as a weapon against me, to undermine my achievements or power.
- I can turn on the television or go to the movies and be assured of seeing characters, news reports and stories that reflect the reality of my life.
- I can live where I want without having to worry about neighbours who disapprove of my sexual orientation.
- I can live in the comfort of knowing that other people's assumptions about my sexual orientation are correct.

Identity privilege lists such as this one are important because they encourage us all to consider how our everyday activities and choices contribute to a climate that supports discriminatory practices. Part of the process of challenging privilege at the cultural and structural levels is reflecting on how those of us in dominant groups gain unearned advantages because of some aspects of our identities. While reconstructing ourselves, we also need to transform our institutions (Carbado 2004).

Bunch's (2004: 219) challenge to heterosexuals who are unaware of privilege is to 'go home and announce to everybody that you know . . . that you're queer'. If heterosexuals try being queer for a week, they will get a sense of what it means to have heterosexual privilege. Alternatively, you need only spend some time walking hand-in-hand in public with someone of the same sex to test your commitment to heterosexual privilege. Such practices can be dangerous, of course. Heterosexual men make themselves vulnerable to anti-gay violence that lesbians and gay men face every day.

There is very little acknowledgement of the role played by heterosexuals in maintaining heterosexual privilege. Heterosexuals have some investment in the oppression of gay men and lesbians because of the benefits they receive for having relationships with those of a different sex. It is difficult for many heterosexual people to come to question ideas about sexuality that they have been taught are logical, true and fair when they are actually illogical, false and unfair. Yet, if we really care about a society based on social justice principles, we will have to take personal responsibility for how we conduct our lives (DiAngelo 1997).

Simoni and Walters (2001) illustrate how heterosexual privilege mediates the relationship between heterosexuals and ant-gay attitudes and practices. As with other forms of privilege, heterosexuals may acknowledge the oppression of gay men and lesbians without appreciating the unearned entitlements and advantages they receive from their own sexual identity status. Recognising heterosexual privilege is fundamental to decrease prejudice and increase understanding and empathy for those without such privileges. Russell (1997) also argues that increasing awareness among heterosexuals of the privileges that they accrue from their heterosexuality is likely to encourage greater awareness of the impact of heterosexism and foster commitments to work against homophobia and anti-gay bias.

Heterosexuals are not a homogeneous group, though. Gender, class, race and ability/disability divide them. These divisions will impact on the meaning of heterosexuality and the privileges that accrue to it and thus heterosexual privilege will impact on people's lives differently in relation to these dimensions. These intersections also mean that any critique of heterosexuality must engage with the experience of sexuality in relation to other systems of domination and privilege.

Heterosexuality and gender domination

Heterosexual privilege cannot be understood without analysing its link with gender. Feminists have developed a critique of heterosexuality in terms of its role in subordinating women and its eroticisation of power difference (Kitzinger et al. 1992; Ingraham 2005; Jackson 2005; V. Robinson 2007). Women do not share the same heterosexual privileges as men because of their subordination in marriage and their exploitation in most relationships with men (Jackson 1998). Some feminists have even argued that heterosexuality should replace gender as the primary source of women's oppression (Ingraham 2005).

It is almost thirty years since Adrienne Rich wrote her groundbreaking article 'Compulsory Heterosexuality and Lesbian Existence' (Rich 1980). She was the first writer to formulate the notion of 'compulsory heterosexuality' to describe the many ways in which heterosexuality was imposed upon women. She argued that women were coerced into heterosexuality and she highlighted the way in which sexuality was socially constructed as opposed to being natural. In her view, all women were positioned on a 'lesbian continuum'.

The other early feminist writer to challenge heterosexuality as an institution was Monique Wittig. In *The Straight Mind* (1992) she argued that the heterosexual marriage contract was a basis for the reproduction of women's subservience. She maintained that heterosexuality as a discourse was all-pervasive and oppressed all women who refused to locate themselves within it. In her view, a 'straight mind' was unable to conceive of an alternative to heterosexuality and unable to identify the mechanisms that socially produce it.

Since the 1970s, heterosexual feminists have been debating the place of heterosexuality with lesbian feminists. Heterosexual women have sought to defend their sexual relationships with men against the charge of 'sleeping with the enemy'. Of course, many heterosexual feminists were offended by the charge that they were coerced into heterosexuality. Many women's experience of sex with men is pleasurable and chosen freely rather than compulsorily (Wilkinson and

Kitzinger 1994). It is perhaps more accurate to conceive of heterosexuality as involving both constraint *and* choice (P. Johnson 2005).

In the special edition of *Feminism and Psychology* on heterosexuality, first published in 1992, many heterosexual feminists expressed ambivalence about identifying with the label 'heterosexual' because it did not in their experience describe their lifestyles. It was not a part of their political identity and this stood in contrast with lesbian feminists who claimed a lesbian identity as a self-naming and oppositional stance against institutionalised heterosexuality (Kitzinger et al. 1992). Jackson (1999) argues that heterosexual feminists cannot claim an oppositional political identity because their sexual practices conform to the institutionalised norm.

Some heterosexual feminists recognised that their heterosexuality was privileged in comparison with lesbian feminists. For Kitzinger et al. (1992), this raised the question of whether their interests in patriarchy may influence their theorising of their heterosexuality and, further, how they gauge the impact that institutionalised heterosexuality has upon them and other women.

Certainly, heterosexual women experience contradictory effects from heterosexuality. On the one hand, they benefit from the privileges associated with its normative and superior status. On the other hand, many of them are subjected to dangerous contraception, date rape and rape in marriage (Kitzinger and Wilkinson 1994). Thus women's experience of heterosexual privilege is problematical because they are on the receiving end of privileges but also penalties in hierarchical relationships with men.

Queer theory and the heterosexual/homosexual binary

An alternative theoretical and political challenge to heterosexual dominance comes from queer theory. Queer theory aims to destabilise categories of identity and to expose the heterosexual/homosexual binary as culturally constructed as opposed to being naturally based (Yep 2003). In contrast to feminist challenges to male dominance in heterosexuality, queer theory focuses on the processes by which homosexuality is rendered marginal by the normativity of heterosexuality (Jackson 2005). Queer theory highlights the ways in which heterosexuality depends on the production of homosexuality to reaffirm its identity. Ironically, heterosexuality reproduces its dominant status through its dependence on homosexuality. It needs to be constantly affirmed and protected to sustain itself (Yep 2003).

By challenging the opposition between heterosexuality and homosexuality, the social construction of both types of sexual identities become more visible. The aim is to disturb, trouble and destabilise heterosexuality in order to make space for non-heterosexual identities (Jackson 1999). This entails challenging the notion of a fixed homosexual identity, which has been the foundational concept underpinning gay affirmative identity politics.

While queer theory has been very important in deconstructing heterosexuality, its dismissal of structural theories has ignored struggles in relation to the state and changing social practices (Adam 1998). Queer theorists have also been criticised for ignoring the material conditions of women's lives and for not addressing male dominance within heterosexuality (Jeffreys 2003; Jackson 2005).

Gay politics and equal rights

As Jackson (1999) argues, some of the goals of the gay movement are in conflict with feminism. She challenges the gay equal rights movement for refusing to critique heterosexuality and for ignoring the feminist critique of heterosexuality as a patriarchal institution. M. Rahman (1998) similarly questions the pursuit of an equal rights agenda because it accepts the normalcy and naturalness of heterosexuality. In his view, the campaigns to legalise same-sex marriage reinforce the patriarchal heterosexual marriage contract.

Jackson (1999) argues that equal rights campaigns are aimed at achieving forms of heterosexual privilege rather than challenging it. She maintains that to achieve real equality with heterosexuals, heterosexuality would have to be displaced from its privileged status and institutionalised normalcy. Carter and Mottier (1998) believe that the pursuit of equal rights by lesbians and gays with heterosexuals lends support to heterosexual families. Gay men are accused of wanting to retain male privilege while striving for equality with heterosexual men. Warner (1999) talks about 'the politics of normal', whereby the aim is to blend in and not be too different. The problem of regarding yourself as 'normal' is that it begs the question of whose norm is being used as the standard for determining normalcy.

The difficulty is that by expressing demands in terms that do not threaten the normalcy of heterosexuality, there is greater likelihood of success. Gay marriage is a good example. While Wolf (2009) acknowledges that gay marriage will not eliminate the oppression of gays and lesbians or challenge heteronormativity, she nevertheless defends it as a reform that will bring material benefits to lesbian and gay couples in the interim.

Legalising same-sex relationships through marriage, and changing the law to recognise entitlement to tax allowances and pensions, offers the promise of greater respectability and acceptance, but at what price? Jackson (1999) asks why gay men and lesbians would want to emulate the unequal relationship between men and women in the marriage contract. Kelly (2009) argues that the state-recognised institution of marriage marginalises all non-marital relationships. This not only disadvantages gay men and lesbians, but also many non-white and poor people who do not marry. She proposes instead an extension of full marital benefits to all who want them.

Challenges to heterosexuality must analyse both male dominance and heteronormativity. Any critique of heterosexuality should address the normative status of heterosexuality and how it marginalises gay and lesbian sexualities. It should also challenge the male-dominated gender hierarchy in which heterosexuality functions in patriarchal societies.

Heterosexuality and masculinity

Since men predominantly perpetrate homophobic violence, we must examine the relationship between masculinity and heterosexual dominance. Research demonstrates a strong relationship between the holding of traditional gender role beliefs and negative attitudes towards homosexuality (Whitley and Aegistottir 2000). Furthermore, men tend to adhere more to traditional gender role beliefs than women (Flood and Pease 2009). Theodore and Basow's (2000) research confirmed that traditional heterosexual masculinity fosters anti-gay prejudice. They found that men who defined their identity in these terms were more likely to express homophobic attitudes towards gay men (Flood and Hamilton 2008).

Masculinity is conveyed through how men walk, hold their bodies, use hand gestures and voice, through to how they wear clothes, groom themselves and live their life. For many men, such identity practices are as much about projecting a heterosexual identity as a masculine one (Dean 2006). Homophobia can help to bolster heterosexual masculinity. Often, this involves expressing a hyper-masculine or exaggerated form of masculinity. According to Hopkins (2004), homophobia would not exist if there were not a need to confirm masculine identity.

Masculinity plays a key role in naturalising and privileging heterosexuality to the point where masculinity is regarded as being heterosexual by definition. While heterosexuality is portrayed as natural, many heterosexual men experience it as fragile and feel so insecure about it that they are easily threatened by homosexuality (Beneke 2004). That is why so many straight men are threatened if they are mistaken as gay. As A. Johnson (2006) argues, most heterosexual men who engage in violence against gay men and lesbians feel uneasy and threatened just by the existence of homosexuals.

Heterosexuality and intersections with other forms of privilege

Heterosexual dominance also needs to be seen in the context of other forms of oppression such as racism, class elitism and ableism. Connecting whiteness with heterosexuality is also important (Stokes 2001; Yep 2003; Stokes 2005; Ward 2008). Stokes (2001; 2005) argues that heterosexuality and whiteness are 'normative co-partners' and he explores the connections between sexuality and white supremacy. Other writers have started to explore the parallels between anti-racist struggles and gay politics (Dixon 2001). Clarke (2004) identifies homophobic statements by many black intellectuals and argues that the black liberation movement has not come to terms with its own sexual politics.

Marxists have argued that acknowledgement of any form of gender and sexual difference would dilute the struggle against class (Smart 1996). In the Marxist view, any movement that fosters identity beyond class will constitute a barrier to challenging class-based oppression (Wolf 2009). Marxists maintain that the economic disadvantages of homosexuals are related to the social relations of capitalism. In this view, gay and lesbian oppression is derivative of capitalist exploitation of workers and consequently struggles against heterosexism are less important than struggles against the capitalist exploitation of workers (ibid.). However, Fraser (1997) maintains that gay and lesbian oppression are best understood in relation to heterosexism. She argues that capitalism benefits from compulsory heterosexuality. Thus some argue that struggles against heterosexual dominance are directly related to struggles against capitalism.

Recently, some writers have also started to explore the relationship between compulsory heterosexuality and able-bodied privilege (Kafer 2003; McRuer and Berube 2006; Barounis 2009). McRuer and Berube (2006) analyse heterosexuality and able-bodiedness as parallel sites of privilege. Kafer (2003) explores the ways in which compulsory able-bodiedness and compulsory heterosexuality work together to maintain both forms of privilege. Given that compulsory heterosexuality is experienced differently among different groups of women, Kafer (ibid.) examines how it impacts on disabled women. Barounis (2009) suggests that queer theory and disability studies have much to learn from each other in understanding how homosexuality and disability are regulated.

From heterosexism awareness to destabilising heterosexuality

Heterosexuals need to recognise their privilege as a necessary first step to becoming involved in a struggle against heterosexual dominance. If straight people do not address their heterosexual privilege, their capacity to pursue social justice is compromised.

Evans and Broido (2005) identify five overlapping stages of awareness among heterosexual people about homophobia and heterosexism. At the first stage, *naivety*, heterosexuals are generally unaware of their sexual orientation. At the second level of *acceptance*, they take their heterosexuality for granted. Third, at the level of *resistance*, they recognise heterosexism but believe that they cannot do anything about it. Fourth, at the *redefinition* stage, they establish a positive heterosexual identity that moves beyond a rejection of heterosexual beliefs. Finally, at the fifth stage of *internalisation*, they establish an identity that is independent of normative definitions of heterosexuality. Other educators identify similar stages of development. DiAngelo (1997), for example, identifies six stages of awareness: contact, disintegration, reintegration, pseudo-independent, immersion/emersion and autonomy.

However, heterosexism training workshops continue to focus on the individual (Peel 2001). Hopkins (2004) points out that because homophobia and heterosexism are not just prejudices, they cannot be eliminated by workshops that encourage greater tolerance and acceptance. To adequately address homophobia and heterosexism, we would have to eliminate the binary of heterosexuality and homosexuality and consequently they would have no meaning. By challenging the binary divide of heterosexuality and homosexuality, as Katz (1995) and others have advocated, we can begin to destabilise the normative basis of heterosexuality.

Reconstructing heterosexuality

Given the reality that heterosexuality is a relationship of power, Seidler (1994) has asked whether it is possible to consider it as legitimate sexual orientation. Some lesbian feminists have expressed doubt about the possibilities for reconstruction towards more egalitarian sexual practices (Kitzinger et al. 1992). Jackson (1996) has noted that there are material constraints on establishing egalitarian forms of heterosexuality within existing gender divisions. Thus our capacity to undo heterosexual dominance is limited by the structural social relations in which it is embedded (Jackson 2005).

Seidler (1992) believes that while heterosexuality is manifested as an oppressive norm, it should not be renounced. Many feminists have argued that heterosexuality does not necessarily represent oppression to women (Smart 1996; Segal 1994; Hollway 1996). A number of feminist writers have argued that heterosexuality can be reconstructed towards a non-oppressive form. Hollway (1996), for example, argues against the notion of compulsory heterosexuality because it is overly determinist. She articulates a form of female sexual desire that is able to resist patriarchal relations.

Smart (1996) has suggested that we should differentiate between oppressive and empowering heterosexualities. Some feminists believe that men can resist patriarchal expressions of sexuality and that women can choose non-oppressive forms of heterosex (Richardson 1996; Van Every 1996; Hollway 1996). Since the dominant form of heterosexuality has prioritised penetration, one project has been to problematise penetrative sex and promote alternatives to penetration (Jackson 1999).

In challenging the normative status of heterosexuality, it does not mean that we should reject heterosexuality per se. Rather, we should reposition it as simply one form of sexual expression among others. And we should avoid presenting heterosexuality as a unitary and monolithic concept. As some writers have argued, we should think in terms of 'heterosexualities' because there is more than one heterosexual identity (Kitzinger and Wilkinson 1994; Segal 1994; Smart 1996). In response to the challenge 'How dare you assume that I am heterosexual', Segal (1994) has encouraged heterosexuals to come out and proclaim 'How dare you assume what it means to be straight'.

C. Johnson (2002) believes that it is possible to construct non-heteronormative notions of heterosexuality that do not inevitably produce homosexuality as the 'other'. Such expressions of heterosexuality would not privilege heterosexual identity over lesbian and gay identities and may not require adherence to a strong sexual identity.

Duggan (1995) argues that heteronormativity is best understood as those forms of heterosexuality that are hegemonic; that is reproductive, legally married, peer aged and monogamous. She points out that many heterosexual people do not subscribe to that dominant form of sexual experience. Queering heterosexuality would involve the validation of non-hegemonic forms of heterosexual practice, including *ménage à trois*, non-monogamy, non-reproductive partnerships and de facto relationships.

Some writers have expressed concern that by pluralising heterosexuality, it may lead to the evasion of heterosexual dominance (Smart 1996; Yep 2003). Yep wonders whether acknowledging the differences in heterosexuality will mean that we cannot hold heterosexuals responsible for heterosexual dominance. Similar concerns have been expressed by some feminists who have been reluctant to acknowledge race, class and sexuality issues because it may take the focus off what they see as the primary division of gender oppression. Critics argue that homogenising struggles erase significant differences within identity groups and can lead to a hierarchy of oppressions (Yep 2003).

Queering heterosexuality

When straight men get involved in challenging heterosexual privilege, their own sexuality is likely to be called into question. Most heterosexual men are afraid of being mistaken as gay. Even straight men who are gay affirmative may be reluctant to take a public stand against heterosexism because of concern about being perceived as gay (Carbado 2004). This means that many heterosexuals who support gay rights are not willing to relinquish the status of their heterosexuality (Dean 2006). Consequently, they perpetuate clear divisions between heterosexuals and homosexuals and thus maintain the privileges associated with heterosexuality. I have to admit that there have been times when I have been involved in challenging heterosexual dominance that I was concerned about being perceived as gay. These experiences confronted me with my own homophobia and my former reluctance to relinquish the privileges I get from being heterosexual.

Whether or not you reveal your heterosexuality is an important strategic question to which there is not an easy answer. Ayres and Brown (2005) differentiate between exercising and disabling privilege. Exercising privilege for social justice involves speaking out as a heterosexual in support of gay and lesbian issues. To do so can have the effect of disrupting the assumptions that people make about the way heterosexuals are likely to view gay rights. In writing this chapter, I have acknowledged that I write from a heterosexually privileged position. Disabling privilege requires heterosexuals to display ambiguity about their sexual identity when they are challenging heterosexual privilege. In other words, we need to allow ourselves to be thought of as gay. If people cannot tell whether you are heterosexual or not, you relinquish some of your heterosexual status. So there are situations where heterosexual people should not necessarily clarify their sexual identity.

Speaking out against heterosexism as a heterosexual conveys that homosexual rights is an issue for straight people as well (Ryder 2004). At the same time, heterosexuals need to be aware that there are politics in coming out as straight. Carbado (2004) is suspicious of heterosexuals who are quick to speak of their spouses when homosexuality is raised. We must ensure that when we point out our heterosexual privilege, we do it in ways that do not reinforce heterosexual dominance.

Some heterosexual allies purposefully blur the boundaries between heterosexual and homosexual identities. By allowing themselves to be seen as homosexual, they contest and subvert the norm of heterosexuality. Thomas (in Thomas and MacGillivray 2000) argues that it is more subversive of heterosexuality for him to walk down the street holding hands with a man he was not in a sexual relationship with than it would be to have sex with another man and not disclose it.

Some writers refer to these practices as 'queer heterosexuality' (Wilkinson and Kitzinger 1994), 'straight queers' (Heasley 2005) or 'straight queerness' (Thomas 2000). Wilkinson and Kitzinger (1994: 83) define queer heterosexuals as 'those people who do what is contentiously known as "heterosexuality", nonetheless do so in ways which are transgressive of "normality"'. A queer heterosexual is someone who does not have to be seen to be heterosexual to feel self-esteem (Smith 2000).

Heasley (2005) has developed a typology of straight queer masculinities, detailing a variety of ways in which men can cross the borders of traditional heterosexual masculinity. He refers to straight men who take public action against homophobia and heterosexism as 'social justice queers'. Heasley identifies queer straight men as those who disrupt the normative constructions of heterosexuality and what it means to be heterosexual. They try to find ways to be a man outside of the hegemonic representations of heterosexual masculinity. In so doing, they extend the boundaries of what it is to be heterosexual.

Conclusion

This chapter has problematised gendered heterosexuality. As in all forms of privilege, the question arises about why heterosexuals might want to challenge their privilege. What would motivate heterosexuals to struggle against heterosexual dominance? Also, since men's heterosexual privileges are usually at the expense of women, straight men are likely to have less motivation than women to challenge heterosexual dominance (Yep 2003).

Some writers argue that heterosexuals pay a price for heterosexual privilege and that they do not benefit in an unqualified way (Crowhurst 2002). For Beneke (2004), since homophobia hurts heterosexual men as well, they should see it as being in their self-interest to challenge it.

Thomas (in Thomas and MacGillivray 2000) is not so sure that the privileges of heterosexuality do harm heterosexuals. He promotes social justice when arguing why heterosexuals should get involved. Irrespective of motivation, however, it is clear here that this struggle will involve some discomfort, if not pain, as heterosexuals confront the taken-for-granted truths about the nature of their sexuality.

EIGHT

Ableist relations and the embodiment of privilege

Oppression and privilege are not simply manifested in terms of differential access to resources; they are also embodied (Shilling 2003). As we have seen in earlier chapters, many forms of privilege are legitimated on the basis of a belief in naturalist views of social stratification and inequality. That is, gendered, racialised and class-based social relations are seen to be a result of our natural bodies rather than being socially constructed. Privileged groups often justify their dominant status on the basis of claimed inferior biological characteristics of the oppressed. They do so because if the causes of social divisions are located in biological bodies, then attempts to transform these inequalities can be seen as misguided.

Human bodies can be used to legitimate privilege and oppression. We need to give attention to the physicality of privilege in relation to class, gender, sexuality, race and especially in relation to disability. Bodies are implicated in the reproduction of privilege because they are granted social value on the basis of their socially constructed class, gender, race, able-bodied and sexuality markers (Tangeberg and Kemp 2002). It is important to become aware of how marginality and privilege are experienced in the body because if the body is a site for *doing* privilege, it has implications for how we *undo* it.

Cassuto (1999) raises the question of whether you can talk about disability without addressing your own disability status. All of those involved with this field need to reflect upon their own positionality in relation to disability and to consider the impact it can have on their research and teaching (Campbell 2009). My own experience of being a temporarily able-bodied man shapes this chapter. Even though my sixtieth birthday looms and chronic back pain continues to plague my life, along with the health scares I have had and my impaired vision, I still write as a man who has not experienced oppression through disability. This means that I do not speak as disabled man or on behalf of disabled people.

I am writing this at a time when there is a growing interest in the body. From features on body image in popular magazines and newspapers through to the fitness and weight loss industry, many people regard the body as a project to be developed as part of their identity. Concerns about obesity and preventable illnesses add weight to this agenda. We are all encouraged to take responsibility for maintaining a healthy and fit body that is free of excess fat and cholesterol. Physical beauty in Western culture is equated with health, fitness and youthfulness and there is a moral imperative towards achieving these characteristics.[1] Images of the perfect body are continually highlighted in fashion and in media representations of the body.

It is said that one attains a beautiful body by engaging in exercise and diet control. Jogging and gym membership are an integral part of many middle-class people's lives. While exercise can be healthy and good for us, Murphy (1995) argues that zealotry about fitness has emerged. The current preoccupation with slimness and the self-regulation of fitness, often leads to aesthetic aspects of the body being promoted above those of health and resistance to disease. Simonsen (2000) considers our interest in health and appearance as an 'obsession' that leads to eating disorders and other psychological illnesses.

The struggle to mould and shape the perfect body through exercise and fitness regimes has class dimensions. Those who have the financial resources, time and knowledge to work on their bodies already belong to an elite group. Health, slimness and beauty have now become equated with money, power and control (ibid.). Maintaining the body is thus a way of emphasising your occupational success and social status.

When people in subordinate groups fail to achieve these privileged bodily norms, they are judged as lacking self-discipline and moral standards. If you believe that being fit and healthy is totally within your control, you are also likely to judge those who are ill or disabled as not taking care of themselves (Wendell 1996). Disability and illness are framed as forms of individual failure rather than society failing the individual. Understanding the ways in which bodies are implicated in maintaining social difference is therefore crucial.

---

1. In this chapter my focus is on the representation of able-bodiedness and disability within Western culture. I acknowledge that these constructions are culturally specific and that we must be careful not to impose a Eurocentric framing of disability on non-Western societies.

Cultural views on attractiveness and beauty negate the potential for a disabled body to be regarded as attractive. Those who adhere to the dominant social norms devalue, if not reject, disabled people's bodies because they are unable to attain many of the qualities associated with beauty (Gordon and Rosenblum 2001). Because their bodies will never meet the cultural ideals, disabled people are negatively affected by the idealisation of the body (Wendell 1996).

Embodied privilege as physical capital

Bourdieu's concept of 'physical capital' can be utilised to understand how the body reproduces privilege and various forms of social inequality (Shilling 2003). Physical capital is part of cultural capital and it can be converted into other forms of capital. Socially valued body markers influence not only social status but also life opportunities (Imrie 2001). Depending upon your social location, you can manage the body for the purpose of acquiring further status and power. Beauty and sporting prowess are good examples as both are socially valued and they enable people to use their bodies to accumulate other forms of capital. Research demonstrates a link between those regarded as beautiful and those in highly paid careers (Habibis and Walter 2009). In this instance, the body can be used as a resource for economic and social gain (Bourdieu 1986).

Throughout this book, I have shown that not everyone has the same opportunity to acquire physical capital. Edwards and Imrie (2003) believe that the concept of physical capital is also useful in understanding the marginalisation of disabled people. Physically disabled people are unable to attain bodily prestige or corporeal value because their bodies are designated to be abnormal and abject. They are unable to acquire physical capital because of the perceptions and reactions by non-disabled people. Bourdieu's concept of physical capital usefully describes the embodiment of privilege and power.

Revisiting the body in the social model of disability

In response to disabled people's critiques of the medical model of disability, Michael Oliver (1983; 1990; 1996) developed the social model of disability in the early 1980s. Informed by materialist and Marxist perspectives, the social model posits disability as a form of social oppression similar to sexism, racism and class domination. It is contrasted with individual bio-medical models of disability that locate disability within the biological body.[2] Oliver (1990) refers to the traditional model of disability as 'the tragedy model'. Underpinning the tragedy model is the view held by most able-bodied people that disabled people cannot enjoy an adequate quality of life and that they all desire to be 'normal'. This personal tragedy theory of disability is most evident in the charity response to disabled people.

The social model distinguishes between impairment and disability.[3] In the social model, people are not disabled by their bodies but by society. Oliver (ibid.) argued that disablement did not have anything to do with the body. The focus thus shifts from disability as a deficit of the body to understanding it as a product of the social relations of capitalism.

From a materialist perspective, the oppression of disabled people cannot be understood solely on the basis of discriminatory and prejudiced perceptions and beliefs (Gleeson 1997). The social model challenges the emphasis on changing the negative attitudes of able-bodied people towards people with impairments. By giving too much attention to negative attitudes as a source of disabled people's oppression, the concern is that attitudes may be seen as the *only* cause of disability oppression and structural barriers will be ignored (Tregaskis 2004). In the previous chapter, a similar concern was raised about homophobia.

---

2. In most instances in this chapter, I use the term 'disabled people' in preference to 'people with disability'. Titchkosky (2001) argues that people-first language of referring to 'people with disabilities' rather than 'disabled person' obscures the social and political understanding of disability. While the intent is to avoid the objectification of people on the basis of their disability, it ignores the socio-political understanding of people being disabled by their culture. With the emphasis on disabled people as people first, it inhibits our understanding of disabling processes and practices in society. In this view, ableist practices and processes produce disabled people. While it is primarily able-bodied professionals working with disabled people who prefer people-first language, I acknowledge that some disabled activists also prefer this language.

3. There is immense difficulty in defining disability and dispute about whether it should include all forms of impairments. Many people with cognitive, psychiatric and sensory impairments do not consider themselves to be disabled. Many people who experience chronic forms of illness do regard themselves as disabled. While I address these definitional issues in the chapter, my focus is on physical impairments and physical disability because I am interested in the embodiment of privilege.

If the economic and political relations of capitalism shape disability, changing prejudiced attitudes will be only a small part of addressing disabled people's oppression. The focus will need to shift to transforming material structures that marginalise people with impairments. In this view, social inclusion of disabled people will only be achieved with a move towards a more egalitarian social order that provides both equal access and equal rights to social, political and economic goods (ibid.). This means going beyond ensuring that doorways are wide enough to accommodate wheelchairs.

The social model has contributed significantly to the rise of the disability people's movement because it validated the intellectual and practical contributions of disabled people. However, the social model has also come under considerable contestation and criticism from within some segments of the disability movement and by some progressive disability studies academics. Many of these critics have challenged the emphasis on the capitalist economy as the main cause of disability and argued that it has failed to acknowledge the critique of modernity (Hughes 1999; Tregaskis 2002; Shakespeare 2006).

The social model has highlighted institutional discrimination and excluded physical spaces in producing disability. However, the experiences of impairment in the oppression of disabled people have been given limited attention (Hughes 1999). The experiences of chronic illness and pain, which are often connected to impairments, are also ignored in the social model (Swain and French 2000).

Progressive critics of the social model point out that in emphasising that most of the problems faced by disabled people are located in the social context of their lives rather than in their own impaired bodies, they end up denying that disability has anything to do with bodily impairment. Disabled people not only experience social oppression; they also experience compromised physical functioning. Morris (1991) says that many disabled people downplay their experiences of bodily distress because they do not want to reinforce able-bodied people's views of how awful disabled people's bodies are. Those who are disabled are likely to experience their bodies as being more constrained than those who are able-bodied. However, Morris (ibid.) has noted that the social model does not address the bodily experiences of pain and affliction that disabled people experience.

If disability is defined as a social category and impairment as a biological category, there is the danger that impairment will always be framed within the bio-medical model. The social model's emphasis on the social and political causes of disability oppression can sit alongside the bio-medical view of impairment that is concerned with missing limbs and/or defective mechanisms of the body (Turner 2002). In this view, the body is conceded to medicine. The social model inadvertently contributes to the reproduction of the individualistic perspective because there is no sociological framing of individual experience (D. Marks 1999b).

We need to develop a social understanding of impairment as well as disability. From a poststructural perspective, it is not possible to separate disability that is caused by social restrictions from impairment that designates aspects of the body (Hughes 2005; Thomas 2007). Paterson and Hughes (1999) put it simply: disability is embodied and impairment is social.

Disability and intersections with other forms of oppression

The social model has also been charged with ignoring gender, race, sexuality and age oppression within the disability movement. Vernon (1999) criticises the social model of disability for ignoring experiences of difference among disabled people due to the focus on the common experiences of disability and the need to reinforce the common humanity and shared identities with non-disabled people.

As with all other social groupings, disabled people are not a homogeneous group. Gender, race, class, sexuality and age also shape their individual experiences. Understandably, the intersections of disablism with other forms of oppression is important (Thompson 2006). An approach that recognises only one form of oppression is not likely to acknowledge that able-bodied people can also be oppressed by class, gender, race and sexuality (Swain and French 2000).

As already noted, feminist disability writers have drawn attention to the gendered nature of disability (Morris 1991; Wendell 1996; Fawcett 2000). Disabled male activists have mostly failed to engage with the issues facing disabled women. Vernon (1999) links the social model's emphasis on structural oppression to the masculinist viewpoint of disabled men. While feminists have addressed the experiences of disabled women, very few male writers have focused on the intersections of masculinity and disability (Gerschick 2007).

In relation to class, disabled people are more likely to be located in lower socio-economic groups (Oliver 1990). They are more vulnerable to war, violence and occupational health hazards and are more likely to be trapped in poverty. Vernon (1999) points out that disabled people who do have access to financial resources can afford to pay for personal assistants and taxis and will not face the same experience of structural discrimination. Some disabled people with financial resources can pass as non-disabled (D. Marks 1999b).

Disablism is linked with ageism, racism and heterosexism. Older age groups are more likely to experience impairment (Thompson 2006). While disabled people of colour have to struggle against disablism and racism in the able-bodied community, they also experience racism and marginalisation within the disability movement (Vernon 1999). Queer disability writers have focused on the relationship between disablism and heterosexual dominance (McRuer and Berube 2006).

Morris (1991) has pointed out that disabled people can be as racist, heterosexist, sexist and class elitist as able-bodied people. Disabled, white, straight, middle- and upper-class men are not likely to think of themselves as having privilege. However, Vernon (1999) says that male privilege applies to all men irrespective of other social divisions. The same can be said about straight, white and class privilege within the disability movement. Thus disabled people must also reflect on their respective privileges to ensure that other forms of oppression are addressed within the disability movement.

The cultural construction of disablism and ableism

In contrast to the materialist emphasis on capitalist social relations in the social model, critical poststructuralists focus on the cultural construction of disability and emphasise the importance of discourse and language in sustaining disablism and the role of cultural beliefs, attitudes and prejudices in shaping disability (Tregaskis 2002; Hughes 2005; Thomas 2007; Sheldon 2007).

Disablism refers to 'the social beliefs and actions that oppress/exclude/disadvantage people with impairments' (Thomas 2007: 13). Campbell (2008a: 152) defines disablism as 'a set of assumptions (conscious and unconscious) and practices that promote the differential or unequal treatment of people because of actual or presumed disabilities'. Disablism forms the ideological dimension of disabled people's oppression and should be regarded as a form of social oppression similar to racism, ageism and sexism.

Thompson (2006: 123) defines disablism as 'the combination of social forces which marginalises disabled people, portrays them in a negative light and thus oppresses them'. Thus, for Thompson, disablism operates on three levels. At the structural level, public policies and inaccessible buildings discriminate against disabled people. At the cultural level, dominant cultural norms privilege the able-bodied and construct disabled people as victims of personal tragedy. At the personal level, individuals express prejudice against disabled people through a range of attitudes from patronising concern to dismissiveness and revulsion.

Beyond explicit forms of prejudice, many non-disabled people also have specific investments and identifications in their own able-bodiedness that perpetuate structures that are disabling (D. Marks 1999a). Much of the prejudice that disabled people experience is subtle rather than overt and thus less easy to identify. Deal (2007) uses the language of 'aversive disablism' to describe the subtle forms of prejudice towards disabled people. The distinction between blatant and subtle forms of prejudice can be understood through differentiating between prejudiced views that break the norms of acceptable behaviour and forms of prejudice that are socially legitimated. The latter may take the form of simply affirming non-disabled behaviour as opposed to expressing explicit prejudiced views about disabled people.

Campbell (2008b) challenges the interchangeability of the terms 'ableism' and 'disablism', arguing that they involve a different understanding of the status of disability in relation to the norm. While disablism, she says, relates to the production of disability, ableism is associated with the production of ableness and the perfect body. Ableism is defined as 'an attitude that devalues or differentiates disability through the valuation of able-bodiednesss'. It is concerned with practices and beliefs that construct an image of the perfect able body, where human worth and value are equated with ability (Hughes 2007).

From an ableist perspective, impairment is inherently negative and devalued. The existence of impairment is something to be tolerated and accommodated but never celebrated as part of human difference. Ableism can also be internalised by disabled people and then used to reinforce their own lack of self-worth.

Many progressive non-disabled people have come to accept the premises of the social model because it does not in itself challenge their own able-bodied privilege. However, non-disabled people have more difficulty in accepting that disabled people may be satisfied with their lives (Morris 1991; Swain and French 2000). Evans (cited in Morris 1991) identifies various prejudiced attitudes that non-disabled people hold about disabled people, most of which assume that disabled people want to be normal.

Swain and French (2000) argue for an affirmative model of disability that emphasises the positive experiences of being impaired and disabled. They talk about the greater level of empathy with the oppression of others and the release from many of the expectations of having to conform to able-bodied society.

These critical poststructural approaches to disability are in my view consistent with a social oppression approach to disability. Thus the social model should be strengthened rather than abandoned, as Shakespeare (2006) argues. Materialist and post-structural perspectives are both relevant to understanding disability and they should not be polarised in an either/or fashion (Hughes and Paterson 1997; Dandermark and Gellerstedt 2004; Boxall 2007). In this regard, Fraser's (2003) work on integrating redistribution (the social model) and recognition (the cultural model) offers some promise.

In previous chapters I have argued that the oppression of working-class people is rooted primarily in an unjust social order and that the oppression of gay and lesbian people is more related to misrecognition. This is not to deny that their experiences are cultural *and* economic. Furthermore, I have argued that the experiences of women and people of colour are shaped equally by political economy and by the dominant culture. I suggest that the experiences of disabled people are similar in this regard to those of women and people of colour (Dandermark and Gellerstedt 2004) and that both realist and poststructural perspectives are important in challenging ableism.

The construction of able-bodied privilege

Ableism is so deeply embedded within our culture that we are often unable to recognise it. That is why we should focus our study on the production of able-bodiedness rather than disability to learn more about how ableism is practised. Campbell (2008b) talks about the notion of 'compulsory ableness' to describe how the ableist viewpoint is sustained. Earlier, I mentioned this in relation to compulsory heterosexuality (see Chapter 7).

The sociological literature on disability has typically focused on how disability oppression is produced by the attitudes of able-bodied people and the environmental and social barriers that restrict their social participation and mobility. Disability is predominantly investigated from the perspective of able-bodiment. We need to consider, however, what our understandings of disability tell us about the production of able-bodiedness (ibid.).

It may be more important to examine the production of a non-disabled identity in challenging disability oppression than to continue to explore disabled subjectivities. This is a call to interrogate the assumed normality of the able-bodied. My concern here is with how ableism is produced and performed. In shifting the focus of scholarship away from disability towards the able-bodied, I want to examine how ableist regulatory norms function to subordinate disabled people (ibid.). In transferring the focus of study to able-bodied people, we may gain a new perspective on disability.

Campbell (2009) provides an epistemology and ontology of ableism to shift the gaze away from disability to the processes that produce ableist regulatory norms. For her, the disciplinary field of disability studies should be replaced by studies in ableism. Such a project has implications not only for the rethinking of disability, but also for understanding the nature of all bodies within our culture.

We might start this project by asking how able-bodied status contributes to or undermines progressive politics. Kafer (2003) has noted that feminist theorists outside disability studies rarely address disablism in their work, nor do they reflect upon the status of being 'non-disabled' and investigate the implications for their feminist politics. This charge may be levelled at other progressive activists as well. On the whole, able-bodied activists have not been critically reflective about their own non-disabled privilege.

A. Johnson (2006: xi) refers to 'non-disabled' privilege as 'the privilege of not being burdened with the stigma and subordinate status that go along with being identified as disabled'. Like other forms of normativity, able-bodiedness is culturally presumed. If you are not clearly marked as disabled, you will be assumed to be able-bodied. This has particular implications for people with invisible disabilities in terms of their access to services and their inclusion within relevant disability communities (Kafer 2003).

Able-bodied privilege allows able-bodied people to maintain experiences of superiority, perfectability, security and comfort. May-Machunda (2005) reminds those of us who are able-bodied that we have not earned our able bodies. We take for granted our able-bodiedness and the privileges that go with it. She identifies forty-nine privileges (not an exhaustive list) accruing to her as an able-bodied woman. Some of these privileges include the following:

- I can ignore the width of doors, the presence of steps and other architectural features of buildings.
- I am not dependent on hiring strangers and acquaintances to assist me with my daily routines and private matters.
- I can be fairly sure that when people look at me, they don't assume that I would be better off dead or that I am a social burden because of my disabilities.
- I can be fairly sure that the first reaction to me is not pity or revulsion due to the condition of my body.
- I can turn on the television, read a book or magazine and be sure that I can see people with similar abilities to me and I can use their experiences as a gauge to understand my own.
- I am not expected to speak for all people who like me are able-bodied.
- I can anticipate being employed and be perceived as capable of working.
- I can expect to succeed or fail in my job or life without it reflecting on all people with similar abilities.
- I can anticipate being able to reach products on the store shelves.
- I can assume that I can physically, emotionally or cognitively handle most situations.
- I can assume that I can select where I sit at the movies, concerts or in church.
- I can assume that when people look at the condition of my body, they will not question the appropriateness of my right to be a sexual being or a parent.
- I do not have to prove myself as a superhuman in order to be respected as a full human being.

Shilling (2003) refers to 'the privileged body' to signify the practice of equating an individual's status with their body. Thus you can say that someone is privileged by their embodiment of the perfect body (Gerschick 2007). To be able-bodied is to be strong, attractive, slim, fit and healthy, all of which comprise the notion of a normal and beautiful body. Gerschick (ibid.) refers to this privilege as being 'bodily normative'. Thus you may be positioned by 'degrees of normativity', which in turn are shaped by one's class, race, ethnicity, gender, age and able-bodiedness. Such judgements locate people within further systems of stratification. Your body can be regarded as a form of 'social currency' designating your worth. The less normative your body, the greater your vulnerability to experiencing misrecognition. Those who are designated as 'disabled' will be furthest away from the normative ideal and will be subject to the exercise of power by those with more normative bodies (Gerschick 2007).

Able-bodied privilege, of course, is impossible to sustain over a lifetime. Even if we are lucky enough to avoid serious accidents or illnesses, we will all experience some level of impairment if we reach old age. That is why it is more appropriate to use the term 'temporarily able-bodied' (D. Marks 1996) or 'temporarily non-disabled' (Gerschick 2007). Since many of us will be subjected to accidents, injury and chronic illness along the way, the boundary between able-bodied people and disabled people is better seen as permeable.

Beyond the binary of able-bodied and disabled?

As in other arenas of identity politics, the disability movement is faced with the dilemma of how much to emphasise respect for their difference and how much to challenge the binary divide of able-bodied and disabled. Poststructuralists argue that reinforcing an identity of being 'disabled' relegates them to the category of the 'other' because the normative status will always be superior (Thomas 2007).

The distinction between disabled and non-disabled people is certainly unclear. Many disabled people's impairments fluctuate over time and some people's impairments are invisible (Gabel and Peters 2004). Some people who experience chronic illness experience some form of disability flowing from it (Wendell 1996). People whose impairments fluctuate sit somewhere between the identities of disabled and non-disabled (Ducket 1998). Also, many of us who are considered able-bodied experience physical limitations and barriers.

Since non-disabled people experience impairment and physical limitation, and since many aspects of disability are transient, Shakespeare and Watson (1996) argue that able-bodied people cannot be easily distinguished from disabled people. Noting how people's embodied experiences change over time, they try to normalise impairment.

However, 'non-disabled' may be an oxymoron because it does not acknowledge the fluctuating experience of impairment for most disabled people and because few people can be classified as totally healthy (Harris n.d.). While Harris resists the label of non-disabled, perhaps because it implies an oppressor role, I think that the refusal to acknowledge able-bodiedness blocks the examination of your own able-bodied privilege.

The benefit of framing impairment as part of the human condition is to encourage able-bodied people to recognise aspects of the 'other' in our own lives (Hughes 2007). When we emphasise the similarities between disabled and non-disabled people, we blur the boundaries and reduce the otherness of those who are not able-bodied. Able-bodied people who reflect upon their own mental and physical limitations are more likely to identify with the struggles of disabled people. The disadvantage is that by extending the category of disability to include everyone we decentre the suffering and struggle of those whose lives are significantly more constrained. It cannot be a stand-alone strategy because it does not, in itself, challenge the dominant paradigm of compulsory able-bodiedness (Wendell 1996). So how do able-bodied people acknowledge their lived experiences without oppressing those who are different?

The pathology of non-disablement

For non-disabled people to understand the experience of disabled people's oppression, we need to understand the way in which disabled people experience the able-bodied oppressive gaze. The able-bodied gaze is similar to the male gaze and the colonial gaze that feminist and postcolonial writers have written about. Dominant groups are able to look without being seen. Disabled people, like other subordinate groups, report what it feels like to be subject to the gaze of the other; how it disempowers and wounds them (Hughes 1999). The challenge for able-bodied people is to allow ourselves to experience what it is like to be seen.

Since the social model's focus on the elimination of the economic sources of oppression does not acknowledge the intercorporeal relationships reflected in the able-bodied gaze, Hughes (ibid.) considers it a 'pathology of non-disablement' because it conveys deficit. The able-bodied gaze is pathological because able-bodied people mostly think of it as neutral. Failing to recognise the damage it does, able-bodied people remain ignorant of their own assumptions in relation to beauty, perfection and normality. They are unable to see how their perception of disabled people is, itself, disfiguring. If we are to effectively address ableism, we must unsettle this perception.

Garland-Thomson (2009) explored ways in which disabled people can turn the disablist gaze back on those who stare. Different forms of staring are distinguished, from benign and attentive staring to malign domination staring, as she encourages able-bodied readers to reflect upon how they gaze at others. It is an important practice for all those concerned with dismantling unearned able-bodied privilege.

Non-disabled people often fear physical difference. Acknowledging the legal and social rights now available to disabled people and the anti-discrimination legislation to prevent the expression of prejudice in employment, Shildrick (2002) maintains that bodily difference still creates unease among many able-bodied people. This is because disabled people's bodies threaten normative embodiment.

Hughes (2005) argues that many non-disabled people are troubled by the frailty of the human condition and that such people experience a deep fear of the possibility that they may become disabled themselves. For them, to suffer a major impairment would be a tragedy that they hope they will never have to experience. People with normative bodies are also loath to be reminded of how fragile their bodies are. This is even more evident among men who adhere to hegemonic notions of masculinity because they want to view their bodies as indestructible (Hughes 2007). As a result of this refusal to recognise and come to terms with this frailty, there is an uneasy ambivalence in the experience of many able-bodied people in their relations with disabled people (Murphy 1995). This ambivalence fuels disabling attitudes and prejudices because it buys into the ableist paradigm.

Aronowitz (2004) attributes this unease about our own fragility to the fantasy of eternal youth that he believes has pervaded our culture. Our own physical and mental well-being is historically specific, a point that many of us would prefer to deny. Disabled people bring us face to face with the arbitrariness and the temporal dimension of our current able-bodiedness. As Deal (2007) notes, while men do not worry about becoming women and white people do not worry about becoming black, many non-disabled people are concerned about the possibility of becoming disabled.

Swain and French (2000) argue that the tragedy mode of disability reflects the deep fears of non-disabled people about their own vulnerability to impairment. When non-disabled people refuse to contemplate the possibility of disability, they maintain the divide between themselves and the disabled. Fear of disability is often then projected on to the subjectivities of disabled people. Not coming to terms with prospective impairment in the lives of able-bodied people is the real tragedy. Able-bodied people need to reclaim their own physical vulnerability and understand how it relates to their responses to bodily difference (Shildrick 2002). They need to study the pathology of non-disablement because it is so destructive to the lives of disabled people (Hughes 2007).

Role of non-disabled people in challenging ableism

Is there a role for non-disabled people in disability politics? Early formulations of the social model did not seem to posit a place for non-disabled people. Branfield (1999) says that most non-disabled allies do not understand either the experience of disability or the impact of disablism.

Many able-bodied people have taken a charitable rather than a political approach to disability. That is why many disability activists and academics remain sceptical of the possibilities of able-bodied people developing non-oppressive alliances with disabled people.

Exploring the contributions that non-disabled people could make to the disability movement (Drake 1997) suggested that the most legitimate focus for non-disabled people is to interrogate the disabling aspects of social policy. Branfield (1998) acknowledged that non-disabled people needed to change to remove the disabling attitudes and barriers that discriminate against disabled people. However, she argued that being non-disabled inevitably carried with it domination and appropriation. She emphasised the dangers of non-disabled people co-opting the disability movement for their own ends.

Ducket (1998) challenges the view that non-disabled people have no place in the disability movement, believing it sets up a binary opposition between disabled people and non-disabled people. He also challenges the view that all disabled people are oppressed and all non-disabled people are oppressors. As we have seen, disabled people are not free from enacting oppression, as the experiences of older, black, female and working-class disabled people can attest.

Non-disabled people often play key roles in the lives of disabled people, as parents, as carers, as professionals, as support workers and as researchers (Shakespeare 2006).[4] Such experiences may provide the impetus for them to become allies in support of disabled people. While most disabled people have experienced oppression at the hands of non-disabled people, Shakespeare (ibid.) explores the possibilities for them to play supportive and non-oppressive roles in the lives of disabled people. He points out the irony that in putting

4. Some proponents of the social model of disability regard the term 'carers' as problematical because it is embedded with power imbalances.

disabled people in the foreground of disability studies and disability politics, the role of non-disabled people in reproducing or challenging disability oppression has not been considered. Space is needed to understand more about how ableist practices may be challenged. A renewed and extended social model of disability could help.

Conclusion

While disabled people have experiences of the world that are different from the able-bodied, it is possible for able-bodied people to generate a non-ableist counter-discourse from which they can challenge both disablism and ableism. Such a project will involve making visible the ableist culture and the power and privileges flowing from this. It means moving beyond disability awareness education.

Disability awareness programmes heighten people's awareness of what it might be like to experience some form of impairment. However, such programmes reinforce an individual deficiency model of disability and fail to capture the most difficult aspects of disability (Griffin et al. 2007). Even disability equality training in the social model, which aims to educate non-disabled people about the ways in which environments can be disabling (D. Marks 1999b), has failed to promote an awareness of ableism as a form of privilege.

Evans and Broido (2005) also question what it means to be a disability ally. The first step, they propose, is awareness among non-disabled people that they derive privilege and power from their able-bodied identity. Challenging ableism and the dominant cultural norms about what constitutes the normal body is part of the work, as is redefining body normativity and accepting their own fragility.

Those of us who are able-bodied need to learn how to engage in dialogues with disabled people in ways that value differences. Very few people are able to fully embody able-bodied norms. Inahara (2009) says that the perfect body is an unattainable ideal that even most able-bodied people fail to achieve. Instead, we need to develop other discursive frames that recognise the multiplicity and fluidity of bodies and to encourage respect for bodily differences.

As with many attitude-change campaigns, some advances in the recognition of disabled people's rights also promote the interests of non-disabled people. While win-win outcomes for all are not in themselves problematic, it raises the question about how non-disabled people will deal with advances for disabled people when they conflict with their own self-interest (Deal 2007).

While non-disabled people will vary in terms of their active involvement in the forces that sustain disablism, non-disabled people still benefit from disablism. Furthermore, while they may be actively engaged in challenging disablism, it does not mean that they are free of disabling practices in their own lives (Branfield 1999). It is important for all progressive people that we critically reflect upon our own position within the framework of able-bodied privilege and take action against it.

PART THREE
Undoing privilege

NINE

Challenging the reproduction of privilege from within

The various forms of privilege examined in the previous six chapters have distinctive dynamics and institutional forms. Nevertheless, there are sufficient similarities across the domains of privilege to warrant an outline of common strategies and processes for challenging privilege. Some of these strategies may play out in different ways in relation to different groups because they are not parallel forms of domination, but rather they intersect and reinforce each other in complex ways.

There is no shortage of strategies in challenging oppression. Mullaly (2002) has outlined strategies at personal, cultural and structural levels. Anti-oppressive practice at the personal level involves empowerment, consciousness raising and involvement in groups of similarly situated others to organise against oppression. At the cultural level, the importance of developing counter-discourses of feminism, black nationalism, Marxism and gay liberation to challenge the oppressive discourses of male domination, white supremacy, capitalism and heterosexism are advocated. At the structural level, laws, social policies and institutions that benefit the dominant group need to be confronted. Mullaly proposes new social movements, alternative organisations, critical social policy analysis and progressive electoral politics to challenge the social, economic and political relations of oppression.

Although Mullaly (ibid.) encourages the development of multi-issue coalitions comprised of groups who are multiply oppressed, he does not acknowledge that inevitably these coalitions will be formed by people who are both privileged as well as oppressed. Consequently, none of his strategies for challenging oppression engages or addresses this group. Oppression and privilege need to be addressed by both marginalised *and* privileged groups.

Just as systems of oppression operate at personal, cultural and structural levels, privilege is reproduced at these levels as well. This means that if the eradication of oppression requires us to transform material conditions, demystify dominant culture and empower those who are oppressed, then complementary strategies need to be developed to address the reproduction of privilege by those in dominant groups.

It has been the argument of this book that structural and discursive levels of privilege are sustained and reproduced by the conscious and unconscious beliefs and the habitual practices of individuals in privileged groups. By focusing on what individual members of privileged groups can do, I am not suggesting that privilege is predominantly an issue facing individuals. Privilege is located in institutions, policies, laws and professional knowledge, as well as normalised cultural practices. Therefore, changing people in privileged groups will not in itself abolish privilege any more than empowering the oppressed will eliminate oppression.

We should be under no illusion that changing individual consciousness among the privileged will in itself be enough to address structural privilege. Clearly, structural changes need to be introduced to address privilege that is embodied in laws, social policies and organisational practices. We need to engage in processes that challenge the institutionalisation of privilege within political, economic, religious and educational systems.

D. Smith's (2005) concept of 'relations of ruling' usefully captures the way in which social relations and forms of social organisation are constituted by professional, bureaucratic and academic knowledge. These forms of knowledge lead to textualised concepts and categories which frame people's lived experiences. Relations of ruling are reproduced by the subjectivity and consciousness of privileged groups and the dominant ideologies that naturalise privilege and entitlement. Dominant groups use ruling relations to regulate subordinate groups. Understanding how our practices in the world either challenge or reproduce these relations of domination helps us to realise how changing our participation in these relations can impact on the wider structures.

Challenging the normalisation of privilege

O'Connor (2002) locates oppression and privilege within the context of 'social practices'. Social practices are practices governed by principles and rules that frame what we say and do. They enable us to make sense of our lives. As I have shown, oppressive actions by individuals are legitimated by these wider social practices. For

O'Connor, the issue of responsibility for oppressive acts is not just in relation to individual actions, but also in relation to the practices that shape them. In this view, responsibility moves beyond the individual to collective and shared responsibility (May 1993) or what Card (2002) calls 'relational responsibility', where the wider community of individuals needs to address their support for those practices.

The question arises as to how conscious individuals are of supporting normative oppressive social practices. If some oppressive attitudes and actions are habituated to the extent that individuals are not aware of holding or expressing them, to what extent can individuals be held responsible and culpable for them? (O'Connor 2002).

Calhoun (1989) observes that social acceptance of oppressive practices often prevents individuals from being aware of the harmful consequences of their practices. If individuals are not responsible then we cannot defend our use of moral reproach when challenging such practices.

The notion of an 'oppressor' does not seem to equate with ordinary people simply going about their lives who are blithely unaware of the implications of their everyday practices for the reproduction of oppressive regimes. We have witnessed throughout history, however, that it is ordinary people's participation in the routines of life that enable oppression and exploitation to take hold. The premise of this book is that there are millions of people of good will who are aware of inequalities but do not see themselves implicated in them and consequently do not feel that they are responsible to do anything about them. It is their inaction that enables privilege to be sustained (A. Johnson 2006).

Individuals need to acknowledge their responsibility for oppression that occurs at the level of social practice if they are going to be able to listen to moral reproach for their actions (O'Connor 2002). Individuals can come to recognise oppressive practices and the role they play in reproducing oppression. It is possible to interrupt these oppressive practices and form moral social practices. My hope for this book is that it may contribute to that awareness. Whether individuals will have the moral courage to act in light of this awareness is another question.

Towards a pedagogy of the privileged

What is the role of the privileged in working for social change? Can enlightened members of privileged groups be effective allies in combating oppression? The premise underlying much progressive politics is that only the oppressed can address oppression. Many writers have portrayed oppressors as incapable of personal change or sustained activism in relation to social change. Little attention has been given to how we might develop a pedagogy to transform the oppressors and the privileged. Challenging oppression from below should be the foundation for social change movements, yet such movements can be complemented by developing strategies to engage and address those who hold power that stand in the way of these movements.

Many members of privileged groups are already involved in progressive social movements in relation to refugees, the anti-war movement, environment politics, international solidarity movements and human rights-based work. However, the privileged status of many of these activists is often not problematised. Many of those who write about challenging oppression do not acknowledge how advantaged they are by it.

So, how do oppressors move towards a critical consciousness of their own status? Recent years have witnessed the emergence of a pedagogy for the privileged (Curry-Stevens 2004; 2007) and a pedagogy of the oppressor (Lee 2002; Breault 2003; Kimmel 2003; Van Gorder 2007; Frueh 2007).[1] These developments provide us with a conceptual and pedagogical framework for engaging members of privileged groups about their unearned entitlements. Much of this work also takes these strategies out of the university classroom and into government and community-based forums where privilege-holders can be challenged about their advantages.

Curry-Stevens (2007) identifies six steps in educating members of privileged groups about oppression and privilege:

1. Developing awareness of the existence of oppression.
2. Understanding the structural dynamics that hold oppression in place.
3. Locating oneself as being oppressed.
4. Locating oneself as being privileged.
5. Understanding the benefits that accrue to one's privileges.
6. Understanding oneself as being implicated in others' oppression and acknowledging one's oppressor status.

---

1. Pedagogy of the privileged is inspired by Paulo Freire's (1970) groundbreaking work on the pedagogy of the oppressed.

She notes that the latter stage is perhaps the most difficult task to take on because it requires acknowledging one's culpability in the oppression of others.

The starting point is to recognise that oppression and privilege exist. Privilege blinds many people in dominant groups to the realities of oppression, so we need to awaken our sense of injustice among those who do not experience the pain and hardship that is the basis for developing a critical consciousness among the oppressed. Under what conditions might we be able to encourage members of privileged groups to engage with the knowledge of oppression and open themselves to hearing the voices of the oppressed (Fine 2006)?

Some approaches to engaging people with privilege focus on acknowledging their experience of oppression from other positionings. For example, it may occur when working with gay men, non-white men and working-class men in relation to gender privilege. The premise is that by acknowledging men's experience of oppression in other social divisions they will see the links with sexism and patriarchy.

According to Bishop (2002), all oppressors have personally experienced oppression, otherwise they would not become oppressors. For her, you must be engaged in challenging your own oppression before you can become an ally to the liberation of others. She also believes that members of privileged groups can only be effective allies when they work for their own liberation and address their own oppression.

This is a contentious issue that is the subject of heated debate. Not all of those who occupy oppressor roles have been oppressed. Also, it is much easier for those who occupy both oppressed and oppressor statuses to concentrate on struggling against their oppression and to ignore the privileged statuses they occupy. As Magnet (2006) reflects, it is easy to neglect our own participation in the maintenance of the oppression that we are struggling against.

In focusing on one's own oppression, we need to be careful not to 'race to innocence'. This occurs when members of privileged groups discount their privilege and frame themselves as oppressed (Fellows and Razack 1998). To effectively challenge privilege from within, we must accept our oppressor status. This is crucial, given how privileged readers with a social justice consciousness have a tendency to read books about oppression from the standpoint of the oppressed (Lee 2002). Experience of oppression can filter the reading experience and consequently make us less likely to acknowledge our own acts of domination. As a white man from a working-class background,

I can always use my previous experience of class-based oppression to locate myself among the oppressed rather than acknowledge my white male privilege. It has been a challenge to construct a narrative in this book that contests this reading orientation.

Developing emancipatory interests

It is important to reflect on why those of us in privileged groups engage in social justice so as to be clear about our motivations (Reason and Broido 2005). A key question here is whether it is in the interests of the dominant group to change. Lichtenberg (1988) argues that those at the top of exploitative relationships are also miserable. Wineman (1984) says that equal relations are more rewarding and fulfilling than hierarchal relations. Hierarchy dehumanises people and denies our capacity for emotional connectedness.

Others have written about the damaging effects privilege has on those in dominant groups. Goodman (2001) identifies a number of costs to privileged groups as a result of oppression, including: psychological costs, where privileged group members are unable to develop their full humanity; relational costs, where members of privileged groups experience barriers to authentic relationships and isolation and lack of trust by those who are different; moral and spiritual costs associated with the inability to live up to principles of fairness and justice; and the physical costs resulting from illnesses associated with dominating behaviour.

If systems of oppression harm members of privileged groups as well as those who are oppressed, we could cultivate the self-interest of the privileged in involving them in social justice campaigns (Edwards 2006). Goodman (2001) believes that an awareness of these costs can lead people from privileged groups to regard their privileges as not necessarily being in their self-interests. They may be motivated to change to improve their interpersonal relationships and their own sense of integrity and authenticity.

These self-interests need to be seen alongside empathy for those who are oppressed and adherence to moral principles and belief in human rights and social justice for all people. Hoy (2004) talks about how people can develop 'ethical resistance' to challenge relations of domination. This requires making these exploitative relations visible and encouraging the privileged to see their 'real interests' as being furthered by challenging oppression.

For some, these motivations are seen as suspect and controversial.

Appealing to self-interests may lead to trivialisation and co-opting of the issues to fit in with the needs of privileged groups (Goodman 2001). While appealing to ethical and moral arguments on their own may not engage members of privileged groups to overcome their material interests in defending their privilege (McMahon 1999).

I have previously argued in relation to male privilege that men can move beyond their socially constructed patriarchal interests to develop emancipatory interests (Pease 2002b) and I believe that this argument can be adapted to other privileged groups as well.

Constructing a traitorous identity

For oppressed groups, reconstructing one's identity is a positive and affirmative project. Members of oppressed groups need to gain a sense of self-respect and pride associated with their identity (Mullaly 2002). However, for those in privileged groups, the process by which people become conscious of their internalised domination and react against it involves the construction of a 'negative identity'.

Developing a negative identity entails challenging our internalised moral superiority and rejecting the sense of entitlement that so many of us are socialised into. This means refusing part of who we are and constructing a traitorous relationship with our dominant subject position (A. Ferguson 1998).

Many writers have described the process of coming to oppose the dominance of our own identity group as becoming a traitor to our group (Harding 1995; Bailey 1998; Lee 2002). Traitorousness involves being disloyal to the parts of ourselves that are privileged and rejecting the expectations that having such privilege entails (Heldke and O'Connor 2004). Bailey (1998) discusses traitorous identities as developing an awareness of privilege and refusing to be faithful to the world views that members of privileged groups are expected to hold.

Harding (1995) believes that members of privileged groups can reinvent themselves by learning about their own social location and by taking responsibility for their dominant subject positions. She argues that privileged traitors can develop liberatory knowledge by being critically reflective of their privilege rather than being oblivious to it. The aim for traitors is to search for ways to disrupt the process of coercion into dominant subject positions. Bailey (1998) regards the process of becoming traitorous as similar to Aristotle's idea of acquiring moral virtue.

While the point of view of men in dominant groups has represented

Western thought as universal, it too is socially situated and partial (Harding 1995). We all need to recognise the multiple subjectivities we inhabit and to locate ourselves in relation to privilege and oppression in our lives. Those who are most unmarked (white, heterosexual, middle-class able-bodied men), need to understand how their subjectivities are constructed through the marking of others (Fellows and Razack 1998).

Those who are privileged across a number of different domains have greater responsibility to address privilege and domination than those who experience privilege in fewer domains of life. I am someone who is close to the top of the matrix of privilege and dominance; I find it easier to address those readers who share all of my privileged statuses, as I believe these readers have the greatest responsibility to examine their privilege. It is also important that I challenge readers who possess some oppressed as well as privileged statuses. All people with relative privilege must take responsibility for their intermediate structural location in relation to privilege as well as their oppressed positioning (Lee 2002). For those who are oppressed and privileged, it means constructing both affirmative and negative aspects of one's identity at the same time (A. Ferguson 1998).

To develop a traitorous identity we must become a 'world traveller' to learn about the lives of those who are oppressed (Bailey 1998). 'World travelling' is a metaphor developed by Lugones (1987) to describe the process of locating ourselves outside our comfort zone and immersing ourselves in other worlds where our privileged identities will be challenged.

Engaging in dialogue across difference and inequality

Many members of privileged groups are disconnected from the lived experiences of people who are oppressed. Thus another strategy for the transformation of the privileged is through critical dialogue with those who are oppressed (Lee 2002; Van Gorder 2007). Curry-Stevens (2004) argues that critical dialogue can bring about changes in relations of ruling.

Critical dialogue is seen to offer the promise of respectful and responsive engagements about difference and inequality. However, it is not inherently liberatory and at times those engaged in critical dialogue have not always been sufficiently aware of the impact of power relations and privilege on the interactions of participants (Barbules 2000). Cross-cultural dialogue is difficult to do well because privileged voices can easily undermine the necessary conditions for an emancipatory process. Certainly, structural inequalities can create obstacles to constructive dialogue. Dialogue may be difficult, if not impossible, if there is resentment, suspicion and hostility arising from years of oppression and suffering (Singh 2001). Yet, some people believe that '*any* attempt to establish reasonable and consensual discourse across difference inevitably involves the imposition of dominant groups' values, beliefs and modes of discourse upon others' (Burbules and Rice 1991: 401).

If equality is predicated on participants being equals first, a non-oppressive dialogue between oppressed and dominant groups will not be possible. This precondition for dialogue can be paralysing, because no action can take place before the precondition is met. The only way forward is to enter into the dialogue and grapple with the contradictions in the unequal power situation. As Grob (1991: 141) puts it, 'there is no way to dialogue, dialogue is the way'.

Even so, it is important for members of dominant groups to earn the right to dialogue. Different opinions exist in relation to how this right may be earned: for Pheterson (1986) it involves the identification of 'internalised domination'; for Harding (1993: 69) it means listening to marginalised people and critically examining 'dominant institutional beliefs and practices that systematically disadvantage them'; for Ellsworth (1989: 324) it means dominant groups understanding that their knowledge of marginalised groups 'will always be partial . . . and potentially oppressive to others'. To enable dialogue to occur, we must recognise the obstacles to it. Members of privileged groups need to demonstrate an understanding that their knowledge and perception of the world is socially situated and only partial if they are going to avoid oppressive practices in their encounters (ibid.).

Some writers have attempted to identify the best conditions to frame dialogue and the best rules to guide it (Alcoff 1995; Singh 2001). Habermas (1987) developed criteria for determining an ideal speech situation where the power of participants was equalised. Curry-Stevens (2004) suggests that if the privileged problematise their own dominant subject positions, they could contribute to the conditions for an ideal speech situation. The privileged need to acknowledge their structural and discursive positioning of dominance if they are going to be able to counter some of its damaging effects.[2]

2. It should be remembered that the mechanism of dialogue through

In the context of multi-racial dialogue, such encounters must involve a critical engagement with whiteness (Rodriguez 2000). Whites must problematise their own social location in any cross-cultural dialogue. Whites also need to confront their prejudice and develop their ability to understand others' perspectives. In the Australian context, whites need to acknowledge the dispossession of land and the ongoing colonisation of Indigenous people.

As part of a project on exploring profeminist men's subjectivities, I organised dialogues with feminist women and gay men to explore male and heterosexual privilege respectively (Pease 2000). The men listened to the women's suspicions about their work, their doubts about how men could overcome their dominant subjectivities and why men would want to change. They also heard from the gay men about their reluctance to engage in an open dialogue with straight men because of their reluctance to acknowledge their heterosexual privilege and the concern that straight men's gay affirmative stance may marginalise gay men's voices. Due to the issues of lack of trust and power inequality, these dialogues were difficult to conduct but charting our way through them left me with some hope for the future of such conversations.

Listening across difference

I. Young (1997) challenges the suggestion that we can fully understand the experiences of others by imagining ourselves in their place because it obscures the differences between us. For her, this involves simply a projection of our own perspective on to others – what she calls 'symmetrical reciprocity'. In contrast, she proposes the notion of 'asymmetrical reciprocity' whereby those in dominant positions in relation to gender, race and class acknowledge and take account of the other without taking on their perspective. This involves adopting a position of moral humility on the part of the privileged. It also entails, for those of use who are privileged, learning to see ourselves as others see us (La Caze 2008).

---

speaking can privilege certain people and marginalise others. Some groups have very different ways of speaking, while others might 'speak' better through art, music, drama, poetry or story-telling. It may be more subtle, circular and indirect than what we assume when we talk about 'dialogue'. It does not all have to be serious verbal exchange and if it is confined to this, it will inevitably privilege the most articulate in Western terms. I am grateful to Jim Ife for alerting me to this issue.

Much of the focus on developing conditions for dialogue across difference is about how oppressed groups can find their voice and speak up about their experiences. Little attention has been given to the responsibility of the privileged to shut up and listen to hear their experiences. Dreher (2009) talks about the right of oppressed groups to be understood and to have their experience comprehended. This involves a sense of obligation for members of privileged groups to listen to those who are oppressed in ways other than those they already understand. We need to find ways to facilitate the hearing of these experiences of the oppressed.

Lloyd (2009) refers to listening as a necessary condition for democratic dialogue and believes that it entails an ethical responsibility on the part of the privileged. Listening across difference and inequality requires an attention to privilege and a preparedness to undo it (Dreher 2009). Dreher refers to this as 'ethical listening'. This involves not only the ability to understand the other, but also to be receptive to our own complicity with systems of privilege. Listeners from dominant groups need to be challenged.

Perhaps best-known for her practice of locating herself in public places in different cities of the world with a sign that says 'American willing to listen', Peavey (2003) formulated the concept of strategic questioning as a way to facilitate listening. She suggests asking questions that open our thinking to new ideas that arise within ourselves.

Listening attentively to the experiences of people who are oppressed is not easy for members of privileged groups (A. Johnson 2006). In part, this is because it means relinquishing our perception of ourselves as knowers rather than as listeners (O'Donnell et al. 2009). It can be quite destabilising to have our dominance, knowledge or expertise contested (Fellows and Razack 1998). It requires us to listen to the pain and suffering of others and to allow ourselves to feel that pain in our heart (Peavey 2003). This fits with Rowan's (1997) belief that men need to allow themselves to be wounded by the challenge of feminism if they are going to be able to heal.

This does not mean that we need only to teach better listening skills. Rather, we need to ensure that more responsive listening on the part of the privileged leads to challenges to the structural inequalities within which listening and dialogue take place (Lloyd 2009).

Becoming an ally

Increased awareness of the injustice of our privilege will hopefully lead to members of privileged groups becoming allies with oppressed groups. Ayvazian (1995: 1) defines an ally as 'a member of a dominant group in our society who works to dismantle any form of oppression from which she or he receives the benefit'. Similarly, Borshuk (2004) discusses ally activism as 'outgroup activism', where those involved are not direct beneficiaries.

Many models of ally identity development have been presented and explored (Bishop 2002; Aveline 2004; Reason and Broido 2005; Jip 2007). Providing support to oppressed groups and advocating for change are central. Much ally building involves challenging other members of dominant groups about their behaviours.

My own involvement as an ally has mainly been involved in challenging men's sexism and violence against women. I co-founded Men Against Sexual Assault (MASA) in 1991 to encourage other men to take responsibility for combating men's violence against women (Pease 1995) and I have conducted numerous Patriarchy Awareness Workshops to examine the impact that patriarchy has on the lives of women and men (Pease 1997a). When I talk to men about women's agency in struggling against sexism and men's violence, I also talk about the historical role of profeminist men in feminist politics (Kimmel and Mosmiller 1992).

In acting as allies to women, profeminist men face a number of challenges. When men become involved with women's campaigns, they often try to move into positions of authority (Luxton 1993: 352). There is a thin line between being a constructive ally and taking over another group's struggle. Even those men who are sensitive to these issues are likely to be acknowledged and praised for taking part.

In spite of their best intentions, allies sometimes perpetuate the oppression they are challenging (Edwards 2006). It is also inevitable that allies will sometimes 'get it wrong'. They must overcome this fear by being willing to learn from oppressed groups and committing themselves to challenging internalised domination. Ongoing challenges that allies face include figuring out when to speak, when to listen and when to remove themselves from the activist space (ibid.). It should also be remembered that it is members of oppressed groups that should be the ones who determine who constitutes an ally and who does not (ibid.).

Forging coalitions against oppression and privilege

Many social change theorists have argued that multi-issue coalitions aimed at addressing all forms of oppression are fundamental for social justice and political change (Reagon 1983; Jakobsen 1998; Bystydzienski and Schacht 2001a; Cole 2008). Coalition politics challenges identity-based social movements that are focused on single issues. Burack (2001) identifies coalitions as operating on three levels:

1. Where groups from different social locations come together to focus on particular issues.
2. Where differences are addressed within groups.
3. Where multiple parts of the self are engaged.

Bystydzienski and Schacht (2001a) have compiled an important collection of practical accounts of 'forging radical alliances across difference'. They emphasise the importance of recognising multiple identities in making dialogues across difference work (Bystydzienski and Schacht 2001b). This means that oppressed groups will also need to engage with their own privileged subjectivities within their own ranks (Cole 2008) and deal with some of the contradictions between espoused positions and enacted behaviours that so often ensue.

In addressing differences in coalitions, it is important to remember that each individual also embodies many of these differences within themselves (Jakobsen 1998). Barvosa-Carter (2001: 21) expresses it as 'identity differences within us enable radical alliances among us'. She argues that the more people acknowledge multiple parts of themselves, the more they will be able to identify with different positions.

For coalitions to work, we must find ways of addressing power differences within them. Bystydzienski and Schacht (2001b) emphasise the importance of creating shared spaces that can assist participants to engage in dialogue without domination. They identify three stages for effective coalitions:

1. An acknowledgement of the impact that social identities have upon the participants.
2. A recognition of how privilege is played out in their relationships.
3. The goodwill to find common ground by honouring perspectives that are different from their own.

Schacht and Ewing (2001: 200) identify six criteria that profeminist men need to address if coalitions with feminist women are going to be forged. These criteria could be adapted to all privileged groups:

1. Acknowledge and give up their male privilege.
2. Be willing to apply feminist principles to their personal lives.
3. Make the elimination of oppression against women and people in general a central priority.
4. Advocate for social and institutional change.
5. Learn non-hierarchical forms of communication and decision-making.
6. Demonstrate respect for women and women's spaces.

For members of privileged groups, coalitional work involves an emotional commitment to process. Reagon (1983: 196) says that privileged members of coalitions will 'feel threatened to the core' most of the time. If they do not, it is unlikely that they are emotionally committed. The attempt to form coalitions across difference will constitute specific sites where oppressive relations are likely to be enacted. When illuminated and challenged, they become microcosms of the larger struggle against privilege.

Developing models of accountability

My experience in the men's violence sector in Australia has been that many men who work with violent men have been reluctant to make their work accountable to women who work with the survivors of men's violence. When we organised campaigns against men's violence in Men Against Sexual Assault, we always engaged in consultations with feminist groups. Similarly, when we facilitated Patriarchy Awareness Workshops, we invited and paid feminist women to observe the workshops and offer critical feedback on their observations.

Because oppression and privilege are more visible to those who are oppressed, they must always be the leaders in social movements for change. The extent to which the privileged have been able to transform themselves will be evaluated by the oppressed (Lee 2002; Van Gorder 2007).

Accountability usually occurs when those with less power are accountable to those with more power. In challenging privilege and oppression, this is reversed. Oppressed groups have more legitimacy to identify oppressive practices than privileged groups because they suffer the injustices of oppression (I. Young 1997). Hence, the work against privilege and oppression by members of privileged groups must be accountable to the oppressed.

Tamasese and Waldegrave (1996) at the Family Centre in New

Zealand developed a model of cultural and gender accountability to enable people from different cultures and men and women to address cultural and gender bias in their work. They reversed the traditional mode of accountability where white people and men control the decision-making. In this model, the privileged need to be able to listen to the experiences of those who are marginalised.

In the Family Centre model, dominant and dominated groups form into separate caucuses who meet on their own prior to and after dialogue group meetings (Tamasese et al. 1998). The dominant group listens to the dominated groups' issues and hears their ideas on how best to respond to their concerns. Hall (1996), at the Dulwich Family Therapy Centre in Adelaide, outlined how this model of partnership accountability was operationalised in relation to women workers' concerns about men's practices.

In the context of emancipatory participatory action research, Wadsworth (1997) has argued that research should be accountable to critical reference groups comprised of people whose interests are to be served by the research. This transforms the role of professionals and activists from experts to participants who work alongside the oppressed as partners to address the issues they identify as important.

In these models of accountability, the more privileged group has to hear the concerns of the less privileged group and together they must find a way to resolve the issues. The premise is that the dominant group is committed to shifting their attitudes and practices towards equality with the dominated group. For this process to work, the dominant group must privilege the views of the dominated group above their own.

Relinquishing privilege?

Some radical critics will no doubt see a project such as this as fitting within a neo-liberal agenda and will question what potential there is for privileged activists to contribute anything meaningful to progressive social change. I have taken these criticisms seriously and I write about the dangers and limitations of involving men as allies in men's violence prevention (Pease 2008). Nevertheless, I maintain that there is a place for this work within a wider social change orientated movement.

Those who argue that change from the top is unlikely to produce any meaningful outcomes and that only change initiated from below can generate significant structural change have often challenged my focus on privilege. It is understandable that many social activists will question whether the privileged can step out of their dominant subjectivities and can transform themselves (Curry-Stevens 2004).

Some critics doubt that members of privileged groups will voluntarily commit themselves to challenge their own privilege (Curry-Stevens 2007). They certainly raise the issue of not expecting the privileged to do so. One of the forms of privilege is the ability to ignore calls for involvement in social justice campaigns. Those who do make a commitment still have the privilege at any point of changing their mind and allowing their commitment to wane. Awareness of privilege can be reversed, but my experience in campaigns tells me that there comes a point of no return for allies. Significant reconstruction of subjectivities can occur to the point where turning away from activist involvements is no longer viable.

Furthermore, if oppressed groups continue to maintain pressure on privileged groups to transform themselves and to take responsibility for action against their privilege, they will not be taking this course of action solely from internalised motivations (ibid.). So, if one is sceptical of the ability of the privileged to transform themselves and relinquish their privilege, how might they respond more positively to the demands of the oppressed? We need to understand how resistance to change can operate to lessen the obstacles to social change activities (Pease 2008). If those with privilege do not yield power, the gains achieved by the oppressed can more easily be co-opted (Curry-Stevens 2004).

Anyone brought up in a patriarchal, racist, class-elitist, heterosexist, ableist Western society is not likely to eliminate oppressive attitudes and practices entirely, just as the privileged cannot fully relinquish privilege. While the structural relations that advantage the privileged remain, unearned benefits will follow. Knowing that they cannot get rid of their privilege, and that they cannot use it without perpetuating the dominant–subordinate relations to which they are opposed, is not an easy thing to live with (Bailey 1999).

Since privilege cannot be completely abandoned by those on the receiving end, some activists argue that we should focus less on giving up privilege and more on mitigating the harmful effects of privilege (ibid.). Here, privilege is used for progressive rather than exploitative or dominating purposes. In a personal communication, Michael Kimmel said: 'I don't share the view that the only choice is to challenge or reproduce privilege. I think that we can acknowledge the privileges we have and then choose to use that privilege to empower others.'

McIntosh's (1992) two types of privilege discussed earlier are worth remembering: unearned advantages that all people should have, but are restricted to dominant groups; and conferred dominance, where one group of people is given power over another group through claimed superiority. The former privileges should be spread throughout society and would become the norm in a just society. It is the latter form of privilege that reproduces hierarchy that needs to be challenged and rejected.

While some aspects of privilege cannot be renounced or given up because they are structurally conferred, a socially just society would restructure so that this no longer occurred. Privileged groups will experience this as a loss. When members of privileged groups say that they want everyone else to have privilege, but do not want to relinquish the privileges they have, they often want to hold on to their conferred dominance.

Conclusion

Almost thirty years ago, Therborn (1980) outlined three modes of ideological justification for defending a social order. They are our perceptions of:

1. What exists and what does not exist.
2. What is good, right and just.
3. What is possible and impossible.

Defenders of the social order can argue that privilege and oppression do not exist. If they are acknowledged as existing because of the overwhelming evidence of inequality, they can argue that such inequalities are justified because those with privilege have earned their entitlements and those who are marginalised are to blame for their situation. If this can be demonstrated to be untrue, then the final line of defence is to acknowledge the injustice but to maintain that there is no possibility for being able to bring about a more equal and socially just world. The logic of social change requires the antithesis of this position. We must acknowledge that privilege exists, that it represents unearned advantages and conferred dominance and *that it can be changed*.

Eisler and Loye (1990) have developed a partnership model of social organisation to stand against the dominator model that governs most societies. I have previously argued that the partnership model provides a valuable way to frame alternative visions for society (Pease 2002b). We can use this model to analyse dynamics at institutional, cultural, interpersonal and individual levels. At the individual level, many of us may espouse partnership principles but be unaware of how deeply embedded the dominator principles may be in our psyches. We are not short on analysis and strategy for social change and yet we seem to lack the political and personal will to undo the relations of domination.

It is now an axiom that those of us who pursue social justice at the public and institutional levels of society need to 'walk the talk' in our personal lives. We need to live out the changes we want to see in the wider society in our own relationships and ways of life (Mullaly 1997). This is an admirable exhortation. However, those of us in privileged groups who have endeavoured to make the political personal in our own lives know how difficult it can be.

Mullaly (2002) concludes his book on challenging oppression by emphasising the constructive use of anger by oppressed groups to channel their discontent and moral outrage into effective strategies of collective resistance. All readers are encouraged to identify themselves as oppressed to enable them to share and articulate this anger about social injustice. It is a fine point on which to finish a book about oppression if you are oppressed. However, what is the place of anger for those of us who are white, economically privileged, heterosexual, Western able-bodied men who embody that which the oppressed are struggling against? In the place of, or alongside anger, we need to articulate our distress about our complicity in oppression. We need to feel this distress to shatter our complacency.

I have mounted a case for rebellion against privilege from within. I have argued that members of privileged groups do not have to maintain their dominance; they can be responsive to the claims of the oppressed and loosen their connections to dominant subject positions (Pease 2000).

In this book I have introduced various intersecting systems of privilege. I hope that it will encourage activist readers to extend their thinking and reading beyond the particular sites in which they struggle against their own oppression. I encourage members of dominant groups to set up reading and study groups to interrogate privilege similar to those organised by the Dulwich Centre (Raheim et al. 2007) and the Reconciliation circles in Australia (Patten and Ryan 2001).

They can provide spaces for critical self-reflection and collective conscientisation for privileged and oppressed identities.

Writing and talking against privilege on its own is insufficient to undo privilege. However, there is a place for analysis and critical reflection as well as mobilisation and collective action. While I began the book with some level of understanding about the workings of privilege, it took me to new places and taught me about aspects of privilege that I had taken for granted. I hope that it also performs this function for many readers.

Unsettling unearned privilege is difficult because it is the privileged who make the rules and construct the norms that govern our actions. It would be utopian to suggest that the structures of privilege can be dismantled solely by actions from within. Challenging privilege has to be projected from below as well. We also know how the struggles of the oppressed can be co-opted and that new oppressive systems will replace old ones if those in dominant groups are not challenged to relinquish their privilege. Meaningful and lasting change in the world, at personal, cultural and structural levels, will only occur through the combined efforts of the oppressed and those willing to forgo and challenge their privileges. I hope that this book makes a contribution to that necessary transformation.

Bibliography

Acker, J. (1999) 'Rewriting Class, Race and Gender', in M. Ferree, J. Lorber and B. Hess (eds) *Revisioning Gender*, Sage, Thousand Oaks, CA.

— (2006a) 'Inequality Regimes: Gender, Class and Race in Organisations', *Gender and Society*, vol. 20, no. 4, pp. 441–64.

— (2006b) *Class Questions, Feminist Answers*, Rowman and Littlefield, Lanham, MD.

Adam, B. (1998) 'Theorizing Homophobia', *Sexualities*, vol. 1, no. 4, pp. 387–404.

Adams, P., Gavey, N., and Towns, A., (1995) 'Dominance and Entitlement: The Rhetoric Men Use to Discuss Their Violence Towards Women', *Discourse and Society*, vol. 6, no. 3, pp. 387–406.

Ahmed, S. (2004) 'Declarations of Whiteness: The Non-Performativity of Anti-racism', *Borderlands e-journal*, vol. 3, no. 2.

Akbar, N. (1992) *Visions for Black Men*, Mind Productions and Associates, Tallahassee, FL.

Akinyela, M. (1995) 'Rethinking Afrocentricity: The Foundation of a Theory of Critical Afrocenticity', in A. Darder (ed.) *Culture and Difference: Critical Perspectives on the Bicultural Experience in the United States*, Bethon and Garvey Press, New York.

Alcoff, L. (1995) 'The Problem of Speaking for Others', in J. Roof and R. Wiegman (eds) *Who Can Speak?: Authority and Critical Identity*, University of Illinois Press, Chicago, IL.

— (2000) 'What White People Should Do', in S. Harding and U. Narayan (eds) *Decentering the Centre: Philosophy for Multicultural, Postcolonial, and Feminist World*, Indiana University Press, Bloomington, IN.

Alden, H., and Parker, F. (2005) 'Gender Role Ideology, Homophobia and Hate Crime: Linking Attitudes to Macro-level Anti-Gay and Lesbians Hate Crimes', *Deviant Behaviour*, vol. 6, no. 4, pp. 321–43.

Allen, J. (2002) 'Men Interminable in Crisis: Historians on Masculinity, Sexual Boundaries and Manhood', *Radical History Review*, vol. 82, pp. 191–207.

Amin, S. (1989) *Eurocentrism*, Zed Books, London.

Anderson, M. (2003) 'Whitewashing Race: A Critical Perspective on Whiteness', in A. Doane and E. Bonilla-Silva (eds) *White Out: The Continuing Significance of Racism*, Routledge, London.

Appleby, G. (2006) 'Lesbian, Gay, Bisexual and Transgender People Confront Heterocentrism, Heterosexism and Homophobia', in G. Appleby, E. Colon and J. Hamilton (eds) *Diversity, Oppression and Social Functioning: Person in Environment Assessment and Intervention*, Allyn and Bacon, New York.

Aptheker, H. (1975) 'The History

of Anti-Racism in the US', *Black Scholar*, vol. 6, no. 5, pp. 16–22.

Aronowitz, S. (1979) 'The PMC or Middle Strata?', in P. Walker (ed.) *Between Labour and Capital*, Harvester Press, Sussex.

— (2004) *How Class Works: Power and Social Movement*, Yale University Press, New Haven, CT.

Asante, M. (2007) *An Afrocentric Manifesto*, Polity Press, Cambridge.

Auerbach, P. (1992) 'On Socialist Optimism', *New Left Review*, no. 192, pp. 5–35.

Aveline, N. (2004) 'Critical Whiteness Studies and the Challenges of Learning to be a "White Ally"', *Borderlands E Journal*, vol. 3, no. 2, pp. 1–10.

Ayres, I., and Brown, J. (2005) *Straightforward: Mobilizing Heterosexual Support for Gay Rights*, Princeton University Press, Princeton, NJ.

Ayvazian, A. (1995) 'Interrupting the Cycle of Oppression: The Role of Allies as Agents of Change', *Fellowship*, Jan–Feb, pp. 7–10.

Bahl, V. (1997) 'Relevance (or Irrelevance) of Subaltern Studies', *Economic and Political Weekly*, vol. 32, no. 23, pp. 1333–44.

Bailey, A. (1998) 'Privilege: Expanding on Marilyn Fry's Oppression', *Journal of Social Philosophy*, vol. 29, no. 3, pp. 104–19.

— (1999) 'Despising an Identity They Taught Me to Claim: Exploring a Dilemmas of White Privilege Awareness', in C. Cuomo and K. Hall (eds) *Whiteness: Feminist Philosophical Assumptions*, Totowa, New Jersey.

— (2000) 'Locating Traitorous Identities: Towards a View of Privilege-Cognizant White Character', in S. Harding and U. Narayan (eds) *Decentering the Centre: Philosophy for a Multicultural, Postcolonial and Feminist World*, Indiana University Press, Bloomington, IN.

Bakari, R. (1997) 'Epistemology from an Afrocentric Perspective: Enhancing Black Students' Consciousness through an Afrocentric Way of Knowing', University of Nebraska, Lincoln, NB.

Barbules, N. (2000) 'The Limits of Dialogue as a Critical Pedagogy', in P. Trifonas (ed.) *Revolutionary Pedagogies: Cultural Politics, Instituting Education and the Discourse of Theory*, Routledge Falmer, London.

Bar-On, A. (1999) 'Social Work and the "Missionary Zeal to Whip the Heathen Along the Path of Righteousness"', *British Journal of Social Work*, vol. 29, pp. 5–26.

Barone, C. (1998) 'Political Economy of Classism: Towards a More Integrated Multilevel View', *Review of Radical Political Economy*, vol. 30, no. 2, pp. 1–30.

Barounis, C. (2009) 'Cripping Heterosexuality and Queering Able-Bodiedness', *Journal of Visual Culture*, vol. 8, no. 1, pp. 54–75.

Barrett, M. (1980) *Women's Oppression Today*, Verso, London.

Barvosa-Carter, E. (2001) 'Multiple Identity and Coalition Building: How Identity Differences Within Us Enable Radical Alliances Among Us', in S. Schacht and J. Bystydzienski (eds) *Forging Radical Alliances Across Difference: Coalition Politics for the New Millennium*, Rowman and Littlefield, Lanham, MD.

Bayley, S. (1990) *Caste, Society and Politics in India from the Eighteenth Century to the Modern Age*, Cambridge University Press, New York.

Bella, L. (2002) 'What "Straight" Social Workers Need to Know About Heterosexism and Well-being', School of Social Work, Memorial University of Newfoundland, NF.

Beneke, T. (2004) 'Homophobia', in L. Heldelke and P. O'Connor (eds) *Oppression, Privilege and Resistance: Theoretical Perspectives on Racism, Sexism and Heterosexism*, McGraw-Hill, New York.

Bentley, M. (2007) *A Primary Health Care Approach to Men's Health in Community Settings*, Flinders University, Adelaide, SA.

Berlant, L., and Warner, M. (1998) 'Sex in Public', *Critical Inquiry*, vol. 24, no. 2, pp. 547–66.

Beynon, J. (2002) *Masculinities and Culture*, Open University Press, Buckingham.

Biddulph, S. (2008) *Raising Boys: Why Boys are Different and How to Help Them Become Happy and Well-balanced Men*, Celestial Arts, Berkeley, CA.

Bishop, A. (2002) *Becoming an Ally: Breaking the Cycle of Oppression*, Allen & Unwin, Sydney, NSW.

Blaut, J. (1993) *The Colonizer's Model of the World: Geographical Diffusionism and Eurocentric History*, Guilford Press, New York.

Bolten, G. (2008) *Aid and Other Dirty Business*, Ebury Press, Reading.

Bonnett, A. (2000) *Anti-Racism*, Routledge, London.

— (2004) *The Idea of the West: Culture, Politics and History*, Palgrave Macmillan, Houndmills, Basingstoke.

Borshuk, C. (2004) 'An Interpretive Investigation into the Motivation of Outgroup Activism', *Qualitative Report*, no. 9, pp. 300–19.

Boulet, J. (2003) 'Globalising Practice in the International Context', in J. Allan, B. Pease and L. Briskman (eds) *Critical Social Work: An Introduction to Theories and Practices*, Allen & Unwin, Sydney, NSW.

Bourdieu, P. (1977) *Outline of a Theory of Practice*, Cambridge University Press, New York.

— (1986) 'The Forms of Capital', in J. Richardson (ed.) *Handbook of Theory and Research for the Sociology of Education*, Greenwood Press, New York.

— (1987a) 'What Makes a Social Class? On the Theoretical and Practical Existence of Groups', *Berkeley Journal of Sociology*, vol. 32, pp. 1–18.

— (1987b) *Distinction: A Social Critique of the Judgement of Taste*, Harvard University Press, New York.

— (2001) *Masculine Domination*, Polity Press, Cambridge.

Boxall, K. (2007) Review Symposium Disability Rights and Wrongs? *Disability and Society*, vol. 22, no. 2, March 2007, pp. 209–34.

Branfield, F. (1998) 'What are You Doing Here? "Non-disabled" People and the Disability Movement: A Response to Robert F. Drake', *Disability and Society*, vol. 13, no. 1, pp. 143–4.

— (1999) 'The Disability Movement: A Movement of Disabled People – A Response to Paul Duckett',

Disability and Society, vol. 14, no. 3, pp. 399–403.

Brantley, C., Frost, D., Pfeffer, C., Buccigrossi, J., and Robinson, M. (2003) *Class: Power, Privilege and Influence in the United States*, Wetware, Workforce Diversity Network, New York, pp. 2–5.

Braverman, H. (1975) *Labor and Monopoly Capital: The Degradation of Work in the Twentieth Century*, Monthly Review Press, New York.

Breault, R. (2003) 'Dewey, Freire, and a Pedagogy for the Oppressor', *Multicultural Education*, vol. 10, no. 3, pp. 2–7.

Brickell, C. (2001) 'Whose "Special Treatment"? Heterosexism and the Problems with Liberalism', *Sexualities*, vol. 4, no. 2, pp. 211–35.

— (2005) 'The Transformation of Heterosexism and Its Paradoxes', in C. Ingraham (ed.) *Thinking Straight: The Power, the Promise and the Paradox of Heterosexuality*, Routledge, New York.

Briskman, L. (2007) *Social Work with Indigenous Communities*, Federation Press, Sydney, NSW.

Brittan, A. (1989) *Masculinity and Power*, Blackwell, Oxford.

— and Maynard, M. (1984) *Sexism, Racism and Oppression*, Blackwell, Oxford.

Brod, H. (1989) 'Work Clothes and Leisure Suits: The Class Basis and Bias of the Men's Movement', in M. Kimmel and M. Messner (eds) *Men's Lives*, Macmillan, New York.

Bryant, K., and Vidal-Ortiz, S. (2008) 'Introduction to Retheorising Homophobias', *Sexualities*, vol. 11, no. 4, pp. 387–96.

Bryson, V. (2007) *Gender and the Politics of Time*, Policy Press, Bristol.

Bulbeck, C. (1998) *Re-Orienting Western Feminisms: Women's Diversity in Postcolonial World*, Cambridge University Press, Cambridge.

Bunch, C. (2004) 'Not for Lesbians Only', in L. Heldelke and P. O'Connor (eds) *Oppression, Privilege and Resistance: Theoretical Perspectives on Racism, Sexism and Heterosexism*, McGraw-Hill, New York.

Burack, C. (2001) 'The Dream of Common Differences: Coalitions, Progressive Politics and Black Feminist Thought', in J. Systydzienski and S. Schacht (eds) *Forging Radical Alliances across Difference: Coalition Politics for the New Millennium*, Rowman and Littlefield, Lanham, MD.

Burbules, N., and Rice, S. (1991) 'Dialogue Across Differences: Continuing the Conversation', *Harvard Educational Review*, vol. 61, no. 4, pp. 393–416.

Burgmann, V., Connell, R. W., Mayne, S., and McGregor, C. (2004) 'Class in Contemporary Australia', in N. Hollier (ed.) *Ruling Australia: The Power, Privilege and Politics of the New Ruling Class*, Australian Scholarly Publishing, Melbourne, Vic.

Bush, M. (2004) *Breaking the Code of Good Intentions: Everyday Forms of Whiteness*, Rowman and Littlefield, Oxford.

Butler, J. (2008) 'Merely Cultural', in K. Olson (ed.) *Adding Insult to Injury: Nancy Fraser Debates Her Critics*, Verso, London.

Bystydzienski, J., and Schacht, S. (2001a) (eds) *Forging Radical Alliances Across Difference:*

Coalition Politics for the New Millennium, Rowman and Littlefield, Lanham, MD.
— (2001b) 'Introduction', in J. Bystydzienski and S. Schacht (eds) *Forging Radical Alliances Across Difference: Coalition Politics for the New Millennium*, Rowman and Littlefield, Lanham, MD.
Calhoun, C. (1989) 'Responsibility and Reproach', *Ethics*, no. 99 (January), pp. 389–406.
Campbell, F. (2008a) 'Exploring Internalized Ableism Using Critical Race Theory', *Disability and Society*, vol. 23, no. 2, pp. 151–62.
— (2008b) 'Refusing Able(ness): A Preliminary Conversation About Ableism', *M/C Journal*, vol. 11, no. 3, pp. 1–13.
— (2009) *Contours of Ableism: The Production of Disability and Abledness*, Palgrave, Houndmills, Basingstoke.
Canaan, J., and Griffin, C. (1990) 'The New Men's Studies: Part of the Problem or Part of the Solution', in J. Hearn and D. Morgan (eds) *Men, Masculinities and Social Theory*, Unwin Hyman, London.
Canagarajah, A. (2002) *A Geopolitics of Academic Writing*, University of Pittsburgh Press, Pittsburgh, PA.
Cannadine, D. (1999) *The Rise and Fall of Class in Britain*, Columbia University Press, New York.
Carabine, J. (1996) 'Heterosexuality and Social Policy', in D. Richardson (ed.) *Theorising Heterosexuality*, Open University Press, Buckingham.
Carbado, D. (2001) 'Men, Feminism and Male Heterosexual Privilege', in J. Delgado and J. Stefancic (eds) *Critical Race Theory: An Introduction*, New York University Press, New York.
— (2004) 'Straight Out of the Closet: Men, Feminism and Heterosexual Privilege', in L. Heldelke and P. O'Connor (eds) *Oppression, Privilege and Resistance: Theoretical Perspectives on Racism, Sexism and Heterosexism*, McGraw-Hill, New York.
Card, C. (2002) 'Responsibility Ethics, Shared Understanding and Moral Communities', *Hypatia*, vol. 17, no. 1, pp. 141–55.
Carlton, E. (1996) *The Few and the Many: A Typology of Elites*, Scholar Press, Aldershot.
Carter, S. (1979) 'Class Conflict: The Human Dimension', in P. Walker (ed.) *Between Labour and Capital*, Harvester Press, Sussex.
Carver, T., and Mottier, V. (1998) 'Introduction', in T. Carver and V. Mottier (eds) *Politics of Sexuality: Identity, Gender, Citizenship*, Routledge, London.
Cashwell, A. (2005) 'Increasing Awareness of Heterosexism and Homophobia', in S. Anderson and V. Middleton (eds) *Explorations in Privilege, Oppression and Diversity*, Thompson, Belmont, CA.
Cassuto, L. (1999) 'Whose Field is It Anyway? Disability Studies in the Academy', *Chronicle of Higher Education*, vol. 45/28, pp. A60–3.
Chakrabarty, D. (2000) 'Voices from the Edge: The Struggle to Write Subaltern Histories', in V. Chaturvedi (ed.) *Mapping Subaltern Studies and the Postcolonial*, Verso, London.
Chang, H. (2007) *Bad Samaritans*, Business Books, London.
Clark, C. and O'Donnell, J.

(1999) 'Rearticulating a Racial Identity: Creating Oppositional Spaces to Fight for Equality and Social Justice', in C. Clark and J. O'Donnell (eds) *Becoming and Unbecoming White: Owning and Disowning a Racial Identity*, Bergin and Garvey, Westport, CT.

Clarke, C. (2004) 'The Failure to Transform Homophobia in the Black Community', in L. Heldelke and P. O'Connor (eds) *Oppression, Privilege and Resistance: Theoretical Perspectives on Racism, Sexism and Heterosexism*, McGraw-Hill, New York.

Class Acts (2007) *The Invisibility of Upper Class Privilege*, Women's Theological Center, Boston, MA.

Clatterbaugh, K. (1990) *Contemporary Perspectives on Masculinity*, Westview Press, Boulder, CO.

Cole, E. (2008) 'Coalition as a Model for Intersectionality: From Practice to Theory', *Sex Roles*, vol. 59, pp. 443–53.

Collins, P. (1991) *Black Feminist Thought: Knowledge, Consciousness and the Politics of Empowerment*, Unwin Hyman, London.

Collins, P., Madonado, L., Takagi, D., Thorne, B. , Weber, L. and Winnant, H. (2002) 'Symposium on West and Fenstermaker's "Doing Difference"', in S. Fenstermaker and C. West (eds) *Doing Difference, Doing Gender: Inequality, Power and Institutional Change,* Routledge, New York.

Collinson, D., and Hearn, J. (2005) 'Men and Masculinities in Work, Organizations and Management', in M. Kimmel, J. Hearn and R. Connell (eds) *Handbook of Studies on Men and Masculinities*, Sage, Thousand Oaks, CA.

Connell, R. (1977) *Ruling Class, Ruling Culture: Studies of Conflict, Power and Hegemony in Australian Life*, Cambridge University Press, Cambridge.

— (1987) *Gender and Power: Society, the Person and Sexual Politics*, Polity Press, Cambridge.

— (1993) 'The Big Picture: Masculinities in World History', *Theory and Society*, vol. 22, no. 5, pp. 597–623.

— (1995) *Masculinities*, Allen & Unwin, Sydney, NSW.

— (2000a) *The Men and the Boys*, Allen & Unwin, Sydney, NSW.

— (2000b) 'Men, Relationships and Violence', keynote address to Men and Relationships Forum, Sydney, November.

— (2001) 'Studying Men and Masculinity', *Resources for Feminist Research*, Fall–Winter, pp. 43–55.

— (2002) *Gender*, Polity Press, Cambridge.

— (2003a) 'Scrambling in the Ruins of Patriarchy: Neo-liberalism and Men's Divided Interests', in U. Pasero (ed.) *Gender: From Costs to Benefits*, Westdeutsch Verlag, Germany.

— (2003b) 'The Role of Men and Boys in Achieving Gender Equality', consultant's paper for The Role of Men and Boys in Achieving Gender Equality Expert Group Meeting, United Nations Development Program, Brasilia, Brazil, 21–24 October.

— (2004) 'Moloch Mutates: Global Capitalism and the Evolution of the Australian Ruling Class 1977–2002', in N. Hollier (ed.) *Ruling Australia: The Power, Privilege and Politics of the New Ruling Class*, Australian Scholarly Publishing, Melbourne, Vic.

— (2005) *Masculinities*, 2nd edn, Allen & Unwin, Sydney, NSW.

— (2006) 'Northern Theory: The Political Geography of General Social Theory', *Theory and Society*, vol. 35, pp. 237–64.

— (2007) *Southern Theory: The Global Dynamics of Knowledge in Social Science*, Allen & Unwin, Sydney, NSW.

— and Messerschmidt J. (2005) 'Hegemonic Masculinity: Rethinking the Concept', *Gender and Society*, vol. 19, no. 6, pp. 829–59.

Conyers, J. (1996) 'Book Review: Not Out of Africa: How Afrocentrism Became an Excuse to Teach Myth as History', *Journal of Black Studies*, no. 27, pp. 130–1.

Cooper, D. (2004) *Challenging Diversity: Rethinking Equality and the Value of Difference*, Cambridge University Press, Cambridge.

Corrigan P., and Leonard, P. (1978) *Social Work Practice Under Capitalism: A Marxist Approach*, Macmillan, London.

Crowhurst, M. (2002) 'Hetero-privilegism: Three Layers of Discriminatory Practices that Target Non-Heterosexual Subjects', *National Drama Australia Journal*, vol. 26, no. 2, pp. 21–34.

Cuomo, C., and Hall, K. (1999) 'Introduction: Reflections on Whiteness', in C. Cuomo and K. Hall (eds) *Whiteness: Feminist Philosophical Reflections*, Rowman and Littlefield, Lanham, MD.

Currie, D. (1993) 'Unhiding the Hidden: Race, Class and Gender in the Construction of Knowledge', *Humanity and Society*, vol. 17, no. 1, pp. 3–27.

Curry-Stevens, A. (2004) 'Pedagogy for the Privileged: Building Civic Virtues in Political Leaders', unpublished paper, University of Toronto, Ont.

— (2007) 'New Forms of Transformative Education: Pedagogy for the Privileged', *Journal of Transformative Education*, vol. 5, no. 1, pp. 33–58.

Danaher, K. (2001) *10 Reasons to Abolish the IMF and the World Bank*, Seven Stories Press, New York.

Dandermark, B., and Gellerstedt, L. (2004) 'Social Justice: Redistribution and Recognition – A Non-Reductionist Perspective on Disability', *Disability and Society*, vol. 19, no. 4, pp. 339–53.

Daniel, A. (1983) *Power, Privilege and Prestige: Occupations in Australia*, Longman Cheshire, Melbourne, Vic.

Davison, K. (2007) 'Phallocentrism', in M. Flood, J. Gardiner, B. Pease and K. Pringle (eds) *International Encyclopedia of Men and Masculinities*, Routledge, London.

Deal, M. (2007) 'Aversive Disablism: Subtle Prejudice Toward Disabled People', *Disability and Society*, vol. 22, no. 1, pp. 93–107.

Dean, J. (2006) 'The Social Construction of Heterosexual Identities', paper presented at the annual meeting of the American Sociological Association, Montreal Convention Centre, Montreal, Quebec, Que.

Dei, G., Karumanchery, L., and Karumanchery-Luik, N. (2004) *Playing the Race Card: Exposing White Power and Privilege*, Peter Lang, Washington.

Demetriou, D. (2001) 'Connell's Concept of Hegemonic Masculinity: A Critique', *Theory and Society*, vol. 30, no. 3, pp. 337–61.

Dempsey, K. (1997) *Inequalities in Marriage: Australia and Beyond*, Oxford University Press, Melbourne, Vic.

DeRosa, P. (1999) 'Building Blocks: My Journey Toward White Racial Awareness', in C. Clark and J. O'Donnell (eds) *Becoming and Unbecoming White: Owning and Disowning a Racial Identity*, Bergin and Garvey, Westport, CT.

Derrida, J. (1976) *Of Grammatology*, Johns Hopkins University Press, Baltimore, MD.

Deutsch, F. (2007) 'Undoing Gender', *Gender and Society*, vol. 21, no. 1, pp. 106–27.

Dews, C., and Laws, C. (1995) *This Fine Place So Far from Home: Voices of Academics from the Working Class*, Temple University Press, New York.

DiAngelo, R. (1997) 'Heterosexism: Addressing Internalised Dominance', *Journal of Progressive Human Services*, vol. 8, no. 1, pp. 5–21.

Dick, A. (1995) 'The Afrocentric-Eurocentric Debate in Africa: From a Fruitless Dichotomy to Critical Dialogue', *International Information and Library Review*, vol. 27, pp. 195–202.

Dienhart, A. (1998) *Reshaping Fatherhood: The Social Construction of Shared Parenting*, Sage, Thousand Oaks, CA.

Dirks, N. (2001) *Castes of Mind: Colonialism and the Making of Modern India*, Princeton University Press, New York.

Dixon, P. (2001) 'Strange Fruit: On Comparing the Struggles of African-Americans for Civil Rights with the Struggles of Lesbian, Gay, Bi-sexual and Transgendered Peoples', unpublished manuscript.

Dominelli, L. (2002) *Anti-Oppressive Social Work Theory and Practice*, Macmillan, London.

Donaldson, M. (1991) 'What is Hegemonic Masculinity?', *Theory and Society*, vol. 22, pp. 643–57.

— (2006) 'The Working Class', paper presented at the Class: History, Formations and Conceptualisations Conference, University of Wollongong, NSW, 3–4 March.

— (2008) 'New Directions in Class Analysis: Explorations in the Working Class', paper presented at the Re-imagining Sociology: Australian Sociological Association Conference, 2–5 December.

Dragiewicz, M. (2009) 'Why Sex and Gender Matter in Domestic Violence Research and Policy', in E. Stark and E. Buzawa (eds) *Violence Against Women in Families and Relationships*, Praeger, Santa Barbara, CA.

Drake, R. (1997) 'What am I Doing Here? "Non-Disabled" People and the Disability Movement', *Disability and Society*, vol. 12, no. 4, pp. 643–5.

Dreher, T. (2009) 'Listening Across Difference: Media and Multiculturalism Beyond the Politics of Voice', *Continuum: A Journal of Media and Cultural Studies*, vol. 23, no. 4, pp. 445–58.

Ducket, P. (1998) 'What are You Doing Here? "Non-Disabled" People and the Disability Movement: A Response to Fran Branfield', *Disability and Society*, vol. 13, no. 4, pp. 625–8.

Duggan, L. (1995) 'Queering the State', in L. Duggan and N. Hunter (eds) *Sex Wars: Sexual Dissent and Political Culture*, Routledge, New York.

Dumont, L. (1980) *Homo Hierar-*

chicas: The Caste System and Its Implications, University of Chicago Press, Chicago, IL.

Dyer, R. (2002) 'The Matter of Whiteness', in P. Rothenberg (ed.) *White Privilege: Essential Readings on the Other Side of Racism*, Worth Publishers, New York.

Easterly, W. (2007) *The White Man's Burden: Why the West's Efforts to Aid the Rest Have Done So Much Ill and So Little Good*, Penguin, London.

Edley, N., and Wetherell, M. (1995) *Men in Perspective: Practice, Power and Identity*, Prentice Hall, London.

Edwards, C., and Imrie, R. (2003) 'Disability and Bodies as Bearers of Value', *Sociology*, vol. 37, no. 2, pp. 239–56.

Edwards, K. (2006) 'Aspiring Social Justice Ally Development: A Conceptual Model', *NASPA Journal*, vol. 43, no. 4, pp. 39–60.

Ehrenreich, B. (1989) *Fear of Falling: The Inner Life of the Middle Class*, Pantheon Books, New York.

— and Ehrenreich J. (1979a) 'The Professional-Managerial Class', in P. Walker (ed.) *Between Labour and Capital*, Harvester Press, Sussex.

— and Ehrenreich, J. (1979b) 'Rejoinder', in P. Walker (ed.) *Between Labour and Capital*, Harvester Press, Sussex.

Eisler, R., and Loye, D. (1990) *The Partnership Way*, Harper, San Francisco, CA.

Ellsworth, E. (1989) 'Why Doesn't This Feel Empowering?: Working Through the Repressive Myths of Critical Pedagogy', *Harvard Educational Review*, vol. 59, pp. 297–324.

Escobar, A. (1995) *Encountering Development: The Making and Unmaking of the Third World*, Princeton University Press, Princeton, NJ.

Esteva, G., and Suri, M. (1998) *Grassroots Postmodernism: Remaking the Soil of Cultures*, Zed Books, London.

Evans, N., and Broido, E. (2005) 'Encouraging the Development of Social Justice Attitudes and Actions in Heterosexual Students', *New Directions for Student Services*, no. 110, Summer, pp. 43–54.

Eveline, J. (1994) 'The Politics of Advantage', *Australian Feminist Studies*, vol. 19, pp. 129–54.

— (1998) 'Naming Male Advantage: A Feminist Theorist Looks at the Future', in A. Mackinnon, I. Elguist-Saltzman and D. Prentice (eds) *Education in the 21st Century: Dangerous Terrain for Women?*, Falmer Press, London.

Fawcett, B. (2000) *Feminist Perspectives on Disability*, Prentice Hall, Harlow.

Fellows, M., and Razack, R. (1998) 'The Race to Innocence: Confronting Hierarchical Relations Among Women', *Journal of Gender, Race and Justice*, no. 1, pp. 335–52.

Fennell, S., and Arnot, M. (2009) 'Decentring Hegemonic Gender Theory: The Implications for Educational Research', RECOUP Working Paper no. 21, Development Studies and Faculty of Education, University of Cambridge.

Fenstermaker, S., and West, C. (2002) 'Introduction', in S. Fenstermaker and C. West (eds) *Doing Difference, Doing Gender: Inequality,*

Power and Institutional Change, Routledge, New York.

Ferguson, A. (1979) 'Women as a New Revolutionary Class in the US', in P. Walker (ed.) *Between Labour and Capital*, Harvester Press, Sussex.

— (1998) 'Resisting the Veil of Privilege: Building Bridge Identities as an Ethical-Politics of Global Feminisms', *Hypatia*, vol. 13, no. 3, pp. 95–113.

Ferguson, I. (2002) *Rethinking Welfare: A Critical Perspective*, Sage, London.

— (2008) *Reclaiming Social Work*, Sage, London.

Ferree, M., Lorber, J., and Hess, B. (1999) (eds) *Revisioning Gender*, Sage, Thousand Oaks, CA.

Figes, E. (1972) *Patriarchal Attitudes*, Pantheon, London.

Fine, M. (2006) 'Bearing Witness: Methods for Researching Oppression and Resistance: A Textbook for Critical Research', *Social Justice Research*, vol. 19, no. 1., pp. 83–108.

Firestone, S. (1971) *The Dialectic of Sex*, The Women's Press, London.

Fish, J. (2007) 'Far from Mundane: Theorising Heterosexism for Social Work Education', *Social Work Education*, vol. 27, no. 2, pp. 182–93.

Flagg, B. (1997) 'Was Blind but Now I See: White Race Consciousness and the Requirement of Discriminatory Intent', in R. Delgado and J. Stefancic (eds) *Critical White Studies: Looking Behind the Mirror*, Temple University Press, Philadelphia, PA.

Flood, M., and Hamilton, C. (2008) 'Mapping Homophobia in Australia', in S. Robinson (ed.) *Homophobia: An Australian History*, Federation Press, Sydney, NSW.

Flood, M., and Pease, B. (2005) 'Undoing Men's Privilege and Advancing Gender Equality in Public Sector Institutions', *Policy and Society*, vol. 24, no. 4, pp. 119–38.

— (2009) 'Factors Influencing Attitudes to Violence Against Women', *Trauma, Violence and Abuse*, vol. 10, no. 2, pp. 125–42.

Flood, M., Gardiner, J., Pease, B., and Pringle, K. (2007) (eds) *International Encyclopedia of Men and Masculinities*, Routledge, London.

Foley, D. (2002) 'An Indigenous Standpoint Theory', *Journal of Australian Indigenous Issues*, vol. 5, no. 5, pp. 3–13.

Frankenberg, R. (1993) *White Women, Race Matters: The Social Construction of Whiteness*, University of Minnesota Press, Minneapolis, MN.

— (1997) 'Introduction: Local Whitenesses, Localizing Whiteness', in R. Frankenberg (ed.) *Displacing Whiteness: Essays in Social and Cultural Criticism*, Duke University Press, Durham, NC.

— (2001) 'The Mirage of an Unmarked Whiteness', in B. Rasmussen, E. Klineberg, I. Nexia and M. Wray (eds) *The Making and Unmaking of Whiteness*, Duke University Press, Durham, NC.

Fraser, N. (1995) 'From Redistribution to Recognition? Dilemmas of Justice in a "Postsocialist" Age', *New Left Review*, no. 2228, March–April, pp. 140–9.

— (1997) 'Heterosexism, Misrecognition and Capitalism: A

Response to Judith Butler', *Social Text*, no. 52/53, pp. 279–89.
— (2003) 'Social Justice in the Age of Identity Politics: Redistribution, Recognition and Participation', in N. Fraser and A. Honneth, *Redistribution or Recognition? A Political-Philosophical Exchange*, Verso, New York.
— (2008) *Scales of Justice: Reimagining Political Space in a Globalizing World*, Polity Press, Cambridge.
Freire, P. (1970) *Pedagogy of the Oppressed*, Continuum, New York.
Frosh, S. (1994) *Sexual Difference: Masculinity and Psychoanalysis*, Routledge, London.
Frueh, J. (2007) 'Pedagogy of the Oppressors: Challenging Nationalism from a Position of Privilege', paper presented at the International Studies Association Conference, Chicago, IL, March.
Gabel, S., and Peters, S. (2004) 'Presage of a Paradigm Shift? Beyond the Social Model of Disability Toward Resistance Theories of Disability', *Disability and Society*, vol. 19, no. 6, pp. 585–66.
Garland-Thomson, R. (2009) *Staring: How We Look*, Oxford University Press, New York.
Garner, S. (2007) *Whiteness: An Introduction*, Routledge, London.
Garvey, J., and Ignatiev, N. (1997) 'Toward a New Abolitionism: A Race Traitor Manifesto', in M. Hill (ed.) *Whiteness: A Critical Reader*, New York University Press, New York.
George, S. (2004) *Another World is Possible if . . .*, Verso, New York.
Gerschick, T. (2007) 'The Body, Disability and Sexuality', in S. Seidman, N. Fischer and C. Meeks (eds) *Introducing the New Sexuality Studies: Original Essays and Interviews*, Routledge, London.
Gheverghese, J., Reddy, V., and Searle-Chatterjee, M. (1990) 'Eurocentrism in the Social Sciences', *Race and Class*, vol. 31, no. 1, pp. 1–26.
Giddens, A. (1973) *The Class Structure of Advanced Capitalist Societies*, Hutchinson, London.
Gilbert, R. (2008) 'Raising Awareness of Class Privilege Among Students', *Diversity and Democracy*, vol. 11, no. 3, pp. 7–9.
Gilding, M. (2004) 'Superwealth in Australia: Entrepreneurs, Accumulation and the Capitalist Class', in N. Hollier (ed.) *Ruling Australia: The Power, Privilege and Politics of the New Ruling Class*, Australian Scholarly Publishing, Melbourne, Vic.
Gillborn, D. (2006) 'Rethinking White Supremacy: Who Counts in "White World"'?, *Ethnicities*, vol. 6, no. 3, pp. 318–40.
Gleeson, B. (1997) 'Disability Studies: An Historical Materialist View', *Disability and Society*, vol. 12, no. 2, pp. 179–202.
Goddin, G. (2009) 'Disability and the Ethics of Listening', *Continuum: A Journal of Media and Cultural Studies*, vol. 23, no. 4, pp. 489–502.
Goldberg, S. (1973) *The Inevitability of Patriarchy*, William Morrow, New York.
— (1993) *Why Men Rule: A Theory of Male Dominance*, Open Court, Chicago, IL.
Goldthorpe, J. (1980) *Social Mobility and Class Structure in Modern Britain*, Clarendon Press, Oxford.

Goodman, D. (2001) *Promoting Diversity and Social Justice: Educating People from Privileged Groups*, Sage, Thousand Oaks, CA.

Gordon, B., and Rosenblum, E. (2001) 'Bringing Disability into the Sociological Frame: A Comparison of Disability with Race, Sex and Sexual Orientation Statuses', *Disability and Society*, vol. 16, no. 1, pp. 5–19.

Goudge, P. (2003) *The Whiteness of Power: Racism in Third World Development and Aid*, Lawrence and Wishart, London.

Gould, L. (2000) 'White Male Privilege and the Construction of Crime', in The Criminal Justice Collective of Northern Arizona University (eds) *Investigating Difference: Human and Cultural Relations in Criminal Justice*, Allyn and Bacon, Boston, MA.

Gramsci, A. (1957) 'The Southern Question', in *The Modern Prince and Other Writings*, International Publishers, New York.

Gran, P. (1996) *Beyond Eurocentrism: A New View of Modern World History*, Syracuse University Press, New York.

Gray, M., and Coates, J. (2008) 'From Indigenization to Cultural Relevance', in M. Gray, J. Coates, and M. Yellow Bird (eds) *Indigenous Social Work Around the World: Towards Culturally Relevant Education and Practice*, Ashgate, Aldershot.

Griffin, P., D'Errico, B., and Schiff, T. (2007) 'Heterosexism: Curriculum Design', in M. Adams, L. Bell and P. Griffin (eds) *Teaching for Diversity and Social Justice*, 2nd edn, Routledge, New York.

Grimes, S. (2002) 'Challenging the Status Quo: Whiteness in the Diversity Management Literature', *Management Communication Quarterly*, vol. 15, no. 3, pp. 381–409.

Grob, L. (1991) 'Male–Female Relations and the Dialogical Imperative', in L. Grob, R. Hassan and H. Gordon (eds) *Women's and Men's Testimonies of Spirit*, Greenwood Press, New York.

Gronemeyer, M. (1995) 'Helping', in W. Sachs (ed.) *The Development Dictionary*, Zed Books, London.

Grosz, E. (1988) 'The In(ter)vention of Feminist Knowledges', in B. Caine, E. Grosz and M. de Lepervanche (eds) *Crossing Boundaries: Feminisms and the Critique of Knowledges*, Allen & Unwin, Sydney, NSW.

Grusky, D., and Sorensen, J. (1998) 'Can Class Analysis be Salvaged?', *American Journal of Sociology*, vol. 103, no. 5, March, pp. 1187–234.

Habermas, J. (1987) *The Theory of Communicative Action*, vol. 2, *Lifeworld and System*, Beacon Press, Boston, MA.

— (1990) 'What Does Socialism Mean Today? The Rectifying Revolution and the Need for New Thinking on the Left', *New Left Review*, no. 183, pp. 3–21.

Habibis, D., and Walter, M. (2009) *Social Inequality in Australia: Discourses, Realities and Futures*, Oxford University Press, Melbourne, Vic.

Hall, R. (1996) 'Partnership Accountability', in C. McLean, M. Carey and C. White (eds) *Men's Ways of Being*, Westview Press, Boulder, CO.

Hall, S. (1997) *Representation: Cultural Representations and*

Signifying Practices, Sage, London.

Hamilton, C., and Denniss, R. (2005) *Affluenza: When Too Much is Never Enough*, Allen & Unwin, Sydney, NSW.

Hanscombe, G. (1987) 'Preface', in G. Hanscombe and M. Humphries (eds) *Heterosexuality*, GMP Publishers, London.

Harcourt, W. (ed.) (2007) 'Reflections on 50 Years of Development', *Development*, vol. 50, pp. 4–52.

Harding, S. (1993) 'Rethinking Standpoint Epistemology: What is Strong Objectivity?', in L. Alcoff and E. Potter (eds) *Feminist Epistemologies,* Routledge, New York.

— (1995) 'Subjectivity, Experience and Knowledge: An Epistemology for Rainbow Coalition Politics', in J. Roof and R. Wiegman (eds) *Who Can Speak?: Authority and Critical Identity*, University of Illinois Press, Chicago, IL.

— (2004) 'Standpoint Theory as a Site of Political, Philosophical and Scientific Debate', in S. Harding (ed.) *The Feminist Standpoint Theory Reader: Intellectual and Political Controversies*, Routledge, New York.

Harris, J. (n.d.) '"Non-Disabled" – An Oxymoron?: Exploring the Foundations of a Divisive Label', University of York, York.

Harvey, D. (2003) *The New Imperialism*, Oxford University Press, Oxford.

Harvey, J. (1999) *Civilized Oppression*, Rowman and Littlefield, Lanham, MD.

Hatty, S. (2000) *Masculinities, Violence and Culture*, Sage, Thousand Oaks, CA.

Hawthorn, S. (2002) *Wild Politics: Feminism, Globalism, Bio/Diversity*, Spinifex Press, Melbourne, Vic.

Haywood, C., and Mac an Ghaill, M. (2003) *Men and Masculinities: Theory, Research and Practice*, Open University Press, Buckingham.

Hearn, J. (1987) *The Gender of Oppression: Men, Masculinity and the Critique of Marxism*, Wheatsheath, Sussex.

— (1996) 'Current Trends and Challenges for Research', *International Association of the Study of Men Newsletter*, vol. 3, no. 1, pp. 3–4.

Heasley, R. (2005) 'Crossing the Borders of Gendered Sexuality: Queer Masculinities of Straight Men', in C. Ingraham (ed.) *Thinking Straight: The Power, the Promise and the Paradox of Heterosexuality*, Routledge, New York.

Held, D., and Kaya, A. (2007) 'Introduction', in D. Held and A. Kaya (eds) *Global Inequality: Patterns and Explanations*, Polity Press, Cambridge.

Heldke, L., and O'Connor, P. (eds) (2004) *Oppression, Privilege and Resistance: Theoretical Perspectives on Racism, Sexism and Heterosexism*, McGraw Hill, New York.

Helms, J. (1995) 'An Update of Helms's White and People of Colour Racial Identity Models', in J. Ponterotto, J. Casas, L. Suzuki and C. Alexander (eds) *Handbook of Multicultural Counselling,* Sage, Thousand Oaks, CA.

Herek, G. (2004) 'Beyond Homophobia: Thinking About Sexual Prejudice and Stigma

in the Twenty-First Century', *Sexuality, Research and Social Policy Journal of NRSC*, vol. 1, no. 2, pp. 6–24.
Hicks, S., and Watson, K. (2003) 'Desire Lines: "Queering" Health and Social Welfare', *Sociological Research Online*, vol. 8, no. 1, www.socresearchonline.org.uk.
Hiddleston, J. (2009) *Understanding Postcolonialism*, Acumen, Stocksfield, NE.
Hill, M. (2004) *After Whiteness: Unmasking the American Majority*, New York University Press, New York.
Hill-Collins, P. (1990) *Black Feminist Thought*, Routledge, New York.
Hitchcock, J. (2002) *Lifting the Veil: An Exploration of White American Culture in a Multiracial Context*, Crandall, Dostie and Douglas, Roseselle, NJ.
Hobgood, M. (2000) *Dismantling Privilege: An Ethics of Accountability*, Pilgrim Press, Cleveland, OH.
Hobson, J. (2004) *The Eastern Origins of Western Civilisation*, Cambridge University Press, Cambridge.
Hochschild, A. (2005) *Bury the Chains: The British Struggle to Abolish Slavery*, Macmillan, London.
Hollier, N. (2004) 'Introduction: The New Australian Ruling Class', in N. Hollier (ed.) *Ruling Australia: The Power, Privilege and Politics of the New Ruling Class*, Australian Scholarly Publishing, Melbourne, Vic.
Hollway, W. (1996) 'Recognition and Heterosexual Desire', in D. Richardson (ed.) *Theorising Heterosexuality*, Open University Press, Buckingham.
Holvino, E. (2002) 'Class: A Difference that Makes a Difference in Organizations', *Diversity Factor*, vol. 10, no. 2, pp. 28–34.
Honneth, A. (2003) 'Redistribution as Recognition: A Response to Nancy Fraser', in N. Fraser and A. Honneth, *Redistribution or Recognition? A Political-Philosophical Exchange*, Verso, New York.
hooks, b. (1992) *Black Looks: Race and Representation*, South End Press, Boston, MA.
— (2000) *Where We Stand: Class Matters*, Routledge, New York.
— (2003) 'Class and Race: The New Black Elite', in M. Kimmel and A. Ferber (eds) *Privilege*, Westview Press, Boulder, CO.
Hopgood, M. (2000) *Dismantling Privilege: An Ethics of Accountability*, Pilgrim Press, Cleveland, OH.
Hopkins, P. (2004) 'Gender Treachery: Homophobia, Masculinity and Threatened Identities', in L. Heldelke and P. O'Connor (eds) *Oppression, Privilege and Resistance: Theoretical Perspectives on Racism, Sexism and Heterosexism*, McGraw-Hill, New York.
Horrocks, R. (1994) *Masculinity in Crisis*, St Martin's Press, London.
Hossay, P. (2006) *Unsustainable: A Primer for Global Environmental and Social Justice*, Zed Books, London.
Hoy, D. (2004) *Critical Resistance: From Post Structuralism to Post-Critique*, MIT Press, Cambridge, MA.
Hubbard, P. (2000) 'Desire/Disgust: Mapping the Moral Contours of Heterosexuality', *Progress in Human Geography*, vol. 24, pp. 191–217.

Hughes, B. (1999) 'The Constitution of Impairment: Modernity and the Aesthetic of Oppression', *Disability and Society*, vol. 14, no. 2, pp. 155–72.

— (2005) 'What Can a Foucauldian Analysis Contribute to Disability Theory', in S. Tremain (ed.) *Foucault and the Government of Disability*, University of Michigan Press, Ann Arbor, MI.

— (2007) 'Being Disabled: Towards a Critical Social Ontology for Disability Studies', *Disability and Society*, vol. 22, no. 7, pp. 673–84.

— and Paterson, K. (1997) 'The Social Model of Disability and the Disappearing Body: Towards a Sociology of Impairment', *Disability and Society*, vol. 12, no. 3, pp. 325–40.

Humphries, M. (1987) 'Preface', in G. Hanscombe and M. Humphries (eds) (1987) *Heterosexuality*, GMP Publishers, London.

Ife, J. (2010) *Human Rights from Below: Achieving Rights Though Community Development*, Cambridge University Press, Cambridge.

Ignatiev, N. (1996) 'Interview' in N. Ignatiev and J. Garvey (eds) *Race Traitor*, Routledge, London.

Imrie, R. (2001) 'Barriered and Bounded Places and the Spatialities of Disability', *Urban Studies*, vol. 38, pp. 231–37.

Inahara, M. (2009) 'This Body Which is Not One: The Body, Femininity and Disability', *Body and Society*, vol. 15, no. 1, pp. 47–62.

Ingraham, C. (2005) 'Introduction', in C. Ingraham (ed.) *Thinking Straight: The Power, the Promise and the Paradox of Heterosexuality*, Routledge, New York.

Itzin, C. (2000) 'Gendering Domestic Violence: The Influence of Feminism on Policy and Practice', in J. Hanmer and C. Itzin (eds) *Home Truths About Domestic Violence: Feminist Influences on Policy and Practice*, Routledge, London.

Jackson, S. (1996) 'Heterosexuality and Feminist Theory', in D. Richardson (ed.) *Theorising Heterosexuality*, Open University Press, Buckingham.

— (1998) 'Sexual Politics: Feminist Politics, Gay Politics and the Problem of Heterosexuality', in T. Carver and V. Mottier (eds) *Politics of Sexuality: Identity, Gender, Citizenship*, Routledge, London.

— (1999) *Heterosexuality in Question*, Sage, London.

— (2005) 'Sexuality, Heterosexuality and Gender Hierarchy: Getting Our Priorities Right', in C. Ingraham (ed.) *Thinking Straight: The Power, the Promise and the Paradox of Heterosexuality*, Routledge, New York.

Jakobsen, J. (1998) *Working Alliances and the Politics of Difference: Diversity and Feminist Ethics*, Indiana University Press, Bloomington, IN.

James, O. (2008) *The Selfish Capitalist: Origins of Affluenza*, Vermillion, London.

Jameson, F. (1991) *Postmodernism or the Cultural Logic of Late Capitalism*, Duke University Press, Durham, NC.

Jefferson, T. (2002) 'Subordinating Hegemonic Masculinity', *Theoretical Criminology*, vol. 6, no. 1, pp. 63–88.

Jeffreys, S. (1993) *The Lesbian Heresy: A Feminist Perspective on the Lesbian Sexual Revolution*, Spinifex Press, Melbourne, Vic.

— (2003) *Unpacking Queer Politics*, Polity Press, Cambridge.

Jensen, R. (2001) *Writing Dissent: Taking Radical Ideas from the Margin to the Mainstream*, Peter Lang, New York.

— (2005) *The Heart of Whiteness: Confronting Race, Racism, and White Privilege*, City Lights, San Francisco, CA.

Jeyasingham, D. (2008) 'Knowledge, Ingnorance and the Construction of Sexuality in Social Work Education', *Social Work Education*, vol. 27, no. 2, pp. 138–51.

Jip, P. (2007) 'Being a Heterosexual Ally to the Lesbian, Gay, Bisexual and Transgendered Community: Reflections and Development', *Journal of Gay and Lesbian Psychotherapy*, vol. 11, no. 3/4, pp. 173–85.

Johnson, A. (1997) *The Gender Knot: Unravelling the Patriarchal Legacy*, Temple University Press, Philadelphia, PA.

— (2001) *Privilege, Power and Difference*, Mayfield Publishing Company, Mountain View, CA.

— (2006) *Privilege, Power and Difference*, 2nd edn, McGraw-Hill, New York.

Johnson, C. (2002) 'Heteronormative Citizenship and the Politics of Passing', *Sexualities*, vol. 5, pp. 317–36.

Johnson, P. (2005) *Love, Heterosexuality and Society*, Routledge, London.

Jolly, M. (2008) 'The South in Southern Theory: Antipodean Reflections on the Pacific', *Australian Humanities Review*, issue 44.

Jones, A. (ed.) (2006) *Men of the Global South: A Reader*, Zed Books, London.

Jones, C. (1983) *State Social Work and the Working Class*, Macmillan, London.

Jukes, A. (1993) *Why Men Hate Women*, Free Association Books, London.

Kafer, A. (2003) 'Compulsory Bodies: Reflections on Heterosexuality and Able-Bodiedness', *Journal of Women's History*, vol. 15, no. 3, pp. 77–89.

Kasser, T. (2002) *The High Price of Materialism*, MIT Press, Cambridge, MA.

Katz, J. (1995) *The Invention of Heterosexuality*, Dutton, New York.

Kaufman, M. (1994) 'Men, Feminism and Men's Contradictory Experiences of Power', in H. Brod and M. Kaufman (eds) *Theorizing Masculinities*, Sage, Thousand Oaks, CA.

Kelly, R. (2009) 'Gay Marriage: Why Now? Why at All?', in S. Seidman, N. Fischer and C. Meeks (eds) *Introducing the New Sexuality Studies: Original Essays and Interviews*, Routledge, London.

Kendall, F. (2006) *Understanding White Privilege: Creating Pathways to Authentic Relationships Across Race*, Routledge, New York.

Kennedy, M., and Galtz, N. (1996) 'From Marxism to Postcommunism: Socialist Desires and East European Rejections', *Annual Review of Sociology*, no. 22, pp. 437–58.

Kerbo, H. (2003) *Social Stratification and Inequality: Class Conflict in Historical, Comparative and Global Perspective*, McGraw Hill, New York.

Kim, C. (2004) 'Unyielding Positions: A Critique of the "Race" Debate', *Ethnicities*, vol. 4. no. 3, pp. 337–55.

Kimmel, M. (2000) *The Gendered Society*, Oxford University Press, New York.

— (2003) 'Toward a Pedagogy of the Oppressor', in M. Kimmel and A. Ferber (eds) *Privilege: A Reader*, Westview Press, Boulder, CO.

— and Ferber, A. (eds) (2003) *Privilege: A Reader*, Westview Press, Boulder, CO.

— and Mosmiller, T. (eds) (1992) *Against the Tide: Pro-Feminist Men in the United States 1776–1990: A Documentary History*, Beacon Press, Boston, MA.

Kincheloe, J., and McLaren, P. (2005) 'Rethinking Critical Theory and Qualitative Research', in N. Denzin and Y. Lincoln (eds) *The Sage Handbook of Qualitative Research*, Sage, Thousand Oaks, CA.

Kincheloe, J., and Steinberg, S. (2000) 'Constructing a Pedagogy of Whiteness for Angry White Students', in N. Rodriguez and L. Villaverde (eds) *Dismantling White Privilege: Pedagogy, Politics, and Whiteness*, Peter Lang, New York.

Kirkhaum, S., and Anderson, J. (2002) 'Postcolonial Nursing Scholarship: From Epistemology to Method', *Advanced Nursing*, vol. 25, no. 1, pp. 1–17.

Kitzinger, C., and Wilkinson, S. (1994) 'Re-Viewing Heterosexuality', *Feminism and Psychology*, vol. 4, no. 2, pp. 330–36.

Kitzinger, C., Wilkinson, S., and Perkins, R. (1992) 'Theorizing Heterosexuality', *Feminism and Psychology*, vol. 2, no. 3, pp. 293–324.

Knowles, C. (2003) *Race and Social Analysis*, Sage, London.

Kristeva, J. (1980) *Desire in Language*, Basil Blackwell, Oxford.

Lacan, J. (1987) *The Four Concepts of Psycho-Analysis*, Penguin, Harmondsworth, Middlesex.

La Caze, M. (2008) 'Seeing Oneself Though the Eyes of the Other: Asymmetrical Reciprocity and Self-respect', *Hypatia*, vol. 23, no. 3, pp. 118–35.

Laclau, E., and Mouffe, C. (1985) *Hegemony and Socialist Strategy: Towards a Radical Democratic Politics*, Verso, London.

Lakritz, A. (1995) 'Identification and Difference: Structures of Privilege in Cultural Criticism', in J. Roof and R. Wiegman (eds) *Who Can Speak?: Authority and Critical Identity,* University of Illinois Press, Chicago, IL.

Lang, J. (2002) *Elimination of Violence Against Women in Partnership with Men*, Background document for UNESCAP's subregional training workshop on Elimination of Violence Against Women in Partnership with Men, New Delhi, India, 2–5 December.

Lasch-Quinn, E. (2001) *Race Experts: How Racial Etiquette, Sensitivity Training and New Age Therapy Hijacked the Civil Rights Revolution*, Norton and Company, New York.

Lawrence, S., and Tatum, B. (1997) 'White Educators as Allies: Moving from Awareness to Action', in M. Fine, L. Weis, L. Powell and L. Wong (eds) *Off White: Readings on Race, Power and Society*, Routledge, New York.

Lee, R. (2002) 'Pedagogy of the

Oppressor: What was Freire's Theory for Transforming the Privileged and the Powerful?', paper presented at the Annual Meeting of the American Educational Research Association, New Orleans, LA, April 1–5.

Lenski, G. (1966) *Power and Privilege: A Theory of Social Stratification*, McGraw-Hill, New York.

Leonard, P. (1984) *Personality and Ideology: Towards a Materialist Theory of the Individual*, Macmillan, London.

Leondar-Wright, B. (2005) *Class Matters: Cross-Class Alliance Building for Middle-Class Activists*, New Society Publishers, Gabriola Island, BC.

— and Yeskel, F. (2007) 'Classism Curriculum Design', in M. Adams, L. Bell and P. Griffin (eds) *Teaching for Diversity and Social Justice*, 2nd edn, Routledge, New York.

Levine-Rasky, C. (2002) 'Critical/Relational/Contextual: Toward a Model for Studying Whiteness', in C. Levine-Rasky (ed.) *Working Through Whiteness: International Perspectives*, State University of New York Press, Albany, NY.

Lichtenberg, P. (1988) *Getting Equal: The Equalizing Law of Relationship*, University Press of America, Lanham, MD.

Lloyd, J. (2009) 'The Listening Cure', *Continuum: A Journal of Media and Cultural Studies*, vol. 23, no. 4, pp. 477–87.

Loewen, J. (2003) 'Foreword: Challenging Racism, Challenging History', in C. Thompson, E. Schaefer and H. Brod (eds) *White Men Challenging Racism: 35 Personal Stories*, Duke University Press, Durham, NC.

Logan, J., Kershaw, S., Karban, K., Mills, S., Trotter, J., and Sinclaire, M. (1996) *Confronting Prejudice: Lesbian and Gay Issues in Social Work Education*, Ashgate, Aldershot.

Loomba, A. (2005) *Colonialism/Postcolonialism*, 2nd edn, Routledge, London.

Loomis, C. (2005) 'Understanding and Experiencing Class Privilege', in S. Anderson and V. Middleton (eds) *Explorations in Privilege Oppression and Diversity*, Thomson, Belmont, CA.

Lopez, I. (1996) *White by Law: The Legal Construction of Race*, New York University Press, New York.

Lorde, A. (1984) *Sister Outsider: Essays and Speeches*, Crossing Press, Freedom, CA.

Lugones, M. (1987) 'Playfulness, "World" Travelling, and Loving Perception', *Hypatia*, vol. 2, no. 2, pp. 3–19.

— and Spelman, E. (1998) 'Have We Got a Theory for You!', in N. Zack, L. Shrage and C. Sartwell (eds) *Race, Class, Gender and Sexuality: The Big Questions*, Blackwell, Malden, MA.

Luxton, M. (1993) 'Dreams and Dilemmas: Feminist Musings on the "Man Question"', in T. Haddad (ed.) *Men and Masculinities: A Critical Anthology*, Canadian Scholars' Press, Toronto, Ont.

McClintock, A. (1992) 'The Angel of Progress: Pitfalls of the Term "Postcolonialism"', *Social Text*, no. 31/32, pp. 84–98.

McEwan, C. (2001) 'Postcolonialism, Feminism and Development: Intersections and Dilemmas', *Progress in Development Studies*, vol. 1, pp. 93–111.

McGee, T. (1995) 'Eurocentrism

and Geography: Reflections on Asian Urbanization', in J. Crush, (ed.) *The Power of Development*, Routledge, London.

McGregor, C. (1997) *Class in Australia*, Penguin, Melbourne, Vic.

Machery, E., and Faucher, L. (2005) 'Social Construction and the Concept of Race', *Philosophy of Science*, no. 72, pp. 1208–19.

McIntosh, P. (1992) 'White Privilege and Male Privilege: A Personal Account of Coming to See Correspondences Through Work in Women's Studies', in M. Anderson and P. Collins (eds) *Race, Class and Gender: An Anthology*, Wadsworth Publishing Company, Belmont, CA.

McIntyre, S., and Clark, A. (2003) *The History Wars*, Melbourne University Press, Melbourne, Vic.

McKay, B. (ed.) (1999) *Unmasking Whiteness: Race Relations and Reconciliation*, Queensland Studies Centre, Nathan, Qld.

McKinney, K. (2005) *Being White: Stories of Race and Racism*, Routledge, New York.

Mackinnon, C. (1991) 'From Practice to Theory, or What is a White Woman Anyway?', *Yale Journal of Law and Feminism*, vol. 4, no. 13, pp. 13–22.

McLaren, P. (1998) 'Whiteness is ... The Struggle for Postcolonial Hybridity', in J. Kincheloe, S. Steinberg, N. Rodriguez and R. Chennault (eds) *White Reign: Deploying Whiteness in America*, St Martin's Press, New York.

— and Farahmandpur, R. (2001) 'Teaching Against Globalization and the New Imperialism', *Journal of Teacher Education*, vol. 52, no. 2, pp. 136–50.

McLeod, J. (2000) *Beginning Postcolonialism*, Manchester University Press, Manchester.

McMahon, M. (1999) *Taking Care of Men: Sexual Politics in the Public Mind*, Cambridge University Press, Melbourne, Vic.

McRuer, R., and Berube, M. (2006) *Crip Theory: Cultural Signs of Queerness and Disability*, New York University Press, New York.

Magnet, S. (2006) 'Protesting Privilege: An Autoethnographic Look at Whiteness', *Qualitative Inquiry*, vol. 12, no. 4, pp. 736–49.

Magnusson, E. (2000) 'Party Political Rhetoric on Gender Equality in Sweden: The Uses of Uniformity and Heterogeneity, *NORA*, vol. 8, no. 2, pp. 78–92.

Maldonado, L. (2002) 'Symposium on West and Fenstermaker's "Doing Difference"', in S. Fenstermaker and C. West (eds) *Doing Difference, Doing Gender: Inequality, Power and Institutional Change*, Routledge, New York.

Mansbridge, J. (2001) 'The Making of Oppositional Consciousness', in J. Mansbridge and A. Morris (eds) *Oppositional Consciousness: The Subjective Roots of Social Protest*, University of Chicago Press, Chicago, IL.

Mantsios, G. (2003) 'Class in America: Myths and Realities', in M. Kimmel and A. Ferber (eds) *Privilege*, Westview Press, Boulder, CO.

Marks, D. (1996) 'Able-Bodied Dilemmas in Teaching Disability Studies', *Feminism and Psychology*, vol. 6, no. 1, pp. 69–73.

— (1999a) 'Dimensions of Oppression: Theorising the Embodied Subject', *Disability and Society*, vol. 14, no. 5, pp. 611–26.

— (1999b) *Disability: Controversial Debates and Psychosocial Perspectives*, Routledge, London.

Marks, R. (2002) *The Origins of the Modern World: A Global and Ecological Perspective*, Rowman and Littlefield, Lanham, MD.

Martin, J. (1994) 'Methodological Essentialism: False Differences and Other Dangerous Traps', *Signs: Journal of Women in Culture and Society*, vol. 19, no. 3, pp. 630–57.

May, L. (1993) *Sharing Responsibility*, University of Chicago Press, Chicago, IL.

May-Machunda, P. (2005) 'Exploring the Invisible Knapsack of Able-Bodied Privilege', unpublished paper, Minnesota State University, Moorhead, MN.

Mederos, F. (1987) *Patriarchy and Male Psychology*, unpublished manuscript.

Mendelsohn, O., and Vicziary, M. (1998) *The Untouchables: Subordination, Poverty and the State in Modern India*, Columbia University Press, New York.

Messerschmidt, J. (1993) *Masculinities and Crime*, Rowman and Littlefield, Lanham, MD.

— (1997) *Crime as Structured Action*, Sage, Thousand Oaks, CA.

— (2000) *Nine Lives: Adolescent Masculinities, the Body and Violence*, Westview Press, Boulder, CO.

Messner, M. (1992) *Power at Play: Sports and the Problem of Masculinity*, Beacon Press, Boston, MA.

— (2003) 'Men as Superordinates', in M. Kimmel and Abby Ferber (eds) *Privilege: A Reader*, Westview Press, Boulder, CO.

Michels, R. (1962) *Political Parties*, Free Press, New York.

Midgley, J. (1983) *Professional Imperialism in the Third World*, Heinemann, London.

— (2008) 'Promoting Reciprocal International Social Work Exchanges: Professional Imperialism Revisited', in M. Gray, J. Coates and M. Yellow Bird (eds) *Indigenous Social Work Around the World: Towards Culturally Relevant Education and Practice*, Ashgate, Aldershot.

Milanovic, B. (2007) 'Globalization and Inequality', in D. Held and A. Kaya (eds) *Global Inequality: Patterns and Explanations*, Polity Press, Cambridge.

Millet, K. (1972) *Sexual Politics*, Abacus, London.

Mills, C. W. (1956) *The Power Elite*, Oxford University Press, New York.

Mills, M. (1998) 'Challenging Violence in Schools: Disruptive Moments in the Educational Politics of Masculinity', PhD thesis, University of Queensland, Brisbane, Qld.

Milner, A. (1999) *Class*, Sage, London.

Minow, M. (1990) *Making All the Difference: Inclusion, Exclusion and American Law*, Cornell University Press, New York.

Mitchell, J. (1975) *Psychoanalysis and Feminism*, Vintage Books, New York.

Mohanty, C. (1991) 'Under Western Eyes: Feminist Scholarship and Colonial Discourses', in C. Mohanty, A. Russo and L. Torres (eds) *Third World Women and the Politics of Feminism*, Indiana University Press, Bloomington, IN.

— (2004) *Feminism without Borders: Decolonizing Theory, Practising Solidarity,* Duke University Press, Durham, NC.
Moir, A., and Moir, B. (2003) *Why Don't Men Iron? The Fascinating and Unalterable Differences Between Men and Women*, Citadel, New York.
Monteiro-Ferreira, A. (2008) 'Afrocentricity and the Western Paradigm', *Journal of Black Studies*, vol. 20, no. 10, pp. 1–10.
Moreton-Robinson, A. (2000) *Talkin' up to the White Woman: Indigenous Women and Feminism*, University of Queensland Press, Brisbane, Qld.
— (ed.) (2004) *Whitening Race: Essays in Social and Cultural Criticism*, Aboriginal Studies Press, Canberra, ACT.
Morris, J. (1991) *Pride Against Prejudice: Transforming Attitudes to Disability*, Women's Press, London.
Morrison, T. (1993) *Playing in the Dark: Whiteness and the Literary Imagination*, Vintage, New York.
Mortimer, P. (2009) 'Pecking Order Keeps Class System Alive', *Guardian*, Tuesday 3 February, p. 4.
Mosca, G. (1939) *The Ruling Class*, McGraw Hill, New York.
Moser, I. (2006) 'Sociotechnical Practices and Difference: On the Interferences Between Disability, Gender and Class', *Science, Technology and Human Values*, vol. 31, no. 5, pp. 537–64.
Moyo, D. (2009) *Dead Aid: Destroying the Biggest Global Myth of Our Time,* Allen Lane, London.
Mullaly, B. (1997) *Structural Social Work: Ideology, Theory and Practice*, Oxford University Press, Toronto, Ont.
— (2002) *Challenging Oppression: A Critical Social Work Approach*, Oxford University Press, Toronto, Ont.
Munck, R. (1999) 'Deconstructing Development Discourses: Of Impasses, Alternatives and Politics', in R. Munck and D. O'Hearn (eds) *Critical Development Theory: Contributions to a New Paradigm*, Zed Books, London.
Murphy, R. (1995) 'Encounters: The Body Silent in America', in B. Ingstad and S. Whyte (eds) *Disability Culture*, University of California Press, Berkeley, CA.
Mutua, A. (2006a) 'Introduction', in A. Mutua (ed.) *Progressive Black Masculinities*, Routledge, London.
— (2006b) 'Theorising Progressive Black Masculinities', in A. Mutua (ed.) *Progressive Black Masculinities*, Routledge, London.
Mutua, K., and Swadener, B. (2004) *Decolonizing Research in Cross-Cultural Contexts: Critical Personal Narratives*, State University of New York Press, Albany, NY.
Naidoo, A. (1996) 'Challenging the Hegemony of Eurocentric Psychology', *Journal of Community and Health Sciences*, vol. 2, no. 2, pp. 9–16.
Narayan, U. (2000) 'Essence of Culture and a Sense of History: A Feminist Critique of Cultural Essentialism', in U. Narayan and S. Harding (eds) *Decentering the Center: Philosophy for a Multicultural, Postcolonial and Feminist World*, Indiana University Press, Bloomington, IN.
Njeza, M. (1997) 'Fallacies of the New Afrocentrism: A Critical Response to Kawame A. Appiah',

Journal of Theology for Southern Africa, no. 99, pp. 1–8.
Noble, D. (1979) 'The PMC: A Critique', in P. Walker (ed.) *Between Labour and Capital*, Harvester Press, Sussex.
Nzira, V., and Williams, P. (2007) *Anti-Oppressive Practice in Health and Social Care*, Sage, London.
O'Brien, J., and Howard, J. (1998) 'Introduction: Differences and Inequalities', in J. O'Brien and J. Howard (eds) *Everyday Inequalities: Critical Interrogations*, Blackwell, Malden, MA.
O'Brien, J., and Feagin, E. (2004) *White Men on Race: Power, Privilege and the Shaping of Cultural Consciousness*, Beacon Press, New York.
O'Connor, P. (2002) *Oppression and Responsibility: A Wittgensteinian Approach to Social Practices and Moral Theory*, Pennsylvania State University Press, University Park, PA.
O'Donnell, P., Lloyd, J., and Dreher, T. (2009) 'Listening, Pathbuilding and Continuations: A Research Agenda for the Analysis of Listening', *Continuum: A Journal of Media and Cultural Studies*, vol. 23, no. 4, pp. 423–39.
O'Grady, C. (1999) 'Seeing Things as They are', in C. Clark and J. O'Donnell (eds) *Becoming and Unbecoming White: Owning and Disowning a Racial Identity*, Bergin and Garvey, Westport, CT.
O'Hagen, K. (2001) *Cultural Competence in the Caring Professions*, Jessica Kingsly Publications, London.
O'Toole, L., and Schiffman, J. (1997) 'The Roots of Male Violence Against Women', in L. O'Toole and J. Schiffman (eds) *Gender Violence: Interdisciplinary Perspectives*, New York University Press, New York.
Oliver, M. (1983) *Social Work with Disabled People*, Macmillan, London.
— (1990) *The Politics of Disablement*, Macmillan, London.
— (1996) *Understanding Disability: From Theory to Practice*, Macmillan, London.
Omi, M. (2001) '(E)racism: Emerging Practices of Antiracist Organisations', in B. Rasmussen, E. Klineberg, I. Nexia and M. Wray (eds) *The Making and Unmaking of Whiteness*, Duke University Press, Durham, NC.
Osei-Hwedie, K. (1993) 'The Challenge of Social Work in Africa: Starting the Indigenisation Process', *Journal of Social Development in Africa*, vol. 8, no. 1, pp. 19–30.
Oyebade, B. (1990) 'African Studies and the Afrocentric Paradigm: A Critique', *Journal of Black Studies*, vol. 21, no. 2, pp. 233–8.
Pakulski, J., and Waters, M. (1996) *The Death of Class*, Sage, London.
Paranjape, M. (1993) *Decolonization and Development*, Sage, New Delhi.
Pareto, V. (1935) *The Mind and Society*, ed. A. Livingston, Harcourt Brace, New York.
Parker, R. (1972) *The Myth of the Middle Class: Notes on Affluence and Inequality*, Liveright, New York.
Parkin, F. (1983) *Marxism and Class Theory: A Bourgeoise Critique*, Columbia University Press, New York.
Paterson, K., and Hughes, B.

(1999) 'Disability Studies and Phenomenology: The Carnal Politics of Everyday Life', *Disability and Society*, vol. 14, no. 5, pp. 597–610.

Patten, H., and Ryan, R. (2001) 'Research and Reconciliation', *Australian Journal of Indigenous Education*, vol. 21, no. 1, pp. 36–42.

Pease, B. (1995) 'MASA: Men Against Sexual Assault', in W. Weeks and J. Wilson (eds) *Issues Facing Australian Families*, 2nd edn, Longman Cheshire, Melbourne, Vic.

— (1997a) *Men and Sexual Politics: Towards a Profeminist Practice*, Dulwich Centre Publications, Adelaide, SA.

— (1997b) 'Teaching Anti-patriarchal Men's Studies in Social Work', *Issues in Social Work Education*, vol. 17, no. 1, pp. 3–17.

— (1998) 'Critical Men's Studies: Fostering Partnership in Gender Relations' in *Proceedings of the Men and Family Relationships Forum*, Commonwealth Attorney General's Department, Canberra, ACT.

— (2000) *Recreating Men: Postmodern Masculinity Politics*, Sage, London.

— (2002a) *Men and Gender Relations*, Tertiary Press, Melbourne, Vic.

— (2002b) 'Reconstructing Men's Interests', *Men and Masculinities*, vol. 5, no. 2, pp. 165–77.

— (2003) 'Rethinking the Relationship Between Self and Society', in J. Allan, B. Pease and L. Briskman (eds) *Critical Social Work: An Introduction to Theories and Practices*, Allen & Unwin, Sydney, NSW.

— (2006) 'Governing Men and Boys in Public Policy in Australia', in G. Marston and C. McDonald (eds) *Analysing Social Policy: A Governmental Approach*, Edward Elgar, Cheltenham.

— (2008) 'Engaging Men in Men's Violence Prevention: Exploring the Tensions, Dilemmas and Possibilities', *Australian Domestic and Family Violence Clearing House Issues Paper* no. 17, University of New South Wales, Sydney, NSW.

— (2009) 'Racialised Masculinities and the Health of Immigrant and Refugee Men', in A. Broom and P. Tovey (eds) *Men's Health: Body, Identity and Societal Context*, Wiley-Blackwell, Chichester, West Sussex.

— and Pringle, K. (eds) (2001) *A Man's World? Changing Men's Practices in a Globalized World*, Zed Books, London.

Peavey, F. (1995) 'Strategic Questioning: An Approach to Personal and Social Change', *In Context: A Quarterly of Humane Sustainable Culture*, Spring, pp. 36–40.

— (2003) 'American Willing to Listen', in M. Brady, *The Wisdom of Listening*, Wisdom Publications, Somerville, MA.

Peel, E. (2001) 'Mundane Heterosexism: Understanding Incidents of the Everyday', *Women's Studies International Forum*, vol. 24, no. 5, 541–54.

Peet, R., and Hartwick, E. (1999) *Theories of Development*, Guilford Press, New York.

Pellebon, D. (2007) 'An Analysis of Afrocentricity as Theory for Social Work Practice', *Advances in Social Work*, vol. 8, no. 1, pp. 169–83.

Pennycook, A. (1994) 'The Politics of Pronouns', *ELT Journal*, vol. 48, no. 2, pp. 173–8.
Perry, B. (2001) *In the Name of Hate: Understanding Hate Crimes*, Routledge, New York.
Petersen, A. (1998) *Unmasking the Masculine: 'Men' and 'Identity' in a Skeptical Age*, Sage, London.
Pheterson, G. (1986) 'Alliances Between Women: Overcoming Internalized Oppression and Internalized Domination', *Signs: Journal of Women, Culture and Society*, vol. 12, no. 1, pp. 146–60.
Philip, H. (2004) 'White Privilege: For or Against? A Discussion of Ostensibly Antiracist Discourses in Critical Whiteness Studies', *Race, Gender and Class*, vol. 11, no. 4, pp. 63–75.
Pickering, M. (2001) *Stereotyping: The Politics of Representation*, Palgrave, Basingstoke.
Pincus, F., and Sokoloff, N. (2008) 'Does "Classism" Help Us to Understand Class Oppression?', *Race, Gender and Class*, vol. 15, nos 1 and 2, pp. 9–24.
Plummer, D. (1999) *One of the Boys: Masculinity, Homophobia and Modern Manhood*, Harrington Park Press, New York.
Prakash, G. (1994) 'Subaltern Studies as Postcolonial Criticism', *American Historical Review*, vol. 99, no. 5, pp. 1475–90.
— (2000) 'Can the "Subaltern" Ride? A Reply to O'Hanlon and Washbrook', in V. Chaturvedi (ed.) *Mapping Subaltern Studies and the Postcolonial*, Verso, London.
Raheim, S., et al. (2007) 'An Invitation to Narrative Practitioners to Address Privilege and Dominance', Dulwich Centre Website, www.dulwichcentre.com.au/privilege.htm.
Rahman, M. (1998) 'Sexuality and Rights: Problematising Lesbian and Gay Politics', in T. Carver and V. Mottier (eds) *Politics of Sexuality: Identity, Gender, Citizenship*, Routledge, London.
Rahman, N. (2007) 'Patriarchy', in M. Flood, J. Gardiner, B. Pease and K. Pringle (eds) *International Encyclopedia of Men and Masculinities*, Routledge, London.
Ramazanoglu, C. (1989) *Feminism and the Contradictions of Oppression*, Routledge, London.
— (1993) 'Introduction', in C. Ramazanoglu (ed.) *Up Against Foucault*, Routledge, London.
Rasmussen, B., Klinenberg, E., Nexica, I., and Wray, M. (2001) 'Introduction', in B. Rasmussen, E. Klinenberg, I. Nexica and M. Wray (eds) *The Making and Unmaking of Whiteness*, Duke University Press, Durham, NC.
Razack, S. (1998) *Looking White People in the Eye*, University of Toronto Press, Toronto, Ont.
Reagon, B. (1983) 'Coalition Politics: Turning the Century', in B. Smith (ed.) *Home Girls: A Black Feminist Anthology*, Kitchen Table: Women of Color Press, New York.
Reason, R., and Broido, E. (2005) 'Issues and Strategies for Social Justice Allies (and the Student Affairs Professionals Who Work for Them)', *New Directions for Student Services*, no. 110, Summer, pp. 81–9.
Rees, W. (1998) 'Reducing the Ecological Footprint of Consumption', in L. Westra and P. Werhane (eds) *The Business of Consumption: Environmental Ethics and*

the Global Economy, Rowman and Littlefied, Lanham, MD.

Rich, A. (1980) 'Compulsory Heterosexuality and Lesbian Existence', *Signs*, vol. 5, no. 4, pp. 631–60.

Richardson, D. (1996) 'Heterosexuality and Social Theory', in D. Richardson (ed.) *Theorising Heterosexuality*, Open University Press, Buckingham.

— (1998) 'Sexuality and Citizenship', *Sociology*, vol. 32, no. 1, pp. 83–100.

Rideway, C., and Correll, S. (2004) 'Unpacking the Gender System: A Theoretical Perspective on Gender Beliefs and Social Relations', *Gender and Society*, vol. 18, no. 4, pp. 510–31.

Rigney, L. (1999) 'Internationalization of an Indigenous Anticolonial Cultural Critique of Research Methodologies: A Guide to Indigenist Research Methodologies and Its Principles', *Wicazo Sa Review*, vol. 14, no. 2, pp. 109–21.

Riska, E. (2006) *Masculinity and Men's Health: Coronary Heart Disease in Medical and Public Discourse*, Rowman and Littlefield, Lanham, MD.

Robinson, N. (1995) *Ideology and the Collapse of the Socialist System: A Critical History of Soviet Ideological Discourse*, Edward Elgar, Northhampton, MA.

Robinson, V. (2007) 'Heterosexuality', in M. Flood, J. Gardiner, B. Pease and K. Pringle (eds) *International Encyclopedia of Men and Masculinities*, Routledge, London.

Rocco, T., and Gallagher, S. (2006) 'Straight Privilege and Moralizing: Issues in Career Development', *New Directions for Adult and Continuing Education*, no. 112, pp. 29–39.

Rochlin, M. (2003) 'Heterosexuality Questionnaire', in M. Kimmel and A. Ferber (eds) *Privilege: A Reader*, Westview Press, Boulder, CO.

Rodriguez, N. (1998) 'Emptying the Content of Whiteness: Toward an Understanding of the Relation Between Whiteness and Pedagogy', in J. Kincheloe, S. Steinberg, N. Rodriguez and R. Chennault (eds) *White Reign: Deploying Whiteness in America*, St Martin's Press, New York.

— (2000) 'Projects of Whiteness in a Critical Pedagogy', in N. Rodriguez and L. Villaverde (eds) *Dismantling White Privilege: Pedagogy, Politics and Whiteness*, Peter Lang, New York.

Roediger, D. (1991) *The Wages of Whiteness: Race and the Making of the American Working Class*, Verso, New York.

— (2006) 'A Reply to Eric Kaufmann', *Ethnicities*, vol. 6, no. 2, pp. 231–66.

Rosenblum, K., and Travis, T. (1996) 'Experiencing Difference: Framework Essay', in K. Rosenblum and T. Travis (eds) *The Meaning of Difference: American Constructions of Race, Sex and Gender, Social Class and Sexual Orientation*, McGraw-Hill, New York.

Rothenberg, P. (2000) *Invisible Privilege: A Memoir About Race, Class and Gender*, University Press of Kansas, KS.

— (2002) 'Introduction', in P. Rothenberg (ed.) *White Privilege: Essential Readings on the Other Side of Racism*, Worth Publishers, New York.

Rowan, J. (1997) *Healing the Male*

Psyche: Therapy as Initiation, Routledge, London.

— (2007) 'Sexism', in M. Flood, J. Gardiner, B. Pease and K. Pringle (eds) *International Encyclopedia of Men and Masculinities*, Routledge, London.

Rowbotham, S. (1981) 'The Trouble with Patriarchy', in R. Samuel (ed.) *People's History and Socialist Theory*, Routledge & Kegan Paul, London.

Rudd, K. (2008) Apology to Australia's Indigenous Peoples, House of Representatives, Parliament House, Canberra, www.gov.au/media/Speech/2008/speech, accessed 23 June 2009.

Russell, G. (1997) 'Using Music to Reduce Homophobia and Heterosexism', in J. Sears and W. Williams (eds) *Overcoming Heterosexism and Homophobia: Strategies That Work*, Columbia University Press, New York.

— and Barclay, L. (1999) *Fitting Fathers into Families: Men and the Fatherhood Role in Contemporary Australia*, Commonwealth Department of Family and Community Services, Canberra.

Ryan, J., and Sackrey, C. (1996) *Strangers in Paradise: Academics from the Working Class*, University Press of America, Lanham, MD.

Ryde, J. (2009) *Being White in the Helping Professions: Developing Effective Intercultural Awareness*, Jessica Kingsley, London.

Ryder, B. (2004) 'Straight Talk: Male Heterosexual Privilege', in L. Heldke and P. O'Connor (eds) *Oppression, Privilege and Resistance: Theoretical Perspectives on Racism, Sexism and Heterosexism*, McGraw Hill, New York.

Sacks, M., and Lindholm, M. (2002) 'A Room without a View: Social Distance and the Structuring of Privileged Identity', in C. Levine-Rasky (ed.) *Working Through Whiteness: International Perspectives*, State University of New York Press, Albany, NY.

Saco, D. (1992) 'Masculinity as Signs: Poststructural, Feminist Approaches to the Study of Gender', in S. Craig (ed.) *Men, Masculinity and the Media*, Sage, Thousand Oaks, CA.

Sagoff, M. (2008) *The Economy of the Earth: Philosophy, Law and the Environment,* Cambridge University Press, Cambridge.

Said, E. (2003) *Orientalism*, Penguin, London.

Sandoval, C. (2000) *Methodology of the Oppressed*, University of Minnesota Press, Minneapolis, MN.

Santos, B. (2007) 'Preface', in B. Santos (ed.) *Another Knowledge is Possible: Beyond Northern Epistemologies*, Verso, London.

— Nunnes, J., and Meneses, M. (2007) 'Introduction: Opening Up the Cannons of Knowledge and Recognition of Difference' in B. Santos (ed.) *Another Knowledge is Possible: Beyond Northern Epistemologies*, Verso, London.

Sardar, Z. (1999a) *Orientalism*, Open University Press, Buckingham.

— (1999b) 'Development and the Locations of Eurocentrism', in R. Munck and D. O'Hearn (eds) *Critical Development Theory: Contributions to a New Paradigm*, Zed Books, London.

Sayers, A. (2005) *The Moral Significance of Class*, Cambridge University Press, Cambridge.

Schacht, S. (2003) 'Teaching

About Being an Oppressor', in M. Kimmel and Abby Ferber (eds) *Privilege: A Reader*, Westview Press, Boulder, CO.

— and Ewing, D. (2001) 'Feminist Women and (Pro)Feminist Men: Moving from an Uneasy to a Radical Alliance', in J. Bystydzienski and S. Schacht (eds) *Forging Radical Alliances Across Difference: Coalition Politics for the New Millennium*, Rowman and Littlefield, Lanham, MD.

Schiele, J. (1996) 'Afrocentricity: An Emerging Paradigm in Social Work Practice', *Social Work*, vol. 41, no. 3, pp. 286–94.

— (1997) 'The Contour and Meaning of Afrocentric Social Work', *Journal of Black Studies*, vol. 27, no. 6, pp. 800–19.

— (2000) *Human Services and the Afrocentric Paradigm*, Haworth Press, New York.

Schor, J. (1998) *The Overspent American: Upscaling, Downshifting and the New Consumer,* Harper Perennial, New York.

— (1999) 'Blindness as Metaphor', *Differences*, vol. 11, no. 2, pp. 76–105.

Schwalbe, M. (2002) 'The Costs of American Privilege', *Counter Punch*, 4 October.

Schwartz, M., and Milovic, D. (1996) 'Introduction', in M. Schwartz and D. Milovic (eds) *Race, Gender and Class in Criminology: The Intersections*, Garland Publishing, New York.

Scott, J. (2000) 'Class and Stratification', in G. Payne (ed.) *Social Divisions*, Macmillan, Houndmills, Basingstoke.

Scott, S., and Jackson, S. (2000) 'Sexuality', in G. Payne (ed.) *Social Divisions*, Macmillan, Houndmills, Basingstoke.

Searling, H. (2008) 'The Crisis in Social Work: The Radical Solution', *Barefoot Social Worker: A Radical Perspective*, November.

Sedgewick, E. (1985) *Between Men: English Literature and Male Homosexual Desire*, Columbia University Press, New York.

Segal, L. (1987) *Is the Future Female?: Troubled Thoughts on Contemporary Feminism*, Virago, London.

— (1994) *Straight Sex: The Politics of Pleasure*, Virago Press, London.

Seidler, V. (1991) *Recreating Sexual Politics: Men, Feminism and Politics*, Routledge, London.

— (1992) *Men, Sex and Relationships: Writings from Archilles Heel*, Routledge, London.

— (1994) *Unreasonable Men: Masculinity and Social Theory*, Routledge, London.

Sennett, R. (2003) *Respect in a World of Inequality*, W.W. Norton and Company, New York.

— and Cobb, J. (1972) *The Hidden Injuries of Class*, W.W. Norton and Company, New York.

Seshadri-Crocks, K. (2000) *Desiring Whiteness: A Lacanian Analysis of Race*, Routledge, London.

Shakespeare, T. (2006) *Disability Rights and Wrongs*, Routledge, London.

— and Watson, N. (1996) '"The Body Line Controversy": A New Direction for Disability Studies?', paper presented at Hull Disabilities Studies Seminar, University of Hull, Hull.

Sheldon, A. (2007) Review Symposium Disability Rights and Wrongs? *Disability and Society*, vol. 22, no. 2, March, pp. 209–34

Shildrick, M. (2002) *Embodying the Monster: Encounters with the Vulnerable Self*, Sage, London.

Shilling, C. (2003) *The Body and Social Theory*, 2nd edn, Sage, London.

Shiva, V. (1993) 'Decolonizing the North', in M. Mies and V. Shiva (eds) *Ecofeminism*, Spinifex, Melbourne, Vic.

Shohat, E. (1992) 'Notes on the "Postcolonial"', *Social Text*, no. 31/32, pp. 99–113.

Shorne, R. (1999) 'Whiteness and the Politics of Location', in T. Nakayama and J. Martin (eds) *Whiteness: The Communication of Social Identity*, Sage, Thousand Oaks, CA.

Sidanius, J., and Pratto, F. (1999) *Social Dominance: An Intergroup Theory of Social Hierarchy and Oppression*, Cambridge University Press, Cambridge.

Simoni, J., and Walters, K. (2001) 'Heterosexual Identity and Heterosexism: Recognising Privilege to Reduce Prejudice', *Journal of Homosexuality*, vol. 41, no. 1, pp. 157–71.

Simonsen, K. (2000) 'The Body as Battlefield', *Transactions of the Institute of British Geography*, vol. 25, no. 1, pp. 7–9.

Singer, P. (2009) *The Life You Can Save: Acting Now to End World Poverty*, Text Publishing, Melbourne, Vic.

Singh, B. (2001) 'Dialogue Across Cultural and Ethnic Differences', *Educational Studies*, vol. 27, no. 3, pp. 341–55.

Skeggs, B. (1997) *Formations of Class and Gender: Becoming Respectable*, Sage, London.

Slater, D. (2004) *Geopolitics and the Postcolonial: Rethinking North–South Relations*, Blackwell, Oxford.

Smart, C. (1996) 'Collusion, Collaboration and Confession: On Moving Beyond the Heterosexuality Debate', in D. Richardson (ed.) *Theorising Heterosexuality*, Open University Press, Buckingham.

Smith, C. (2000) 'How I Became a Queer Heterosexual', in C. Thomas (ed.) *Straight with a Twist: Queer Theory and the Subject of Heterosexuality*, University of Illinois Press, Chicago, IL.

Smith, D. (2005) *Institutional Ethnography: A Sociology for People*, Alta Mira Press, Lanham, MD.

Smith, L. T. (1999) *Decolonizing Methodologies: Research and Indigenous Peoples*, Zed Books, London.

Smith, R. (2001) *Australian Political Culture*, Longman, Sydney, NSW.

Stark, E. (2007) *Coercive Control: How Men Entrap Women in Personal Life*, Oxford University Press, New York.

Stokes, M. (2001) *The Color of Sex: Whiteness, Heterosexuality and the Fictions of White Supremacy*, Duke University Press, Durham, NC.

— (2005) 'White Heterosexuality: A Romance of the Straight Man's Burden', in C. Ingraham (ed.) *Thinking Straight: The Power, the Promise and the Paradox of Heterosexuality*, Routledge, New York.

Sullivan, S. (2006) *Revealing Whiteness: The Unconscious Habits of Racial Privilege*, Indiana University Press, Bloomington, IN.

Sumara, D., and Davis, B. (1999) 'Interrupting Heteronormativity: Toward a Queer Curriculum

Theory', *Curriculum Inquiry*, vol. 29, no. 2, pp. 191–208.
Sutcliff, B. (1999) 'The Place of Development in Theories of Imperialism and Globalization', in R. Munck and D. O'Hearn (eds) *Critical Development Theory: Contributions to a New Paradigm*, Zed Books, London.
Swain, J., and French, S. (2000) 'Towards an Affirmation Model of Disability', *Disability and Society*, vol. 15, no. 4, pp. 569–82.
Swigonski, M. (1993) 'Feminist Standpoint Theory and the Question of Social Work Research', *Affilia*, vol., 8, no. 2, pp. 171–83.
Tamasese, K., and Waldegrave, C. (1996) 'Cultural and Gender Accountability in the "Just Therapy" Approach', in C. McLean, M. Carey and C. White (eds) *Men's Ways of Being*, Westview Press, Boulder, CO.
— Waldegrave, C., Tuhaka, F., and Campbell, W. (1998) 'Furthering Conversations About Partnerships of Accountability', *Dulwich Centre Journal*, no. 4, pp. 51–64.
Tangeberg, K., and Kemp, S. (2002) 'Embodied Practice: Claiming the Body's Experience, Agency and Knowledge for Social Work, *Social Work*, vol. 47, no. 1, pp. 9–18.
Tappan, M. (2008) 'Reframing Internalized Oppression and Internalized Domination from the Psychological to the Socio-Cultural', *Teachers College Record*, vol. 108, no. 10, pp. 2115–44.
Thandeka (2000) *Learning to be White*, Continuum International Publishing Group, New York.
Theodore, P., and Basow, S. (2000) 'Heterosexual Masculinity and Homophobia', *Journal of Homosexuality*, vol. 40, no. 2, pp. 31–48.
Therborn, G. (1980) *The Ideology of Power and the Power of Ideology*, Verso, London.
Thomas, C. (2000) 'Straight with a Twist: Queer Theory and the Subject of Heterosexuality', in C. Thomas (ed.) *Straight with a Twist: Queer Theory and the Subject of Heterosexuality*, University of Illinois Press, Chicago, IL.
— (2007) *Sociologies of Disability and Illness*, Palgrave, Houndmills, Basingstoke.
— and MacGillivray, C. (2000) 'Afterword(s): A Conversation', in C. Thomas (ed.) *Straight with a Twist: Queer Theory and the Subject of Heterosexuality*, University of Illinois Press, Chicago, IL.
Thompson, N. (2006) *Anti-Discriminatory Practice*, 4th edn, Palgrave, Houndmills, Basingstoke.
Thorne, B. (2002) 'Symposium on West and Fenstermaker's "Doing Difference"', in S. Fenstermaker and C. West (eds) *Doing Difference, Doing Gender: Inequality, Power and Institutional Change*, Routledge, New York.
Tillner, G. (1997) 'Masculinity and Xenophobia: The Identity of Dominance', paper presented to the UNESCO conference, Masculinity and Male Roles in the Perspective of a Culture of Peace, Oslo, Norway.
Titchkosky, T. (2001) 'Disability: A Rose by Any Other Name? People-First Language in Canadian Society', *Canadian Review of Sociology and Anthropology*, vol. 38, no. 2, pp. 125–40.

Tokarczyk, M., and Fay, E. (1993) *Working-class Women in the Academy: Laborers in the Knowledge Factory*, University of Massachusetts Press, Amherst, MA.

Tolson, A. (1977) *The Limits of Masculinity*, Tavistock, London.

Tregaskis, C. (2002) 'Social Model Theory: The Story So Far …', *Disability and Society*, vol. 17, no. 4, pp. 457–70.

— (2004) *Constructions of Disability: Researching the Interface Between Disabled and Non-Disabled People*, Routledge, London.

Tucker, V. (1999) 'The Myth of Development: A Critique of a Eurocentric Discourse', in R. Munck and D. O'Hearn (eds) *Critical Development Theory: Contributions to a New Paradigm*, Zed Books, London.

Turner, B. (1994) *Orientalism, Postmodernism and Globalism*, Routledge, London.

— (2002) 'Disability and the Sociology of the Body', in G. Albert, K. Seelman and M. Bury (eds) *Handbook of Disability Studies*, Sage, Thousand Oaks, CA.

Van Every, J. (1996) 'Heterosexuality and Domestic Life', in D. Richardson (ed.) *Theorising Heterosexuality*, Open University Press, Buckingham.

Van Gorder, A. (2007) 'Pedagogy for the Children of the Oppressors', *Journal of Transformative Education*, vol. 5, no. 1, pp. 8–32.

Verhelst, T. (1990) *No Life without Roots: Culture and Development*, Zed Books, London.

Vernon, A. (1999) 'The Dialectics of Multiple Identities and the Disabled People's Movement', *Disability and Society*, vol. 14, no. 3, pp. 385–98.

Wackernagel, M., and Rees, W. (1996) *Our Ecological Footprint: Reducing the Human Impact on the Earth*, New Society Publishers, Gabriola Island, BC.

Wadham, B. (2001) 'What Does the White Man Want?', PhD thesis, Flinders University, Adelaide, SA.

Wadsworth, Y. (1997) *Do It Yourself Social Research*, Allen & Unwin, Sydney, NSW.

Waite, L. (2001) 'Divided Consciousness: The Impact of Black Elite Consciousness on the 1966 Chicago Freedom Movement', in J. Mansbridge and A. Morris (eds) *Oppositional Consciousness: The Subjective Roots of Social Protest*, University of Chicago Press, Chicago, IL.

Walby, S. (1990) *Theorizing Patriarchy*, Basil Blackwell, Oxford.

Walkowitz, D. (1999) *Working with Class: Social Workers and the Politics of Middle-Class Identity*, University of North Carolina Press, Chapel Hill, NC.

Wallerstein, I. (1974) *The Modern World System*, Academic Press, New York.

— (2004) *World Systems Analysis: An Introduction*, Duke University Press, New York.

Ward, J. (2008) 'Dude Sex: White Masculinities and "Authentic Heterosexuality"', *Sexualities*, vol. 11, no. 4, pp. 414–34.

Warner, M. (1999) *The Trouble with Normal: Sex, Politics, and the Ethics of Queer Life*, Free Press, New York.

Weber, L. (2002) 'Symposium on West and Fenstermaker's "Doing Difference"', in S. Fenstermaker and C. West (eds) *Doing Difference, Doing Gender: Inequality, Power and Institutional Change*, Routledge, New York.

Websdale, N., and Chesney-Lind, N. (1998) 'Doing Violence to Women: Research Synthesis on Victimisation of Women', in L. Bowker (ed.) *Masculinities and Violence*, Sage, Thousand Oaks, CA.

Weinberg, G. (1972) *Society and the Healthy Homosexual*, Alyson Publications, Boston, MA.

Wellman, D. (1993) *Portraits of White Racism*, 2nd edn, Cambridge University Press, Cambridge.

Wendell, S. (1996) *The Rejected Body: Feminist Philosophical Reflections on Disability*, Routledge, New York.

West, C., and Zimmerman, D. (1987) 'Doing Gender', *Gender and Society*, vol. 1, no. 2, pp. 125–51.

Westergaard, J. (1995) *Who Gets What? The Hardening of Class Inequality in the Late Twentieth Century*, Blackwell, London.

Westra, L. (1998) 'Preface', in L. Westra and P. Werhane (eds) *The Business of Consumption: Environmental Ethics and the Global Economy*, Rowman and Littlefield, Lanham, MD.

White, S. (2001) *Communism and Its Collapse: Making of the Contemporary World*, Routledge, London.

Whitehead, S. (2002) *Men and Masculinities: Key Themes and New Directions*, Polity Press, Cambridge.

— (2007) 'Patriarchal Dividend', in M. Flood, J. Gardiner, B. Pease and K. Pringle (eds) *International Encyclopedia of Men and Masculinities*, Routledge, London.

Whitley, B., and Aegistottir, S. (2000) 'The Gender Belief System, Authoritianism, Social Dominance Orientation and Heterosexuals' Attitudes Toward Lesbians and Gay Men', *Sex Roles*, vol. 42, Nos. 11/12, pp. 947–67.

Wildman, S., and Davis, A. (2000) 'Language and Silence: Making Systems of Privilege Visible', in R. Delgado and J. Stefancic (eds) *Critical Race Theory: The Cutting Edge*, 2nd edn, Temple University Press, Philadelphia, PA.

Wilkinson, R. (2005) *The Impact of Inequality: How to Make Sick Societies Healthier*, New Press, New York.

Wilkinson, R., and Pickett, K. (2009) *The Spirit Level: Why More Equal Societies Almost Always Do Better*, Allen Lane, London.

Wilkinson, S., and Kitzinger, C. (1994) 'Dire Straights: Contemporary Rehabilitations of Heterosexuality', in G. Griffin, M. Hester, S. Rai and S. Roseneil (eds) *Stirring It: Challenges for Feminism*, Taylor & Francis, London.

Williams, C. (2005) 'In Defence of Materialism: A Critique of Afrocentric Ontology', *Race and Class*, vol. 47, pp. 35–48.

Willis, P. (1981) *Learning to Labor: How Working-Class Kids Get Working-Class Jobs*, Columbia University Press, New York.

Wineman, S. (1984) *The Politics of Human Services: A Radical Alternative to the Welfare State*, South End Press, Boston, MA.

Wise, T. (2005) *White Like Me: Reflections on Race from a*

Privileged Son, Soft Skull Press, New York.

Wittig, M. (1992) *The Straight Mind and Other Essays*, Beacon Press, Boston, MA.

Wolf, S. (2009) *Sexuality and Socialism: History, Politics and Theory of LGBT Liberation*, Haymarket Books, Chicago, IL.

Wonders, N. (2000) 'Conceptualising Difference', in The Criminal Justice Collective of Northern Arizona University (eds) *Investigating Difference: Human and Cultural Relations in Criminal Justice*, Allyn and Bacon, Boston, MA.

Woods, M. (1998) 'Rethinking Elites: Networks, Space and Local Politics', *Environment and Planning A.*, vol. 30, pp. 2101–19.

Wray, M. (2006) *Not Quite White: White Trash and the Boundaries of Whiteness*, Duke University Press, Durham, NC.

Wright, E. (1979) 'Intellectuals and the Class Structure of Capitalist Society', in P. Walker (ed.) *Between Labour and Capital*, Harvester Press, Sussex.

— (1993) 'Class Analysis, History and Emancipation', *New Left Review*, no. 229, pp. 15–35.

— (1997) *Class Counts: Comparative Studies in Class Analysis*, Cambridge University Press, Cambridge.

— (1998) *The Debate on Classes*, Verso, New York.

Yang, K. (2000) 'Monocultural and Cross-Cultural Indigenous Approaches: The Royal Road to a Balanced Global Psychology', *Asian Journal of Social Psychology*, vol. 3, pp. 241–63.

Yea, S. (1997) 'The "Women" in Women's Studies', *Differences: A Journal of Feminist and Cultural Studies*, vol. 9, no. 3, pp. 31–60.

Yep, G. (2003) 'The Violence of Heteronormativity in Communication Studies', *Journal of Homosexuality*, vol. 45, nos 2/3, pp. 11–59.

Young, I. (1997) *Intersecting Voices: Dilemmas of Gender, Political Philosophy and Policy*, Princeton University Press, Princeton, NJ.

— (2008) 'Unruly Categories: A Critique of Nancy Fraser's Dual Systems Theory', in K. Olson (ed.) (2008) *Adding Insult to Injury: Nancy Fraser Debates Her Critics*, Verso, London.

Young, R. (1990) *White Mythologies: Writing History and the West*, Routledge, London.

Zinn, M., Cannon, L., Higginbotham, E., and Dill, B. (1986) 'The Costs of Exclusionary Practices in Women's Studies', *Signs: Journal of Women in Culture and Society*, vol. 11, no. 2, pp. 290–303.

Index